company's coming

foods for entertaining friends and family

junior league of kansas city, missouri

company's coming

Also by the Junior League of
Kansas City, Missouri:

Beyond Parsley (1984)
Above & Beyond Parsley (1992)

First Printing November 1975
Second Printing November 1977
Third Printing October 1981

Printed in the United States of America

ISBN 0-9607076-0-3

The purpose of the Junior League is to train
volunteers to serve the community. The profit
realized from the sale of *Company's Coming*
will be used for community projects
sponsored by the Junior League of Kansas
City, Missouri.

For information on ordering copies of cookbooks
published by The Junior League of Kansas City,
Missouri, contact:

Cookbook Committee
The Junior League of Kansas City,
Missouri, Inc.
9215 Ward Parkway
Kansas City, MO 64114

ſtaff

chairman	judy hoffman
editor	janet thoma
promotion	prudie true
	barbara milledge
	jannie barron
	vicki massman
	lucy bell
art	ginny graves
	heidi allen
	cindy burcham
testing	barbara adam
	jean smith
selection	mary jane barnes
business manager	susan moeller
indexing	diane sloan
introduction and presentation of foods	ann lombardi
enjoying wine	neil lombardi
napkin folding	doreen carbaugh
proofreading	judy stokes
secretaries	louise kaine
	josie gordon
advisor	mary kay horner
economist	sally carmichael
	kansas city power and light company

contents

entertaining

introduction

Cooking is my bag—it's almost an addiction. For to me, it's one of the most exciting, challenging and rewarding forms of creative expression. It's amusing to read of the woman who's "stuck over a hot stove all day." My kitchen is no more a prison than the studio is for an artist, and to find a whole day to experiment is a treat, not a punishment.

Entertaining is putting this creativity into a different realm, for in this area more things come into play than just the preparation of the food. Think of yourself as director of a play. You carefully gather your "actors", hopefully a blend of old friends and new faces. You set the scene—lighting, sound and decoration all playing a part.

Scene One is the cocktail hour, and you are most involved as director. You greet your guests and help them to feel comfortable in the scene. Sometimes Scene One gets off to a great crescendo, and it's tempting to let it play too long.

The idea is to build the action, so you want to move right ahead into Scene Two, the presentation of the food. The food should fit the scene—a casual menu calls for informal table settings. Choose several special dishes or a whole menu that appeals to you from this book. Try the recipes out ahead so you'll know how much effort is involved and how far in advance you can prepare certain things. Don't overextend yourself—this scene can take only two or three, at the most, great moments. Save something for your next production. You work hard to prepare dishes you know will taste superb. Take time to bring their appearance to the same level. Presentation is as important as taste—food that looks good tastes good. Study magazines for great ideas on how to develop this talent.

The wine is another important facet of your production. It acts as a catalyst. A "big name" is not important, but thoughtful selection is. For suggestions, see the following section, "Enjoying Wine".

By now the "actors" have the feeling of the mood you want to impart. Never slow down the action with an apology or excuse for something that isn't quite as good as you had hoped. Creative cooking means "never having to say you're sorry!" The dessert should be the grand finale of this scene leaving everyone with a glow of well-being.

11

Now the action changes, and the next scene could involve some type of entertainment such as games, music or more often, just good conversation. I'm not in favor of inviting the guests into the backstage activity—why dilute the mood that has been created with too much realism? A kitchen party, however, is a different kind of scene and can be a delightful departure.

If the guests are well-trained actors, they will make their exits at the proper moment, while the action is still high, not waiting until things begin to sag.

Entertaining your own family is one of the most fun ways of developing your style in food preparation. Pick one special new dish to try, and let the rest of your menu be less taxing. Again, set the scene with music, candles, wine and perhaps a different table setting, or even a different room to take things out of the ordinary. The results are immediate and rewarding.

Many satisfying experiences await you in this book. Happy adventuring, and may you, too, become a "hooked cook"!

ann lombardi

enjoying wine

There are three basic approaches to wine—collecting, investing and consuming. I do not knock collecting. It is a nice hobby and has given pleasure to many. Investing can also be a worthwhile pursuit for the astute and unemotional. But the subject which is of most interest to me (and with which this article will, therefore, be concerned) is consuming—consuming and enjoying, particularly as part of a good meal. I do not propose to discuss the classic vintages. Anyone can tell you that a Chateau Margaux 1961 will be marvelous, if you are willing to pay the price. But choosing wines you can enjoy regularly on less-exalted occasions is a different thing, and on this level the information is not so well documented.

There is a lot to learn about wine, and you can pursue it just as far as your interest takes you. The place to start is with the basic literature. Everyone should have one of the rather comprehensive reference books which are available. There are many good ones, such as Alexis Lichine and Frank Schoonmaker's "encyclopedias" and Hugh Johnson's *World Atlas of Wine*. These books are interesting in themselves. After all, wine has played a major role in the economic and cultural history of our civilization. They also provide the general background you will need for your own program of experimentation. For specific selections, however, they are not particularly helpful because they deal in a fantasy world of great vineyards and classified growths. Most of their wines are not available from local sources; and, if available, they command a price far beyond the market for ordinary consumption. It is a little like studying a Rolls Royce catalogue.

Another source of information is word of mouth—just talking to other people who are interested in wine. This can be very informative, and in any event is more rewarding than most cocktail party chatter. It, too, has its hazards, however. The wine snob has already been thoroughly and deservedly taken to task. Equally oppressive is the militant anti-snob, who keeps his favorite jug wine under the radiator and is loudly disdainful of all traditional lore. Don't be over-persuaded by him, either. But the biggest reason why conversation isn't the whole answer is that so many genuine differences exist in taste and opinion. There are really no objective standards. In a blind tasting, experts are frequently unable to identify wines precisely, and their ratings usually disagree. Only the individual can really tell what he likes, when, and with what.

The happy conclusion from all this is that the only way to really learn about wine is by drinking it. You may learn quite a bit just by drinking at random, but it is really more fun, as well as more efficient, to go about it with some degree of organization. The best place to do this is at home. Unfortunately most restaurants not only have uninspired selections, but they feel they are entitled to the same profit margin as on a half-ounce drink of bar whiskey.

Here is what I recommend: most wine merchants have sales during one or more months of the year. At this time, buy a case composed of twelve different wines you wish to sample. Drink them with dinner that month. If you find one or more you like, buy a case to tide you over until the next sale. In this way you will gradually accumulate a supply of wines you *know* you will enjoy.

Better even than trying one wine at a time is sampling two or more to compare them. (An opened and corked red wine is usually still all right the next day; white can be kept several days in the refrigerator.) Start out with a basic comparison, such as a Burgundy with a Bordeaux of about the same price range. Move on to other variations and refinements—regional wine against a classified wine of the same region, California wine of the same grape as its French counterpart, 1966 against a 1967 of the same vineyard. The possibilities are endless. Your encyclopedia and wine conversations will give you leads. If you have guests for dinner, this will provide an opportunity to taste more different wines and get other opinions.

In this tasting process, you will sometimes know the agony of defeat, but you will also know the joy of discovery. Since no scholarly article is worth its salt without an appendix, I am appending notes from a recent wine sale sampling to serve as an example.

A word about the hocus-pocus of wine: A few time-honored maxims (white wine with seafood, red wine at room temperature, etc.) are worth observing because they are generally right. Aside from these, you should really make your own rules, if any. For example, it is probably true that smoking detracts from the fullest appreciation of wine, but it is an even more important rule that you should not be unhappy while drinking wine. Hence, if it *really* makes you unhappy not to smoke, you should smoke. Just try not to pollute the atmosphere of your neighbor, who may have different preferences. As to glasses, relatively large ones with sides sloping inward toward the top will help funnel the aroma of the wine into your nose. Other types of glasses will not, however, spoil the wine. And, there are times when nothing can surpass a furtive slug direct from the bottle. This is not to say that there aren't great wines and grand occasions which should be approached with reverence and ceremony. That is fun, too, in proper perspective.

So, don't let the opportunity pass. Just remember that the two key words are "taste" and "enjoy"!

neil lombardi

APPENDIX A

SAMPLES FROM A RECENT WINE SALE

1. Robert Mondavi 1971 Traminer. An Alsatian style white wine from a very good California vintner. Light and fruity. A fine picnic wine.

2. De Luze 1970 Graves Royale. For years, I assumed that all white Bordeaux was too sweet for anything but dessert. Not so, and it is a nice change from the white Burgundies or Burgundy-types. This particular one is not bad, but I have tasted Dry Semillon from California that I like better.

3. Sonoma Vineyard 1971 Zinfandel. From all I read, Zinfandel has really come into its own. It is a California original of mysterious descent, now receiving critical raves. The only trouble is, every one I try (including this one) seems to bear a strong resemblance to Carignane, the high-volume grape from which most California red jug wines are made. I obviously haven't found the right one yet.

4. Demetrios Retsina. Greek white wine flavored with resin. What ever made me think resin would taste good? It doesn't. Zorba would choke on this stuff. (But, there are obviously those who disagree.)

5. Bon Vin 1970 Crozes-Hermitage. Not from the fabled Rhone Valley vineyard tended by a retired Crusader, but from nearby. An enjoyable wine with a slight spicyness to it.

6. Cantina Sociale di Soave 1970 Soave. (Schoonmaker selection) A lovely white from the shores of Lake Garda, near Verona. Some experts say it lacks character, but I don't agree. Italians probably drink more of it than any other white wine, and who should know better?

7. Ribieros Vihno Verde. (Portuguese) An interesting comparison with the Soave. More pronounced flavor, but not offensively so. I like it.

8. Torres 1962 Gran Coronas. A winner. A full-bodied red, remarkably good for the price, as are many Spanish wines. A bigger wine than those of the Spanish Rioja district which are, however, equally good in their own way.

menu planning

menu selection, ann lombardi
carolyn kroh

wine selection, neil lombardi

Special Breakfast

Sunrise

Citrus Brunch Fruit OR Cantaloupe Rings

Eggs Copenhagen

Pennsylvania Dutch Funnel Cakes

Little Girl's Orange Blossom Party

Orange Straws

Orange Jubilee

Orange Butter Cake

Orange Julius

Coffee for New Neighbor

Pineapple Shell with Fruit

Swedish Apple Cake OR Blueberry Coffeecake

Fresh Ground Spiced Coffee

Children's Backwards Party

Ice Cream Sundaes with Caramel Sauce AND Blender Fudge Sauce

Toppings: Nuts, cherries, whipped cream, crushed peppermint candy, granola

Red Hot Jello Salad

Pizza Loaves

18

Teenage After-Sledding Party

Hot Spiced Punch

Raw Vegetables with Avocado Dip

Chasen's Chili

Rio Grande Cornbread

Watson's Brownies and Monte Carlo Squares

Christening Brunch

Jud's Champagne Punch

Citrus Avocado Molded Salad

Curried Eggs in Shrimp Sauce

Old Fashioned Cinnamon Rolls OR Cranberry Muffins

Ladies' Luncheon

Strawberry Daiquiris

Chipped Beef à la Russe

Green Gage Plum Salad

Refrigerator Bran Muffins

Angel Orange Fluff

French Dinner

Molded Pâté

Boula

Veal in Wine

Spinach on Artichoke Bottoms

Tossed Greens with Vinaigrette Dressing

Coffee Mousse

Wine: Meursault—Lupe Chalet

20

Elegant Dinner

Scampi

Tournedos Henry IV

Broccoli Fritters

Tomato Roquefort Aspic

Baked Alaska OR Coffee Alaska Pie

Wine: Hermitage Blanc—Chante Alouette, Chateau Cantenac Brown, 1966

Large Cocktail Party

Blue Cheese Pastry

Matterhorn

Texas Crabgrass

Salmon Party Ball

Arkansas Hot Pepper Pecans

Raw Vegetables with Curry Dip and Avocado Dip

Engagement Party

Caviar Spread

Chicken and Ham Mornay en Brioche

Zucchini with Spinach Puree

Fresh Mushroom Salad

Crème Caramel

Wine: Tavel Vin Rosé—Chapoutier

Patio Dinner

Tomato Dill Consommé

Green Pea Salad

Butterflied Leg of Lamb

Cheese Potatoes

Peach Blueberry Custard Pie

Wine: La Vieille Ferme (Rhone)

Elegant Garden Picnic

Greek Lemon Soup, chilled

Wine Poached Salmon

Armenian Bread

Chocolate Cinnamon Torte

Wine: Pinot Chardonnay—Wente Brothers

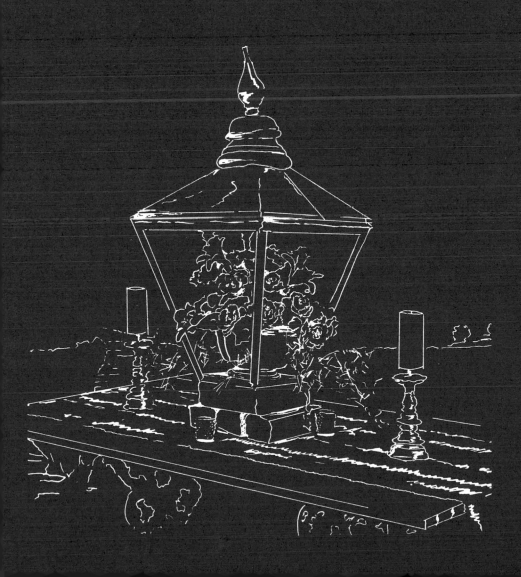

Mexican Dinner

Sangria

Chunky Guacamole OR Jalapeño Crisps

Green Chilies and Cheese

Baked Sour Cream Enchiladas

Mexican Chocolate Soufflé

East Indian Dinner

Chilled Cucumber Soup

Bengal Curry with Pineapple Rice and Condiments

Pineapple Date Chutney

Sliced Fresh Oranges with Vanilla Custard Sauce

Wine: French Colombard—Chateau Souverain

Chinese Dinner

Egg Rolls

Chicken Egg Drop Soup

Cashew Chicken

Chinese Beef and Snow Peas

Chinese Fried Rice

Sour Cream Pudding

Wine: Johannisberger Riesling St. Michelle (Washington State)

Soup Dinner

Canadian Cheese Soup

Rye Bread OR Whole Wheat Batter Bread

Broccoli Salad

Lemon Berry Pie

Wine: Vino Unduraga, Cabernet Reservado (Chile) 1971

Italian Dinner

Capoñata

Cannelloni

Spinach Salad

Biscuit Tortoni

Wine: Valpolicella—Bolla

Autumn Brunch

Toe Warmer OR Sherry's Bloody Mary

Hot Curried Fruit

Woodcock OR Surprise Package

Sausage Ring

Pear Bran Bread

Wine: Piesporter Goldtropfchen (Mosel)

Bridge Luncheon

Bahama Mama

Pineapple Turkey Luncheon Salad OR Sea Dream Salad

Junior League Toast

Marble-Top Chocolate Rum Pie

Wine: Dry Semillon—Fetzer

Easy Dinner for Busy Day

Crock-Pot Old English Short Ribs

Spaghetti Al Burro

Princess Salad

Brandy Royal

Wine: Chianto Classico—Brolio

Wild Game Dinner

Crudités with Special Sauce

Sherried Consommé

Roast Duck with Cumberland Sauce OR Wild Goose with Orange Sauce

Wild Rice

Peas Auberge OR Broccoli with Pine Nuts

Lemon-Lime Ice

Brown Lace Cookies

Wine: Chateau Ripeau—St. Emilion, 1966

Missouri Country Ham Dinner

Fresh Vegetables with Spinach Dip

Missouri Country Ham

Corn Ring with Mushroom Sauce

Mandarin Tossed Salad

Spritz Torte

Wine: Cabernet Sauvignon—Christian Brothers

Late Night Supper

Steak Tartare

Hearty Chicken Gumbo

No-Knead Potato Rolls

Pears Continental

Wine: Champagne—Korbel Brut

After Sporting Supper (Tennis, Golf, etc.)

Chutney and Cream Cheese

Tomato Bisque

Cold Barbequed Loin of Pork

Molded Asparagus Salad

Frozen Lemon Crunch

Wine: Federico Paternina—Banda Azul (Red Rioja)

Special Dinner on Short Notice

Secret Soup

Hollandaise Chicken

Herbed Green Beans

Rice with Chives

Ice Cream with Flaming Westport Room Chocolate Sauce

Wine: Graves—Jouvet

Stag Party

Lentil Bean Soup

Steaks Au Poivre

Fresh Mushroom Salad

Frozen Chocolate Mint Soufflé

Wine: Nuits Saint Georges—Clos de la Marechale—1970

WEEKEND AT THE LAKE

Saturday Lunch

Spritzers

Chilled Summer Soup

Cheese Straws

Seafood Quiche

Fondant Squares

Wine: Soave—Cantina Sociale

Saturday Dinner

Mushroom Rollups

Teriyaki Flank Steak

Tomatoes Vinaigrette

Blueberry Mañana

Wine: Hospices de Beaujeu—Faiveley

Sunday Brunch

Alta Mira Gin Fizz OR Salty Dogs

Cantaloupe Rings

Brunch Eggs with Spanish Sauce

Honey Oatmeal Loaves

Wine: Chenin Blanc—Robert Mondavi

napkin folding

Twenty-four inch napkins are the most effective in the more complicated, larger figures, such as the Lotus or Pyramid.

Use well-starched napkins, linen if possible.

Sharpen edges with a hot iron while folding, or in final stages.

Practice using newspaper before final assembly.

Printed napkins add variety.

Let your children help—many of the figures can be mastered easily.

CANDLE

Easily Done
Festive for Birthdays or Holidays
Can be Decorated

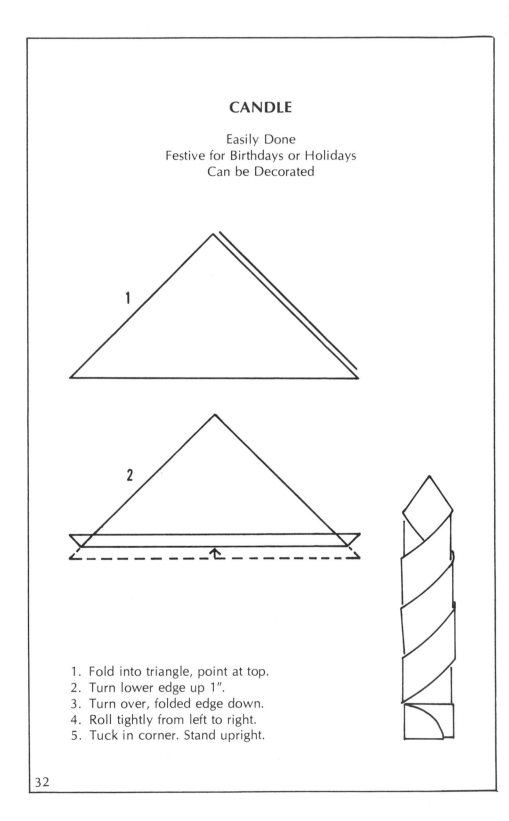

1. Fold into triangle, point at top.
2. Turn lower edge up 1".
3. Turn over, folded edge down.
4. Roll tightly from left to right.
5. Tuck in corner. Stand upright.

ROSETTE

Elegant on Plate

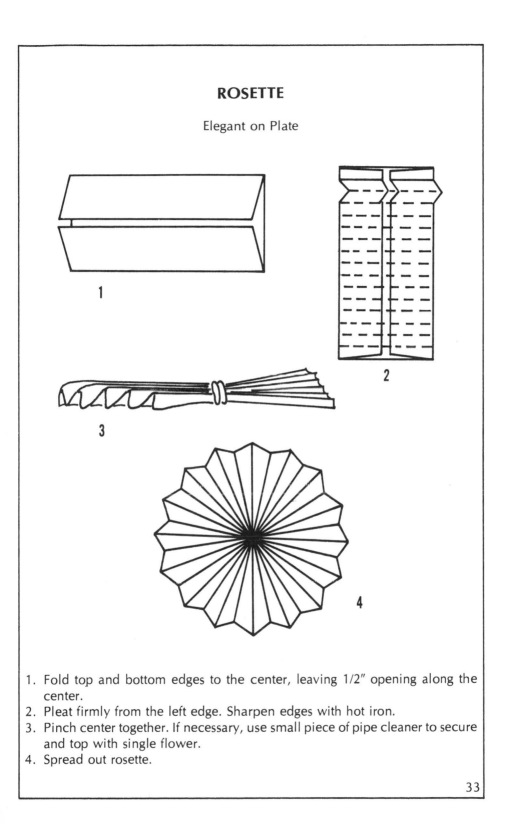

1. Fold top and bottom edges to the center, leaving 1/2" opening along the center.
2. Pleat firmly from the left edge. Sharpen edges with hot iron.
3. Pinch center together. If necessary, use small piece of pipe cleaner to secure and top with single flower.
4. Spread out rosette.

FAN

Pretty at Top of Plate, or in Napkin Ring.

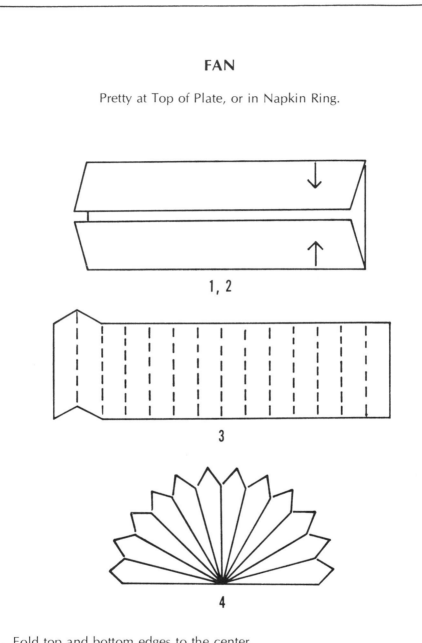

1. Fold top and bottom edges to the center.
2. Fold top and bottom edges to center a second time. (For a smaller napkin, fold in thirds once.)
3. Pleat firmly from the left edge. Sharpen edges with a hot iron.
4. Spread out fan. Balance flat folds on each side on table. Well-starched napkins will hold the shape.

SHIELD

Simple; Always Correct
Pretty with Monogram in Corner or Embroidered

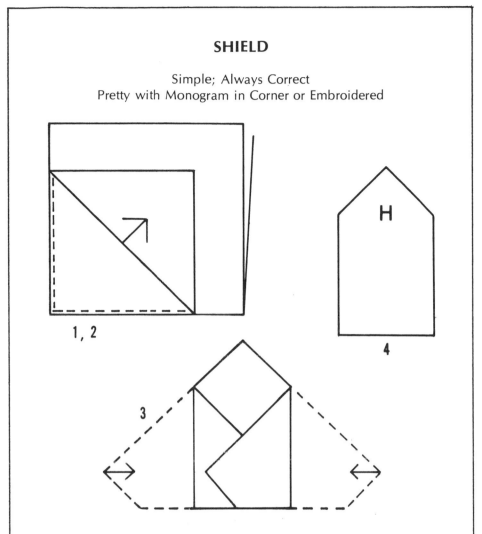

1. Fold into quarter size. If embroidered, ornate corner should face down.
2. Turn up folded corner three-quarters.
3. Overlap right and left side points.
4. Turn over; adjust sides so that they are even, single point in center.
5. Place point up or down on plate; or place to left of plate. If monogrammed, point is usually down.

THE TULIP

A Variation

1. Same as above, but turn up *open* corners at 2. Do not turn over.

JESTER'S CAP

Quickly Done—Use on Plate

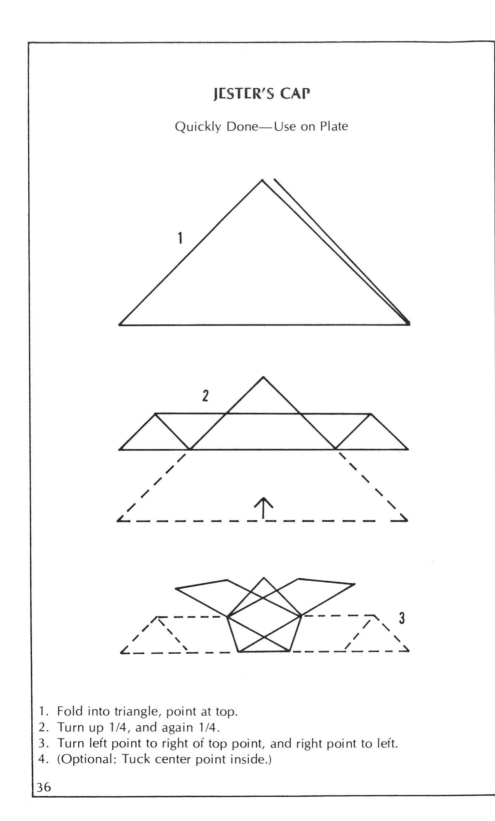

1. Fold into triangle, point at top.
2. Turn up 1/4, and again 1/4.
3. Turn left point to right of top point, and right point to left.
4. (Optional: Tuck center point inside.)

36

BUFFET

Combine Silver with Napkin

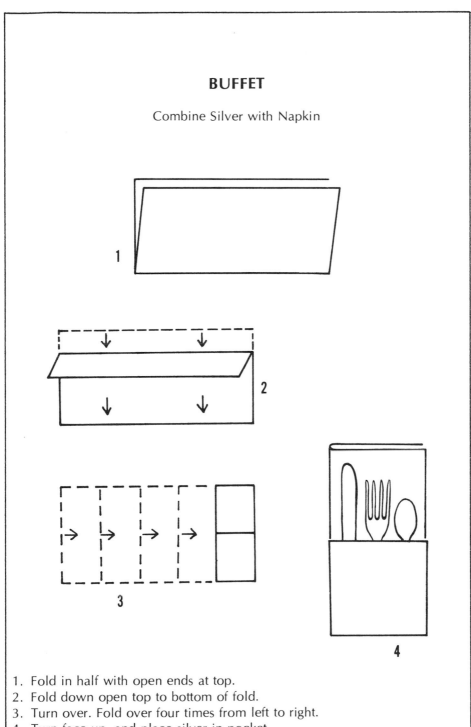

1. Fold in half with open ends at top.
2. Fold down open top to bottom of fold.
3. Turn over. Fold over four times from left to right.
4. Turn face up, and place silver in pocket.

DIAGONAL STRIPE

Attractive for a Name Card, Favor or Flower

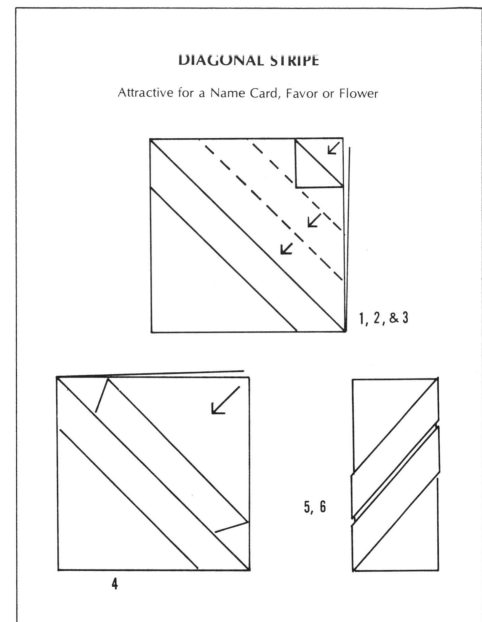

1, 2, & 3

5, 6

4

1. Fold into quarter size, open at upper right.
2. Turn down one upper-right corner 2".
3. Fold over corner twice for diagonal across napkin.
4. Turn down next upper right corner, tucking into the diagonal to the same width as first stripe.
5. Turn under top and bottom of napkin, overlapping underneath.
6. Place vertically on the table.

BISHOP'S HAT

Formal, Standing Fold

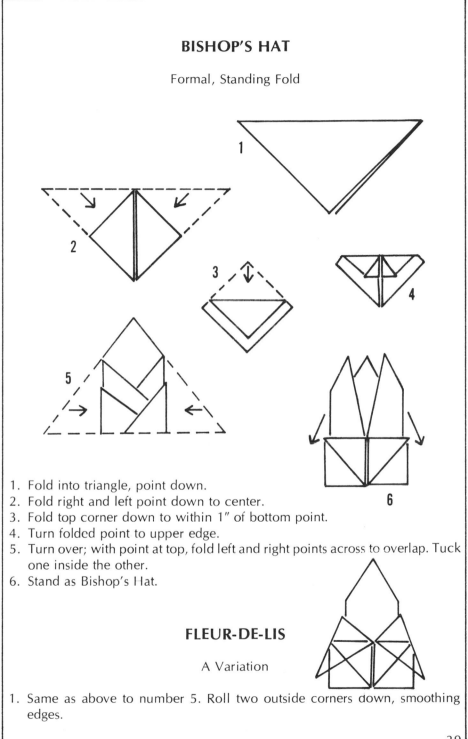

1. Fold into triangle, point down.
2. Fold right and left point down to center.
3. Fold top corner down to within 1" of bottom point.
4. Turn folded point to upper edge.
5. Turn over; with point at top, fold left and right points across to overlap. Tuck one inside the other.
6. Stand as Bishop's Hat.

FLEUR-DE-LIS

A Variation

1. Same as above to number 5. Roll two outside corners down, smoothing edges.

39

PHAROAH'S CROWN

Pretty in a Goblet

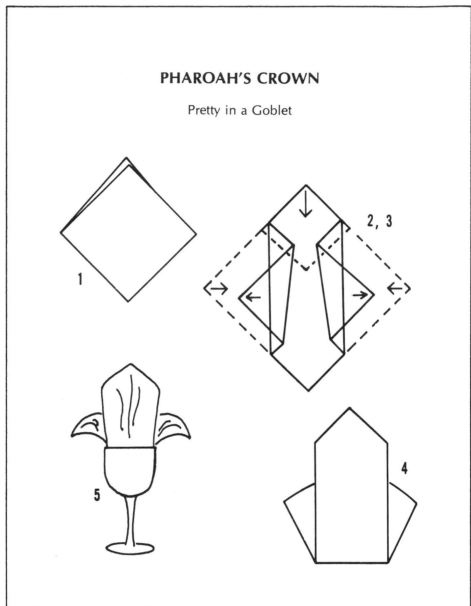

1. Fold into quarters. Turn; open corners at top.
2. Turn over. Fold left and right corners into the middle, forming a pleat on each side, by left corner extending beyond left side and right corner beyond the right side. The opening between the pleats should form a "V" shape, with the bottom open.
3. Turn bottom point up approximately 1/3.
4. Turn face up. Pleat softly using center section and both sides.
5. Insert in wine goblet or napkin ring. Shape folds.

PYRAMID, DUNCE OR WITCH HAT

Nice for Children's Parties

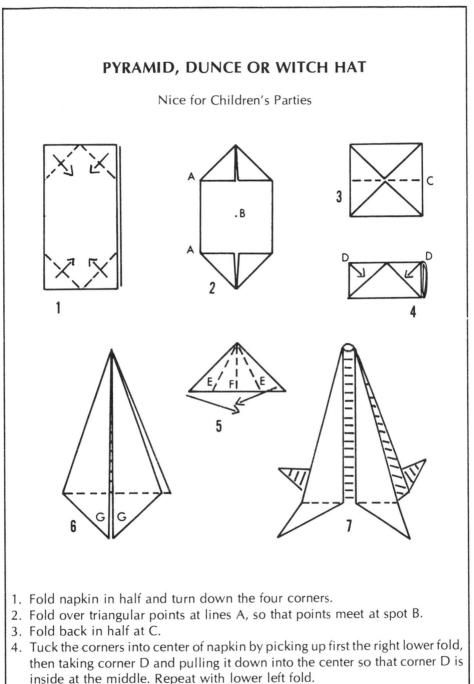

1. Fold napkin in half and turn down the four corners.
2. Fold over triangular points at lines A, so that points meet at spot B.
3. Fold back in half at C.
4. Tuck the corners into center of napkin by picking up first the right lower fold, then taking corner D and pulling it down into the center so that corner D is inside at the middle. Repeat with lower left fold.
5. Turn down the sides (E and E) of the first pleat to the center (F). Turn over and repeat with other pleat.
6. Turn up the points (G) to form a stand or brim.

THE LOTUS

Elegant and Fun for an Oriental Theme

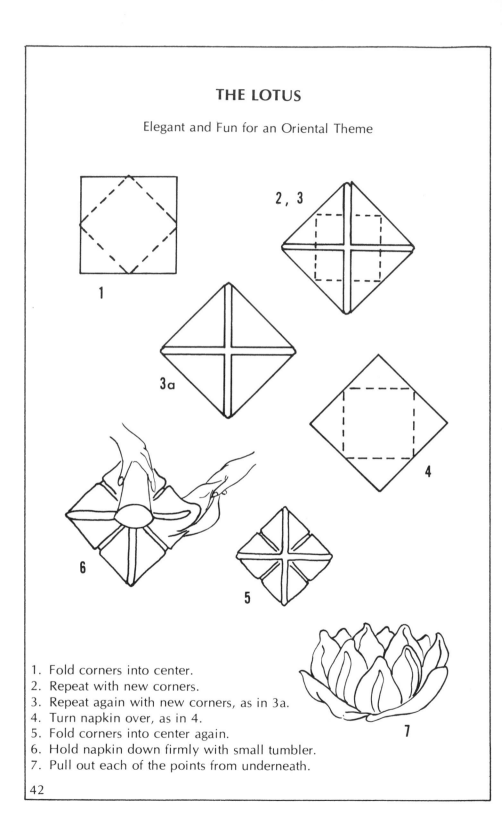

1. Fold corners into center.
2. Repeat with new corners.
3. Repeat again with new corners, as in 3a.
4. Turn napkin over, as in 4.
5. Fold corners into center again.
6. Hold napkin down firmly with small tumbler.
7. Pull out each of the points from underneath.

THE LILY

Pretty and Effective on Table

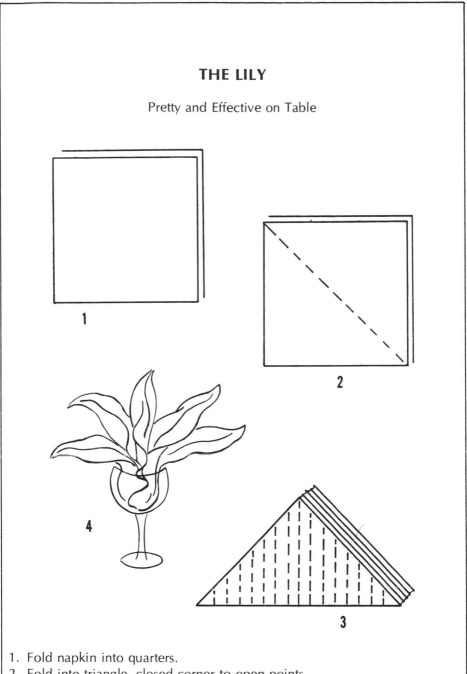

1
2
3
4

1. Fold napkin into quarters.
2. Fold into triangle, closed corner to open points.
3. Turn two points over to other side. (Two points are on either side of closed point.) Pleat.
4. Place closed end in glass; pull down two points on each side and shape.

43

kitchen math

WITH

METRIC TABLES

Measure	Equivalent	Metric (ML)
1 tablespoon	3 teaspoons	14.8 milliliters
2 tablespoons	1 ounce	29.6 milliliters
1 jigger	1-1/2 oz.	44.4 milliliters
1/4 cup	4 tablespoons	59.2 milliliters
1/3 cup	5 tablespoons plus 1 teaspoon	78.9 milliliters
1/2 cup	8 tablespoons	118.4 milliliters
1 cup	16 tablespoons	236.8 milliliters
1 pint	2 cups	473.6 milliliters
1 quart	4 cups	947.2 milliliters
1 liter	4 cups, plus 3-1/3 tablespoons	1,000.0 milliliters
1 ounce (dry)	2 tablespoons	28.35 grams
1 pound	16 ounces	453.59 grams
2.21 pounds	35.3 ounces	1.00 kilogram

/ub/titution chart

When the recipe calls for:	You can use:
1 T. cornstarch	2 T. all-purpose flour (for thickening)
1 whole egg	2 egg yolks plus 1 T. water
1 C. homogenized milk	1 C. skim milk plus 2 T. butter OR 1/2 C. evaporated milk plus 1/2 C. water
1 oz. unsweetened chocolate	3 T. cocoa powder plus 1 T. butter
1 t. baking powder	1/2 t. cream of tartar plus 1/4 t. baking soda.
1 C. sifted cake flour	7/8 C. sifted all-purpose flour (7/8 C. is 1 C. less 2 T.)
1/2 C. butter	7 T. vegetable shortening
1 C. sour milk or buttermilk	1 T. white vinegar plus sweet milk to equal 1 C.
1 clove fresh garlic	1 t. garlic salt OR 1/8 t. garlic powder
2 t. minced onion	1 t. onion powder
1 T. chopped fresh chives	1 t. freeze-dried chives
1 t. dry leaf herb	1 T. chopped fresh herbs
1 C. dairy sour cream	1 T. lemon juice plus evaporated milk to make 1 C.

When the recipe calls for:	You start with:
5-1/2 C. cooked fine noodles	8 oz. pkg. fine noodles
4 C. sliced raw potatoes	4 medium-sized potatoes
2-1/2 C. sliced carrots	1 lb. raw carrots
4 C. shredded cabbage	1 small cabbage (1 lb.)
1 t. grated lemon rind	1 medium-size lemon
2 T. lemon juice	1 medium-size lemon
4 t. grated orange rind	1 medium-size orange
4 C. sliced apples	4 medium-size apples
2 C. shredded Swiss or Cheddar cheese	8 oz. piece Swiss or Cheddar cheese
1 C. soft bread crumbs	2 slices fresh bread
1 C. egg whites	6 or 7 large eggs
1 C. egg yolks	11 or 12 large eggs
4 C. chopped walnuts or pecans	1 lb. shelled walnuts or pecans

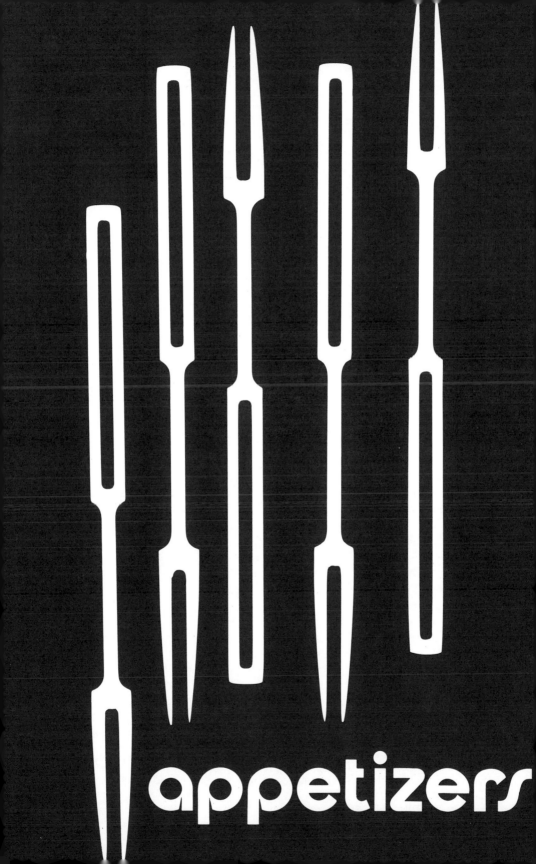

appetizers

Simple and easy to do as a dish of salted nuts and a bowl of olives, or as complicated and difficult as an elegant pâté en croûte—appetizers welcome your guests and stave off hunger before the main attraction, the entrée.

If your entrée is elaborate and filling, keep the appetizer light. Arrange whatever you want to serve before your guests arrive, so that all you need to do is bring it in. Shy away from recipes that require many trips to the kitchen—this is your time to be with your guests.

Appetizers often make a good "first course", if you have plenty of plates and can enlist the aid of a child to help serve. This more formal approach sets up your dinner as a special event. Keep servings quite small, and use salad plates or even bread and butter plates placed on top of the dinner plates to present the first course. At all costs, don't have the hors d'oeuvre sitting all by itself on the plate. If it's cold, place it on a pretty lettuce leaf; if it's hot, garnish with parsley. Often the proper eating utensil can be placed on the plate with the hors d'oeuvre. If appropriate, a small fork stuck into a lemon wedge looks attractive.

Remember, appetizers are just to hint at what lies ahead. Don't overdo, or you'll end up with half the entrée left on the plate and a refrigerator full of leftovers!

hot appetizers

ARTICHOKE HEARTS PIQUANT

10 oz. pkg. frozen artichoke hearts
  OR 14 oz. can artichoke hearts
3 oz. cream cheese, softened
1 C. bottled blue cheese dressing
1/4 C. vermouth
1/2 t. lemon juice
Parmesan cheese

Cook artichoke hearts and drain well (or rinse and drain canned artichoke hearts). Combine cream cheese, blue cheese dressing, vermouth and lemon juice. Add artichoke hearts. Fill 6 ramekins three-quarters full with mixture. Sprinkle top with Parmesan cheese. Place ramekins on foil-lined cookie sheet and bake in 350° oven for 35 to 40 minutes. Cool slightly. Serves 6 as a first course.

SCAMPI

1 lb. large or jumbo shrimp, shelled and deveined
3 T. butter
3 small cloves garlic, crushed
Dash salt
1 T. flour
1/2 C. dry white wine
3/4 C. light cream
1/2 t. salt
Lemon juice
Parsley
Lemon wedges

Sauté shrimp in butter with garlic for 2 minutes. Salt lightly. Remove shrimp; reduce heat and add flour. Cook for 1 minute without browning. Add cream; cook until fairly thick and add wine and shrimp. Add 1/2 t. salt and lemon juice to taste. Heat briefly. Sprinkle with parsley. Serve as first course with lemon wedges. (Allow 4 to 5 shrimp per person if large and 3 per person if jumbo.)

TORTA VERDÉ

10 to 12 Luncheon Crêpes, see pg. 223
10 oz. box frozen chopped spinach
1/4 C. water
Dash salt
1/2 C. onions, finely-chopped
1-1/2 t. butter
1/4 t. nutmeg
1-1/2 t. lemon juice

Sherry Béchamel Sauce:
4 T. butter
5 T. flour
1/2 t. salt
1-1/2 C. milk, heated
3 T. sherry

Mornay Sauce:
3 T. flour
3 T. butter, melted
1-1/2 C. milk, heated
1/2 C. Swiss cheese, grated
1/4 t. nutmeg
1/4 C. sherry
1/4 t. salt
1/4 C. Parmesan cheese, grated

Prepare crêpes, taking care not to make too thin. Cook spinach until just done in 1/4 C. lightly-salted water. Drain in sieve, pressing out as much water as possible. Place in mixing bowl. Sauté onions in butter and add to spinach. Add nutmeg and lemon juice. To prepare Sherry Béchamel Sauce, melt butter; add flour and cook over low heat for 2 minutes. Add salt, heated milk and sherry. Cook until very thick and combine with spinach mixture.

Place 1 crêpe on an ovenproof platter. Spread 1 T. of spinach mixture on crêpe. Alternate layers of spinach and crêpes until all the spinach is used, ending with a crêpe on top. (You will have used about 10 crêpes.) Recipe may be prepared ahead to this point and refrigerated or frozen.

Bring mound of crêpes to room temperature. To prepare Mornay Sauce, cook flour and melted butter without browning for 2 minutes. Add remaining ingredients except for Parmesan cheese. Cook until smooth and thick. (Sauce may be prepared ahead to this point; press wax paper on top of mixture to keep it from forming skin.) Pour Mornay Sauce over mound of crêpes; sprinkle with Parmesan cheese and heat in a 350° oven for 30 minutes, or until light brown on top and sauce is bubbly. Cut into 6 pie-shaped wedges to serve as a first course (or 4 pie-shaped wedges to serve as a luncheon entrée).

STUFFED CHERRYSTONE CLAMS

24 cherrystone clams, well-scrubbed
2 T. butter
1/2 C. green onions, minced
1 clove garlic, minced
1 T. flour
1 C. light cream

1-1/4 C. packaged bread crumbs
1/4 C. parsley, chopped
2 T. lemon juice
1/4 t. pepper
2 T. melted butter
Paprika

Place clams in large kettle with 1 C. water. Cover; bring to boil and steam until all clams are opened. Remove from kettle as soon as they open. Shuck clams; reserve half of the shells. Strain and reserve clam juice. Chop clams finely. Melt butter in skillet. Add green onions and garlic and cook 2 minutes. Sprinkle with flour; cook 1 minute. Add 1/2 C. reserved clam juice. Bring to boil, stirring constantly. Stir in cream. Simmer 1 minute; remove from heat. Stir in 1 C. of the bread crumbs. Mix in parsley, lemon juice, pepper and chopped clams. Mix well and mound filling in reserved clam shells. Sprinkle with remaining bread crumbs. Drizzle melted butter over clams. Sprinkle with paprika. Bake for 15 minutes at 400°. Serves 6 as a first course.

SCALLOP SHELLS

1/4 lb. fresh mushrooms, quartered
3 T. onion, minced
3 T. butter
2 t. fresh lemon juice
1-1/2 t. salt
1/4 t. pepper
1/4 C. flour
1-1/2 C. dairy sour cream
1 C. milk
1/2 C. parsley, chopped
Dash paprika
1 lb. scallops, fresh or frozen
14 oz. can artichoke hearts, drained

Sauté mushrooms and onions in 3 T. butter. Add lemon juice and stir. Add salt, pepper and flour. Add sour cream and milk, stirring until smooth. Stir in parsley and paprika. Simmer scallops in enough water to cover for 5 minutes. Drain well and add. Cut artichoke hearts in half and add. Fill 12 seafood shells and place in 375° oven for 15 minutes, or until heated through. Serves 12 as a first course.

JALAPEÑO CRISPS

1/3 C. Parmesan cheese, grated
3/4 C. mayonnaise
1/2 C. onion, chopped
Dash Tabasco sauce
1 jalapeño pepper
Salt and pepper
Toasted rye rounds OR melba toast rounds

Combine Parmesan cheese, mayonnaise, onion and Tabasco sauce. Remove seeds from jalapeño pepper and chop. Add to mayonnaise mixture. Salt and pepper to taste. Spread mixture on rounds of rye or melba toast and broil for 3 to 5 minutes, or until bubbly. Store spread in refrigerator.

CRABMEAT CANAPÉS

7-1/2 oz. can crabmeat, drained
1/2 C. butter, softened
1 C. cheddar cheese, grated
1 T. Worcestershire sauce
1 small loaf white bread

Combine crabmeat, butter, cheese and Worcestershire sauce. Remove crusts from bread (easier if frozen and partially defrosted). Cut each slice into quarters. Spread bread with crabmeat mixture. Place on cookie sheet and bake at 400° for 5 to 7 minutes. (May be fully prepared and frozen before baking.) Makes 60 canapés.

CHUTNEY AND CREAM CHEESE

6 slices fresh white bread
4 oz. cream cheese
1/4 t. curry powder
2 T. mayonnaise
1/2 C. chutney

Trim bread and cut each slice into quarters. Brown in 350° oven for 10 to 15 minutes. Soften cream cheese and blend with curry and mayonnaise. Spread each square with cheese mixture, and top with small dab of chutney. Place under broiler for a few seconds. Makes 2 dozen canapés.

MOZZARELLA CANAPÉS

12 slices very-thin sliced bread
4 oz. cream cheese
1/4 C. mayonnaise
1 T. lemon juice
Several dashes Tabasco sauce
1 C. black olives, chopped
1/3 C. mozzarella cheese, finely-grated
1 egg
Butter

Remove crust from bread and cut each slice into quarters. Combine cream cheese, mayonnaise, lemon juice, Tabasco sauce, olives, cheese and egg. Blend well. Spread each bread quarter with butter, then cheese mixture. Place on cookie sheet and broil for 3 to 5 minutes, or until browned. Serve hot. Makes 48 canapés.

SAUSAGE ROUNDS

1 lb. hot sausage
1 lb. mild sausage
4 oz. Velveeta cheese
1 loaf white bread

Crumble sausage into skillet and brown. Drain and add cheese. Stir until cheese is melted and mixed with sausage. Cut rounds from bread, and toast on one side in oven. Place sausage mixture on untoasted side of bread and heat in 350° oven for 5 to 10 minutes, or until brown. (May be prepared ahead and frozen.) Makes 3 dozen.

TORTILLA CRISPS

12 large flour tortillas
1/2 C. butter, melted
1 T. Worcestershire sauce
Garlic salt
Parmesan cheese
Chili powder

Fry tortillas in well-oiled skillet, pricking bubbles as they rise. Turn once. Brush crisp, hot tortilla with mixture of melted butter and Worcestershire sauce. Sprinkle with garlic salt, Parmesan cheese and chili powder. Break into pieces and serve immediately. Serves 12.

MUSHROOM ROLLUPS

1/2 C. butter
1 C. flour
1/2 t. salt
4 oz. small-curd cottage cheese
12 oz. fresh mushrooms, chopped
2 T. butter
Salt and pepper to taste
Onion salt to taste
3 T. sesame seeds OR caraway seeds
2 T. butter, melted
1 egg, beaten
Dash onion salt

Cut 1/2 C. butter into flour and salt until lumps are pea-sized. Stir in cottage cheese and press into ball. Refrigerate at least 2 hours. Sauté mushrooms briefly in 2 T. butter. Season to taste with salt, pepper and onion salt. Set aside. Sprinkle floured board with seeds and roll dough to a 15" x 8" rectangle. Cut rectangle in half, lengthwise, and spread each piece with melted butter. Spread half of mushroom filling on each piece of dough. Beginning with longest edge, roll up, jelly-roll fashion. Place rolls on cookie sheet and chill 1 hour.

When ready to bake, brush tops of rolls with egg and sprinkle lightly with onion salt. Cut into 1/2" slices; place slices on cookie sheet and bake at 400° for 15 minutes, or until golden. Makes 4 dozen.

MUSHROOM QUICHE

9" single pastry shell
1/4 lb. fresh mushrooms, sliced
1/2 C. onion, chopped
3 T. butter
4 eggs
1 T. flour
1/8 t. nutmeg
Dash cayenne
2 C. light cream
12 oz. Gruyère cheese, grated

Bake pastry shell for 5 minutes in 375° oven to seal. Remove from oven. Sauté mushrooms and onions in butter. Combine eggs, flour, nutmeg, cayenne and cream. Add mushrooms, onions and Gruyère cheese. Pour mixture into prepared crust and bake at 375° for 40 minutes. Serves 8 as a first course.

54

BLUE CHEESE PASTRY

2 10-oz. boxes frozen patty shells
1 egg, beaten
4 oz. blue cheese OR Roquefort cheese

Soften shell dough at room temperature. Stack 6 shells and roll out to a 12" x 6" rectangle. Trim edges, reserving trimmings. Place on ungreased cookie sheet, and brush edges with egg. Place crumbled cheese over pastry, leaving a 1" border free of cheese on all sides. Roll remaining 6 shells to another 12" x 6" rectangle, and place on top of cheese. Press edges together to seal. Brush with egg. Decorate top of pastry with reserved trimmings. Brush again with egg, and bake at 425° for 30 minutes. Let stand 12 minutes before serving. Cut into 1" slices. (This is good with a clear soup as a first course, or on a Holiday Buffet table.)

MINERS' PASTRIES

2 C. flour
1/4 t. salt
1 C. butter, softened
8 oz. cream cheese, softened
1 egg, beaten
Left-over meat or ground beef, cooked

Sift flour and salt. With pastry blender, cut in butter and cream cheese. Blend well, roll into a ball and chill 1 hour. Roll out very thin on floured board. Cut into shapes with biscuit cutter or cookie cutter. Place 1 T. of well-seasoned cooked meat on dough. Cover with another piece of dough, pressing edges together. Brush with beaten egg. Bake on greased cookie sheet 20 to 30 minutes at 400°. (This is also good with fruit filling.)

TEXAS CRABGRASS

1/2 C. butter, melted
1/2 C. onion, chopped
10 oz. pkg. frozen chopped spinach

1/2 lb. fresh crabmeat
  OR 7 oz. can crabmeat
3/4 C. Parmesan cheese, grated

Melt butter and sauté onions. Parboil spinach; drain and add to butter mixture. Add crabmeat and cheese. Heat and serve in chafing dish. Serves 8.

COCKTAIL PECAN SPREAD

2 T. milk
8 oz. cream cheese, softened
1/2 C. dairy sour cream
2-1/2 oz. jar dried beef, chopped
2 T. onion flakes
1/2 t. garlic salt

1/4 t. pepper
1/4 C. green pepper, finely-chopped
1-1/2 C. pecans, coarsely-chopped
2 T. butter
Ritz crackers

Add milk to cream cheese and blend thoroughly. Blend in sour cream. Add dried beef, onion flakes, garlic salt, pepper and green pepper. Sauté pecans in butter until golden. Stir 1 C. of pecans into cheese mixture. Place in ovenproof serving dish. Sprinkle remaining 1/2 C. nuts on top, and bake at 325° for 25 minutes. Serve with Ritz crackers.

CHILI DIP

1 lb. ground round
1/2 C. onion, chopped
1/2 C. ketchup
1 t. cumin
3 T. chili powder
1 t. salt
15 oz. can red kidney beans, drained
1 C. sharp cheddar cheese, grated
1/2 C. onion, chopped
1/2 C. stuffed green olives, sliced

Brown meat with 1/2 C. chopped onion; add ketchup, cumin, chili powder and salt. Mash kidney beans with fork and add to meat mixture. Simmer 20 minutes. Remove from heat and set aside for 2-1/2 hours, covered. Reheat in chafing dish. To serve, sprinkle grated cheese, chopped onion and sliced olives over top of chili mixture. Do not stir. Serve with tortilla chips for dipping, and replenish cheese, onion and olives over top as needed. Serves 12.

PRAIRIE FIRE BEAN DIP

16 oz. can pork and beans
1/4 C. sharp cheese, grated
1/2 t. garlic salt
1/2 t. chili powder
1/4 t. salt
1/16 t. cayenne
1 t. wine vinegar
1/4 t. liquid smoke
4 slices bacon, fried and crumbled

Combine all ingredients except bacon in chafing dish. Heat and top with bacon. Makes 2 C. dip.

CHINESE EGG ROLLS

1-1/2 C. ground pork, shrimp, ham or chicken,
    cooked and diced (all, or any combination)
1/4 C. bamboo shoots, diced
1/4 C. water chestnuts, diced
4 black Chinese dried mushrooms, chopped
1 T. soy sauce
1/2 t. sugar
2 C. lettuce, finely-chopped OR bean sprouts
4 green onions, finely-chopped
1 pkg. egg roll wrappers
1 egg, beaten
Oil for deep frying

Combine meat, bamboo shoots, water chestnuts and mushrooms. Heat with soy sauce and sugar. Mix with lettuce and green onions. Cool. Place 1/4 C. filling diagonally across center of each egg roll wrapper. Lift lower triangle over filling and tuck point under, leaving upper point of wrapper exposed. Bring each of 2 small side flaps over top of the enclosed filling and tuck points in. Brush the upper and exposed triangle of dough lightly with beaten egg, and roll the wrapper into a neat package. Heat oil to 375°. Deep fry egg rolls, 1 or 2 at a time, and drain on absorbent paper. Serve hot. Makes 18 to 24 egg rolls.

SHERRIED MEATBALLS

3 lbs. ground round
6 eggs, beaten
1/4 C. flour
1 t. allspice
1 T. salt
1/4 t. pepper
1/2 t. oregano
1/2 C. oil
3 T. flour
2 10-1/2-oz. cans beef consommé
2 to 3 T. onion, minced
1 T. Worcestershire sauce
3/4 C. dry sherry

Mix meat and eggs; blend 1/4 C. flour, allspice, salt, pepper and oregano and add to meat mixture. Shape into balls 1/2" in diameter and brown in hot oil. Remove from skillet and drain. Stir 3 T. flour into oil remaining in skillet. Add consommé, onion and Worcestershire sauce and cook until thickened. Add sherry, mix and pour over meatballs. (May be frozen—place frozen meatballs with sauce in 375° or 400° oven for 30 minutes OR place in Crock-pot to thaw and heat.) Serve warm from chafing dish. Makes 150 meatballs.

HOT BROCCOLI DIP

2 10-oz. pkgs. frozen chopped
   broccoli
3/4 lb. fresh mushrooms, chopped
1/4 C. onion, finely-chopped
1/4 C. celery, minced
1/4 C. butter
2 6-oz. rolls garlic cheese, diced

10-1/2 oz. can cream of mushroom
   soup, undiluted
Tabasco sauce to taste
Worcestershire sauce to taste
Seasoned salt to taste
Dash garlic powder
King-size corn chips

Cook broccoli according to package directions. Drain well, all day if possible. Sauté mushrooms, onions and celery in butter. Place in double boiler. Add drained broccoli, cheese and soup, stirring until cheese is melted. Add Tabasco sauce, Worcestershire sauce, seasoned salt and garlic powder. Pour mixture into chafing dish and serve with corn chips. Serves 12.

cold appetizers

MOLDED PÂTÉ

3/4 lb. chicken livers
1/2 C. onions, chopped
1/2 C. butter
1/4 C. brandy
Dash ground cloves

Salt and pepper to taste
Seasoned salt to taste
Toast rounds
Green onions and tops, sliced
Lemon wedges

Sauté chicken livers and onion in butter. Add brandy and seasonings. Cool and puree in blender until very smooth. Cool completely and pour into well-buttered mold. Cover and refrigerate. Spread toast with pâté, add green onions and squeeze a few drops of lemon juice over top. (Also good as a sandwich spread for pumpernickel bread.) Keeps 2 to 3 weeks in refrigerator.

STEAK TARTARE

2 lbs. ground sirloin
2 large onions, minced fine
3 oz. bottle capers, drained
3 oz. tin fillets of anchovies, drained and chopped
1 egg yolk
Garlic salt to taste
Seasoned salt to taste
Worcestershire sauce to taste
Heinz 57 Sauce to taste
Cocktail rye bread
Mustard

Place sirloin, onions, capers, anchovies, egg yolk, garlic salt, seasoned salt, Worcestershire sauce and Heinz 57 sauce in large mixing bowl. Mix thoroughly, using hands. Correct seasonings, and chill for at least 1 hour in round mixing bowl. To serve, invert on serving platter. Serve with cocktail rye bread and mustard. Serves 12 to 16.

MUSHROOM CAVIAR

1 onion, chopped
2 T. butter
1/2 lb. fresh mushrooms
2 T. lemon juice
1 t. Worcestershire sauce
Salt and pepper to taste
2 t. to 1 T. mayonnaise
Toast rounds

Sauté onion in butter until golden. Chop mushrooms very fine; add to onions and sauté 5 minutes. Add lemon juice, Worcestershire sauce, salt and pepper. Remove from heat. Cool and correct seasoning. Add only enough mayonnaise to bind mixture. Pack in jar or small bowl, and refrigerate overnight. Unmold on serving platter, and serve with small toast rounds. Serves 6 to 8.

SALMON PARTY BALL

16 oz. can salmon
8 oz. cream cheese, softened
1 T. lemon juice
2 t. onion, grated
1 t. horseradish
1/4 t. salt
1/4 t. liquid smoke
1/2 C. pecans, chopped
3 T. parsley, snipped
Assorted crackers

Drain and flake salmon, removing skin and bones. Combine with cream cheese, lemon juice, onion, horseradish, salt and liquid smoke. Mix thoroughly and chill. Combine pecans and parsley. Shape salmon mixture into ball, roll in nut mixture and chill. Serve at room temperature with assorted crackers.

SHRIMP-FROSTED CREAM CHEESE

12 oz. bottle chili sauce
2 to 3 dashes Worcestershire sauce
2 7-oz. cans tiny shrimp, drained and rinsed
8 oz. cream cheese
Triscuits or wheat crackers

Combine chili sauce, Worcestershire sauce and shrimp. Chill. Bring block of
cream cheese to room temperature and place on serving dish. Spoon chili-
shrimp mixture over cheese. Some of shrimp mixture as well as cream cheese is
spread on each cracker. Replenish shrimp mixture on top of cheese as needed.
(Two 7-oz. cans crabmeat, flaked, may be substituted for shrimp.) Serves 6 to 8.

FESTIVE CRAB MOLD

1 C. light cream
1 envelope unflavored gelatin
1/4 C. water
1 C. salad dressing
1 t. onion powder OR onion juice
2 T. Worcestershire sauce

1/2 t. salt
Dash pepper
3 7-oz. cans crabmeat
Sliced stuffed green olives
Parsley

Heat cream and stir in gelatin, which has been softened in water. Remove from
heat and add salad dressing. Add onion powder, Worcestershire sauce, salt,
pepper and crabmeat. Place in oiled mold and chill. Unmold, and decorate top
with olives and parsley. Serves 12 to 16.

SHELLFISH HORS D'OEUVRES

2 8-oz. cans water chestnuts
1 lb. fresh crabmeat, flaked
    OR 1 lb. cooked shrimp, chopped
1 C. green onions, sliced
1 C. mayonnaise
2 T. soy sauce
2 T. lemon juice

Chop water chestnuts and mix with remaining ingredients. Spread on crackers to
serve. Serves 12 to 16.

POTTED SHRIMP

1/2 t. dry mustard
Juice of 1/2 lemon
3 oz. cream cheese, softened
1 t. Worcestershire sauce
1/4 C. shrimp sauce
1 t. horseradish
2 to 3 drops Tabasco sauce
1 to 2 T. mayonnaise
7 oz. can medium shrimp

Dissolve dry mustard in lemon juice. Add to cream cheese and blend. Blend in Worcestershire sauce, shrimp sauce, horseradish, Tabasco sauce and mayonnaise. Drain shrimp, and set aside 1 or 2 whole shrimp for garnish. Mash remaining shrimp and add. Place in serving crock. Decorate with sprig of parsley and whole shrimp. Chill. (May be prepared 1 or 2 days ahead.) Remove from refrigerator 1 hour ahead of serving time for easy spreading. Serve with assorted crackers. Serves 10.

CAVIAR SPREAD

5 eggs, hard-cooked
1/2 C. butter, melted
2 T. green onions, sliced
2 C. dairy sour cream
8 oz. caviar
Toast rounds

Press eggs through ricer. Combine with butter. Shape in circle on attractive glass platter. Cover with foil or plastic wrap and refrigerate until set. Sprinkle with finely-chopped onion, spread generously with sour cream and return to refrigerator. To serve, spread with caviar and serve with toast rounds. Serves 12.

OEUFS EN GELÉE

2 T. tarragon vinegar
1 t. salt
6 eggs
1 envelope unflavored gelatin
10-1/2 oz. can chicken consommé
1/4 C. white wine
Vegetable oil
Lettuce
Parsley sprigs
Rémoulade Sauce (made without anchovy paste) see pg. 122

Fill a large skillet with water; add tarragon vinegar and salt. Poach eggs, 3 at a time, in simmering water until firmly set. (Yolks should remain soft.) Remove eggs, rinse in a bowl of cold water, and trim away ragged edges. Soften gelatin in 1/2 C. chicken consommé; add remaining consommé and wine. Heat for 5 minutes and cool. Oil 6 small ramekins or custard cups. Place 1 egg, face-side down, in each cup and fill with cooled consommé. Refrigerate 3 to 4 hours, or overnight. To unmold, place ramekins in hot water and count to 5, slowly. Remove from water; invert on serving plate and garnish with small pieces of lettuce and a sprig of parsley on top. Serve with rémoulade sauce. Serves 6 as a first course.

RAW VEGETABLES WITH CURRY DIP

Cauliflower
Cherry tomatoes
Carrot sticks
Zucchini strips
Artichoke hearts
Celery sticks
Fresh green beans, parboiled

Curry Dip:
1 C. mayonnaise
1 t. curry powder
1 t. soy sauce
1 t. white vinegar
1 t. Worcestershire sauce

Combine dip ingredients and chill. Serve with any or all of suggested raw vegetables. (May also be used as a sauce for hot or cold artichokes.) Makes 1 C. dip.

CRUDITÉS WITH SPECIAL SAUCE

Crudités:
4 carrots
1 bunch fresh broccoli
1 pint cherry tomatoes

Special Sauce:
3/4 t. Coleman's mustard
1 to 2 t. lemon juice
1 t. Worcestershire sauce
1/3 C. chili sauce
1 C. mayonnaise
3 to 4 drops Tabasco sauce

Peel and slice carrots; chill. Break off flowerets of broccoli and blanch in 3 quarts boiling, salted water for 3 minutes. Plunge into ice water immediately to stop cooking process. Wash cherry tomatoes and leave stems on. Drain all crudités and chill.

To make sauce, soften mustard in lemon juice. Add Worcestershire and chili sauce. Mix into mayonnaise. Add Tabasco sauce. Refrigerate, covered, for 1 week to 10 days. To serve, place sauce in dish and arrange vegetables around sauce. Serves 10 to 12.

SAUCED SHRIMP ON ARTICHOKE BOTTOMS

1 recipe Special Sauce (above)
1 lb. fresh small shrimp, shelled, deveined and boiled
   OR 2 7-oz. cans tiny shrimp, drained and rinsed
16 artichoke bottoms
Lettuce leaves
Paprika

Prepare sauce as directed; toss with shrimp. Drain and rinse artichoke bottoms well. For each serving, place 2 artichoke bottoms on lettuce leaves and spoon sauced shrimp over top. Garnish with paprika. Serves 8 as a first course.

ANCHOVY MAYONNAISE DIP

3 oz. can rolled anchovy fillets with capers
3 T. fresh parsley, chopped
1/2 T. chives OR green onions, chopped
Black pepper
1 C. mayonnaise

Place anchovies, parsley, chives and pepper in blender and mix briefly. Remove cover and blend in mayonnaise. Chill and serve.

AVOCADO DIP

28 oz. canned tomatoes
4 ripe avocados
 OR 2 7-3/4 oz. cans frozen avocado dip
3 green onions, sliced
Juice of 1/2 lemon
1/2 t. garlic salt
3/4 C. dairy sour cream
4 oz. can chopped green chilies, drained and seeded
1 lb. bacon
Taco chips

Drain and chop tomatoes. Blend with avocados, green onions, lemon juice, garlic salt, sour cream and green chilies. Chill. Fry bacon; drain and crumble. Sprinkle part of bacon on top of dip, replenishing bacon as needed. Serve with taco chips.

CHUNKY GUACAMOLE

4 avocados, peeled and pitted
1 onion, finely-chopped
1 ripe tomato, peeled and chopped
4 oz. can whole green chilies, drained, seeded and chopped
Dash garlic salt
1 T. lime juice
1 T. olive oil
Salt to taste
Dash Tabasco sauce

Combine all ingredients. Bury avocado pit in mixture to prevent mixture turning dark. Remove pit before serving. Chill or freeze. Serves 6 to 8.

FRESH VEGETABLE SPINACH DIP

10 oz. box frozen spinach
1/2 bunch green onions, chopped
2 C. Hellman's mayonnaise
1 t. garlic powder
1/2 t. lemon juice
1/2 t. Worcestershire sauce
2 t. seasoned salt

Defrost spinach. Drain and squeeze to golf-ball size through cheesecloth. Mix with other ingredients and chill overnight. Serve with fresh, crisp, raw vegetables, such as zucchini, turnips, carrots, celery, or cauliflower. Serves 15 to 20.

MARINATED MUSHROOMS AND ARTICHOKE HEARTS

1 lb. fresh whole mushrooms
Juice of 1 lemon
1 t. salt
1/2 t. freshly-ground pepper
2 T. olive oil
2 t. Dijon mustard OR plain mustard
2 T. parsley flakes
2 T. chives, chopped
1 t. sugar
2 14-oz. cans artichoke hearts, drained

Combine all ingredients in deep skillet and simmer, uncovered, for 15 minutes, stirring occasionally. Chill and serve as appetizer with toothpicks or as an antipasto on a bed of lettuce. Serves 12 to 16.

ARKANSAS HOT PEPPER PECANS

1/4 C. butter
2 C. pecan halves
4 t. soy sauce
1 t. salt
12 dashes Tabasco sauce

Melt butter in baking pan. Spread pecans evenly in pan and bake at 300° for 30 minutes. Combine soy sauce, salt and Tabasco sauce and toss with pecans. Spread on paper towels to cool.

SPICED SHERRIED WALNUTS

1/4 C. sherry
1-1/2 C. brown sugar
1/4 t. salt
1 T. pumpkin pie spice
2 T. light corn syrup
3 C. walnut halves
Granulated sugar

Blend sherry, brown sugar, salt, spice and corn syrup. Add walnuts. Roll nuts in granulated sugar and dry overnight on wax paper.

MATTERHORN

1 large round unsliced loaf pumpernickel OR rye bread
4 oz. carton whipped cream cheese with onions (or any flavor)

Braunschweiger spread: OR   *Deviled ham spread:*
3 oz. braunschweiger   3 oz. can deviled ham
1-1/2 T. mayonnaise   1 t. mustard
1/2 t. mustard   1 t. horseradish
3 drops Tabasco sauce
Salt and pepper to taste

2 hard-cooked eggs, chopped
2 T. mayonnaise
Dash salt
Dash dillweed
Thin slices of cucumber
    OR sliced green onions
4 oz. jar caviar

Slice bread horizontally into 3 slices at least 3/4" thick. Set aside top slice of bread. Spread each of other 2 slices with whipped cream cheese. Prepare either braunschweiger or deviled ham spread. Place meat spread in large circle in center of each slice.

Combine eggs with mayonnaise, salt and dillweed. Spoon egg mixture onto each slice into center of meat spread. Cut cucumber slices into fourths. Arrange in 2 rows around edge of meat spreads. Fill in around cucumber slices with caviar. Stack one layer on top of the other and add top slice of bread. Cut entire loaf into small pie-shaped wedges with a very sharp knife.

beverages

Drinking habits in America are changing, and for the better. I haven't seen a cocktail shaker in years, and people really prefer a shorter cocktail hour. Twenty-five years ago, very few people served wine, and, therefore, there was greater emphasis on cocktails and hard liquor. Too many cocktails may give you a witty tongue, but will also dull and virtually destroy the taste buds. As these are necessary to enjoy fine food skillfully prepared, it doesn't make sense to deliberately deaden them before having a delightful meal. To keep from overextending both physically and financially on liquor, consider serving your guests interesting wines. Adventuring with aperitifs is also enlightening—both will give a definite glow that does not spring into a blaze.

Unusual drinks seem to appear more often at a morning party or late in the evening. Be always on the lookout for interesting garnishes—a bit of cocoa on the top of a Brandy Alexander looks appealing; a celery stick with a topknot of leaves is attractive in a Bloody Mary; and a bit of lemon or orange peel can dress up many a simple aperitif.

While it would be too much to say a drink is as good as the glass it's served in, there's no doubt that the right glass can make a big difference. Choose from the wide selection available today; wine glasses come in all shapes and sizes — — medium, large and gigantic.

For an interesting way to serve wine at a buffet, fill a large punch bowl with crushed ice, and place several bottles of white wine in it. Set the punch bowl on a very large tray and decorate with bunches of grapes and ivy leaves. For an outdoor gathering where wine is to be served, use a large wooden tub or even a huge clay pot as a focal point for the same purpose.

iced beverages

GRAMMIE'S ICED TEA

1 gallon water
3 lemons, juice and rind
7 sprigs fresh mint
2 C. sugar
2 heaping T. tea

Boil water; add remaining ingredients and steep until cool. Strain, squeezing all juice from lemons. Put in quart bottles; store in refrigerator up to 5 days. Makes 1 gallon.

SUN TEA

2 Constant Comment tea bags
3 Lipton tea bags
2 large sprigs fresh mint

Fill half-gallon glass bottle with cold water; add tea bags and mint and set bottle outside in sunlight for 4 hours or more. Makes 1/2 gallon tea.

ORANGE JULIUS

1/3 C. orange juice concentrate
1/4 C. sugar
1/2 C. milk
1/2 C. water
1/2 t. vanilla
6 ice cubes

Place all ingredients in blender and blend for 30 seconds. Serve immediately or freeze for 1 to 2 hours. Makes 3 cups.

JUD'S CHAMPAGNE PUNCH

Ice Ring:
Maraschino cherries
  OR fresh strawberries
Mint leaves

Punch:
1 bottle champagne
1 jigger cointreau
1 jigger brandy

Freeze ice in decorative mold, adding cherries or strawberries and mint leaves. Pour champagne, cointreau and brandy over ice ring in punch bowl. May be made in any quantity and added in 1-bottle increments. Serves 6.

SPRITZER

3 oz. white wine
Club Soda
Fresh Mint

Fill a 12 oz. tumbler with ice cubes. Add wine and fill glass with Club Soda. Garnish with fresh mint. Serves 1.

BAHAMA MAMA

1/2 C. coconut rum
1/2 C. light rum
1/4 C. orange juice
1/4 C. triple sec
1/4 C. pineapple juice
2 T. grenadine syrup
4 orange slices
4 maraschino cherries

Mix rum, orange juice, triple sec, pineapple juice and grenadine syrup in blender and serve over crushed ice in chilled glasses. Garnish with orange slices and maraschino cherries. Serves 4.

SUNRISE

2 t. sugar
1/4 C. apricot nectar
1 C. orange juice
Juice of 1/2 lime
1 C. dry white wine

Mix all ingredients together and chill for several hours before serving. Serve over ice. Serves 4.

ALTA MIRA GIN FIZZ

1-1/2 oz. gin
1 egg white
Juice of 1/2 lemon
2 t. sugar
3 drops orange flower water
1/2 oz. orange Curacao
3 oz. light cream
Dash nutmeg

Place gin, egg white, lemon juice, sugar, orange flower water, Curacao and cream in blender with small amount of shaved ice. Blend and strain into chimney glass. Dust with nutmeg and serve. Serves 1.

SANGRIA

1/2 lemon, sliced thin
1/2 lime, sliced thin
1/2 orange, sliced thin
4 oz. brandy
4 to 6 T. sugar
1 bottle dry red wine
2 T. lemon juice
1/2 C. vodka (optional)
Club Soda

Put lemon, lime and orange slices in large glass pitcher. Mix brandy with sugar and add. Let stand for 1 hour at room temperature. Add wine and lemon juice. Stir thoroughly, and let stand for at least 1 hour. Just before serving, add optional vodka, ice cubes and fill pitcher with Club Soda. Stir briskly until very cold and serve in chilled glasses. Serves 10 to 12.

VELVET HAMMERS

3 pints vanilla ice cream
6 jiggers brandy
6 jiggers creme de cacao (white)

Blend all ingredients in blender. (May be made ahead and refrigerated.) Serves 6.

JAMAICAN DAIQUIRI

6 oz. frozen limeade concentrate
12 oz. rum
18 oz. water

Place all ingredients in blender. Blend, then freeze for 3 to 4 hours. Spoon into 3 oz. glasses and serve with straw. Serves 12.

STRAWBERRY DAIQUIRI

10 oz. box frozen strawberries, undrained
6 oz. frozen daiquiri mix
5 oz. rum
6 to 8 ice cubes

Thaw berries slightly and blend in blender jar. Add daiquiri mix and rum and blend briefly. Add ice cubes, one at a time, until desired consistency is reached and ice is blended in. Serves 6.

MINTED DAIQUIRI

2 T. frozen limeade concentrate
12 mint leaves
4 oz. light rum
1 C. crushed ice

Place all ingredients in blender at high speed for 30 seconds. Serve in iced champagne glasses. Serves 2.

SUMMER SAUCE

2 C. dark rum
6 oz. frozen lemonade concentrate
6 oz. frozen daiquiri mix
6 oz. frozen orange juice concentrate
1 quart Collins mix
1 quart Club Soda
10 sprigs fresh mint

Combine rum, lemonade concentrate, daiquiri mix, orange juice concentrate, Collins mix and Club Soda. Bruise mint leaves and add. Serve over ice. Makes 3 quarts.

SALTY DOGS

1 jigger vodka
1 C. grapefruit juice
Salt to taste
Sliver of grapefruit peel

Fill 12 oz. tumbler with ice cubes. Add vodka, grapefruit juice and several shakes of salt. Garnish with grapefruit peel. Serves 1.

SHERRY'S BLOODY MARY

6 oz. can tomato paste
3-1/2 6 oz. cans water
10 oz. can Snap-E-Tom
1/2 t. salt
1/8 t. pepper
1 t. monosodium glutamate
1 t. celery salt
1/2 t. garlic salt
1/4 C. lime juice
2 t. onion juice
2 T. Worcestershire sauce
1/4 t. Tabasco sauce

Make a base by combining all ingredients. Store in refrigerator. Mix in a ratio of 1 part vodka to 4 parts Bloody Mary base. Makes 6 C. base.

heated beverages

FRESH GROUND SPICED COFFEE

2-1/2 C. roasted coffee beans (8 oz.)
3 inches stick cinnamon
1/4 t. ground nutmeg

Place coffee beans, cinnamon sticks and nutmeg in blender jar. Cover and blend on low speed 30 to 45 seconds, or until beans are crushed. Blend on high speed 15 seconds. Store in covered container and perk as needed. Makes 2-1/4 C. ground coffee. (Use filter in basket for clearer coffee.)

CAPPUCINO

1 oz. hot cocoa mix
1 T. brandy OR half Kahlua and half brandy
1 C. strong hot coffee
Whipped cream for topping

Combine cocoa mix and brandy in coffee mug. (Kahlua and brandy give a sweeter taste than brandy alone.) Fill mug with coffee and top with whipped cream. Serves 1.

HOT APPLE TODDY

3 oranges, studded with cloves
46 oz. can apple juice
1 large cinnamon stick
1/4 t. nutmeg

1/4 C. honey
2 T. lemon juice
1 t. lemon rind, grated
2-1/2 C. unsweetened pineapple juice

Place oranges in a pan with small amount of water. Bake at 325° for 30 minutes. Heat apple juice with cinnamon stick in a large pan. Bring to a boil and simmer, covered, for 5 minutes. Add nutmeg, honey, lemon juice, lemon rind and pineapple juice. Simmer, uncovered, 5 minutes. Add baked oranges. Serves 15.

HOT VODKA

9 C. cranberry juice cocktail
9 C. unsweetened pineapple juice
4-1/2 C. water
1 C. brown sugar
1 quart vodka
4-1/2 t. cloves, whole
4 sticks cinnamon, broken
1/4 t. salt

Pour cranberry juice, pineapple juice, water, brown sugar and vodka into bottom of 30-cup electric coffeemaker. Put cloves, cinnamon sticks and salt into basket and percolate. Makes 30 cups hot vodka.

HOT BUTTERED RUM

1/2 C. sweet butter
1 C. brown sugar, packed
1/4 t. ground cloves
1/4 t. ground cinnamon
Dark rum
Boiling water
Cinnamon sticks
Lemon slices
Cloves

Make a base by creaming butter, sugar and spices until mixture is smooth and puffy. Put 1 T. to 2 T. of base (depending upon mug size) into mug and add 1 jigger of dark rum. Fill mug with boiling water. Garnish with cinnamon stick and lemon slice studded with cloves. Store base tightly covered in refrigerator.

ROSY WASSAIL

1 pint cranberry juice cocktail
6 oz. frozen orange juice concentrate, thawed
2 C. water
1 T. sugar
1/4 t. allspice
3-1/4 C. dry sauterne
Few drops red food coloring (optional)
Orange slices
Cloves

In large kettle, combine cranberry juice, orange juice concentrate, water, sugar and allspice. Bring just to simmer; add sauterne and heat. Do not boil. If desired, add food coloring. Stud orange slices with whole cloves. Pour punch into preheated punch bowl, and float orange slices on top. Serves 12 to 14.

HOT SPICED PUNCH

9 C. unsweetened pineapple juice
9 C. cranberry juice cocktail
4-1/2 C. water
1 C. brown sugar
4-1/4 t. whole cloves
4 cinnamon sticks, broken
1/4 t. salt

Combine pineapple juice, cranberry juice and water in bottom of large electric coffee maker. Place remaining ingredients in basket. Allow to perk until light comes on and serve hot. Makes 30 cups.

HOT TOMATO TODDY

46 oz. can tomato juice
10-1/2 oz. can beef consommé
1 C. vodka
Salt to taste
2 lemons, sliced thin

Simmer all ingredients for 1 hour or more. Serve in punch cups. Serves 8.

TOE WARMER

6 oz. frozen lemonade concentrate
3 6-oz. cans water
6 oz. Scotch OR bourbon
12 cloves
5 sticks cinnamon

Garnish:
Cinnamon sticks
Lemon slices
Whole cloves

In a kettle, mix lemonade, water and Scotch or bourbon. Tie cloves and cinnamon sticks in cheesecloth and add. Simmer 15 to 20 minutes. Serve in mugs with stick cinnamon to stir with and a slice of lemon studded with cloves for garnish. Serves 4.

soups

With the cost of food skyrocketing, the idea of entertaining with an informal soup party has great appeal, and soup may be made with such a great variety of tastes and textures. It can be as tempting and delicious as any entrée. The kitchen is the ideal setting for such a party, accented with low lights and lots of candles.

Soup may be served from all sorts of interesting containers. A glass punch bowl may be called into service for a colorful chilled soup. For hot soups, try a handsome copper pot or earthenware crock placed on a large wooden board surrounded by curly endive, parsley dotted with cherry tomatoes, radish roses or carrot curls. Several types of cheese, a homemade loaf of bread, a green salad and, of course, a bottle of wine round out this festive meal. To finish off, you could serve fruit and a choice of cookies. Bravo soup!

Soup mugs with small napkins pulled through the handle have eye appeal. You might also tie a napkin in the handle of the soup pot lid to look attractive and act as a pot holder.

Garnish for soup can lift it out of the "kids home from school for lunch" category. Try topping soup with chopped parsley, a dollop of sour or whipped cream, a few croutons, a sprinkle of Parmesan cheese, a dash of paprika or a dusting of finely-chopped nuts.

chilled soups

TOMATO MADRILENE

3 13-oz. cans madrilene consommé
18 oz. dairy sour cream
4 oz. jar caviar
8 to 10 lemon slices

Remove madrilene from can and chill until jellied. Layer madrilene alternately with sour cream in parfait glasses. Top each serving with a spoonful of caviar and garnish with a slice of lemon. Serves 8 to 10.

ARCTIC ASPARAGUS SOUP

2 large leeks, chopped
1/4 C. butter
3 cubes chicken bouillon
   OR 1 T. instant chicken broth
3 C. water
2 10-oz. boxes frozen asparagus
1/4 C. flour
1 t. salt
1/8 t. pepper
2 C. light cream
1 C. heavy cream
Salt to taste
Chopped parsley for garnish

Sauté leeks in butter until soft. Combine chicken broth and water in large saucepan. Add asparagus and cook 5 minutes. Remove asparagus and add asparagus to leeks. Stir flour into leek mixture until absorbed. Add chicken broth, salt and pepper. Simmer 3 minutes. Pour part of soup at a time into blender, and blend until smooth. Pour into large bowl and stir in light cream. Chill 4 hours. Whip cream; add salt to taste. Serve soup with dollop of cream, and sprinkle chopped parsley on top. Serves 8.

CHILLED CUCUMBER SOUP

1 clove garlic, minced
2 T. olive oil
1 large cucumber, peeled and diced
2 C. dairy sour cream
2 dashes monosodium glutamate
1 t. grated lemon peel
1/2 t. salt
2 dashes lemon-pepper
Dash dill weed, crumbled
   OR plain yogurt

Place all ingredients except dill weed or yogurt in blender and blend on low speed. Add 6 ice cubes and chill until ready to serve. Remove ice cubes, and garnish with dill weed or yogurt before serving. Serves 6.

GAZPACHO

1-1/2 C. tomatoes, chopped
1/2 C. green pepper, chopped
1/2 C. celery, diced
1/2 C. cucumber, chopped
1/2 C. onion, chopped
2 t. fresh parsley, minced
1 t. chives
1 t. salt
1/2 t. pepper
Small clove garlic, minced
1/2 t. Worcestershire sauce
3 T. tarragon wine vinegar
2 T. olive oil

Garnish:
Chopped green pepper
Chopped celery
Chopped cucumber
Chopped onion

Place tomatoes, green pepper, celery, cucumber and onion, a little at a time, in blender jar and blend until smooth. Add parsley, chives, salt, pepper, garlic, Worcestershire sauce, tarragon wine vinegar and olive oil and chill for 24 hours. Serve with individual bowls of green pepper, celery, cucumber and onion (or any other garnish of your choice) to be spooned into soup for garnish. Serves 4 to 6.

COLD SQUASH SOUP

1 medium onion, sliced
2 T. butter
1 C. chicken broth
6 medium summer squash (yellow), sliced

1-1/2 C. light cream
1/4 t. freshly-grated nutmeg
Salt and white pepper to taste
Chopped parsley or chives

Cook onion in butter until soft but not brown. Add broth and squash. Cover and cook until tender, about 15 minutes. Cool mixture and puree in blender, using some of the cream if necessary. Combine with remaining cream; add nutmeg and season to taste with salt and pepper. Chill until serving time. Garnish with chopped parsley or chives. Serves 8.

CHILLED SUMMER SOUP

1 C. raw potato, diced
1 C. peas, fresh or frozen
1/4 C. green onions, sliced
1-1/2 C. chicken bouillon
1/8 t. celery salt
1/8 t. curry powder
1 C. heavy cream

Add potatoes, peas and green onions to bouillon in saucepan. Bring to boil. Reduce heat, cover and simmer until vegetables are just tender, about 10 minutes. Put mixture in blender and blend until smooth. Mix in celery salt, curry powder and cream. Chill. Serves 4.

VICHYSSOISE GLACÉ

2 T. butter
3 T. onion, chopped
2 C. water
3 Idaho potatoes, peeled and sliced
2 t. salt
1/2 C. milk

1/2 C. light cream
1-1/2 C. dairy sour cream
Salt to taste
White pepper to taste
1/2 C. heavy cream
Chopped fresh chives

Melt butter. Add onions and cook 5 minutes. Add water, potatoes and 2 t. salt. Boil gently until potatoes are tender. Blend mixture in blender. Add milk, light cream and sour cream. Blend again. Add salt and white pepper to taste. Chill thoroughly. To serve, add heavy cream and garnish with chives. Serves 12.

hot soups

SNAPPY TOMATO CONSOMMÉ

20 oz. Snap-E-Tom
2-1/2 C. boiling water
4 envelopes MBT chicken-flavored
  broth (.19 oz. each)
5 whole cloves
2 t. lemon juice
2 shakes seasoned salt
2 shakes Worcestershire sauce

2 shakes butter-flavored salt
1/2 C. dry white wine
Salt to taste
1/4 t. curry powder
1/4 C. dry white wine
Dill weed
1/2 C. Monterrey Jack cheese, grated

Simmer Snap-E-Tom, boiling water, chicken MBT, cloves, lemon juice, seasoned salt, Worcestershire sauce, butter-flavored salt, 1/2 C. dry white wine, salt and curry powder. Remove cloves. (May be made ahead to this point and reheated.) Just before serving, add 1/4 C. dry white wine and dash of dill weed. Pour into soup bowls or cups and sprinkle with grated cheese. Serves 8 to 10. (For a richer consommé, add 2-2/3 T. butter.)

SHERRIED CONSOMMÉ

1/4 C. almonds, chopped
2 t. butter, melted
10-1/2 oz. can beef consommé
1 C. water
2 T. dry sherry

Sauté almonds in butter until golden. In saucepan, heat consommé, water and sherry. Place 1 T. sautéed almonds in each soup bowl. Ladle consommé mixture over almonds. Serves 4.

TOMATO DILL CONSOMMÉ

2 8-oz. cans tomato sauce or 2 16-oz. cans tomatoes
1-1/2 t. dill seed
2 T. onion, chopped
1 T. sugar
1 t. salt
1/8 t. black pepper
2 t. chicken seasoned stock base
2 C. water

Simmer tomato sauce, 1 t. of the dill seed, onion, sugar, salt and pepper for 20 minutes. Rub through strainer. Dissolve chicken stock base in water. Add with remaining 1/2 t. dill seed and heat thoroughly. Cool and refrigerate. (Flavor improves if made the day before serving.) Serves 4.

TOMATO BISQUE

1/4 C. butter
1 onion, chopped
1/4 C. celery, diced
1/4 C. green onions, sliced
3 lbs. canned tomatoes, undrained
10 1/2 oz. can beef bouillon, undiluted
2 t. salt
1/4 t. basil
1/4 C. butter
1/4 C. flour
1/4 C. dry vermouth
1 C. light cream

Melt butter and sauté onion, celery and green onions until soft. Add tomatoes, bouillon, salt and basil. Simmer, uncovered, for 30 minutes. Cool and blend in blender, a little at a time, until smooth. Bring back to boil, and add remaining 1/4 C. butter blended with flour. Stir as soup thickens. Add vermouth and cream; heat, but do not boil. Serves 8 to 10.

CHICKEN EGG-DROP SOUP

4 C. chicken broth, homemade or canned
2 t. salt (optional)
1/2 C. water chestnuts, finely-chopped
2-1/2 T. cornstarch
2-1/2 T. cold water
1/3 C. scallion tops, chopped
1 egg, slightly beaten

If homemade chicken broth is used, combine with salt in saucepan and bring to boil. If using canned chicken broth, omit salt. Add water chestnuts to pan and simmer 1 minute. Mix cornstarch and water together until smooth, and stir into soup. Continue stirring until soup thickens. Add scallions and turn off heat. Slowly pour in beaten egg, stirring gently. Serve at once. Serves 6.

CANADIAN CHEESE SOUP

2 large potatoes, peeled and diced
2 large onions, diced
1/2 C. carrots, finely diced
1/2 C. celery, finely diced
2 C. water
32 oz. canned chicken broth
3 C. sharp cheddar cheese, grated
1 C. light cream
Salt and pepper to taste
1/4 C. chopped parsley

Place vegetables in water. Bring to boil; cover and simmer for 15 minutes. Add remaining ingredients except parsley. Heat and stir for 15 minutes, or until cheese is melted. Garnish with parsley. Serves 8 to 10.

ONION SOUP

1 large onion, sliced
2 T. butter
3 C. boiling water
3 envelopes MBT beef-flavored broth
   (.19 oz. each)
1/2 t. Worcestershire sauce
2 T. vermouth
2 slices French bread
1/2 C. baby Swiss cheese, grated
   OR grated Parmesan cheese

Sauté onion in butter for 30 minutes. Add boiling water, beef MBT and Worcestershire sauce. Cover and simmer for 45 minutes. Add vermouth and return to boil. Toast French bread slices in oven. When ready to serve, divide soup into 2 earthenware bowls or mugs. Float toast on top of soup; sprinkle heavily with cheese and broil to melt cheese. Serves 2.

GREEK LEMON SOUP

8 C. boiling water
8 envelopes MBT chicken-flavored broth
   (.19 oz. each)
1/2 C. rice, uncooked
2 whole eggs
2 egg yolks
Juice of 2 lemons
1/2 t. lemon peel, grated
Salt to taste
Tabasco sauce to taste (optional)

Bring water to boil. Add chicken MBT. Return to boil and add rice. Cook until tender. Beat eggs and egg yolks until light, and slowly beat in lemon juice and rind. Add a little of the hot broth to the lemon-egg mixture, blending in well so that eggs do not curdle. Slowly add to broth in pan, stirring constantly. Heat through, but do not boil. Add salt to taste and Tabasco sauce if desired. Serve hot or chilled. Serves 6.

SECRET SOUP

6 8-1/2 oz. cans peas
6 10 1/2 oz. cans beef consommé
1 large onion, quartered
3/4 C. dry sherry
Parmesan cheese to garnish

Drain peas, reserving liquid from 3 cans. Place peas, liquid, consommé, onion and sherry into blender, 1/3 at a time. Blend until smooth. (May be made ahead to this point and refrigerated. Mixture may become jellied and separate, but it will smooth out when stirred and heated.) Heat and serve from large crock. Sprinkle with Parmesan cheese. Serves 10 to 12.

BOULA

4 13-oz. cans green turtle soup
4-1/2 cans green pea soup, undiluted (10-1/2 oz. each)
2 t. Worcestershire sauce
1 C. heavy cream, whipped
Parmesan cheese

Combine soups and Worcestershire sauce and heat slowly for 10 minutes. Top each serving with a large dollop of whipped cream and sprinkle with Parmesan cheese. Serves 12.

QUICK BORSCHT

16 oz. jar tiny whole red beets
10-1/2 oz. can beef consommé
Salt to taste
1/2 C. dairy sour cream
Chopped chives for garnish

Reserve beet liquid and chop beets well. Combine beets, liquid and consommé, and heat slowly for 10 minutes. Salt to taste and chill. Serve with sour cream on top of each serving and garnish with chives. Serves 6.

POTAGE SANTÉ

10 oz. pkg. frozen spinach
1 onion, sliced
1/2 C. chicken broth, undiluted
1/4 t. nutmeg OR curry powder
Salt to taste
Freshly-ground pepper to taste
1 T. butter, softened
10-1/2 oz. can cream of mushroom soup, undiluted
1/4 lb. mushrooms (optional)
2 T. butter (optional)
1-1/2 C. dairy sour cream

Cook spinach and onion in chicken broth. Add nutmeg (or curry), salt, pepper, 1 T. butter and mushroom soup. Add fresh mushrooms, sautéed in 2 T. butter, if desired. Place ingredients in blender and blend for 30 seconds or until smooth. Add sour cream and blend again. Warm over low heat so that cream does not curdle. Serve warm or cold. Serves 4.

PUREE MONGOLE

2 chicken bouillon cubes
1/2 C. water
10-1/2 oz. can cream of green pea soup
1/2 10-1/2 oz. can cream of tomato soup
1/4 C. light cream (optional)
1 t. curry powder
Salt and pepper to taste
2 T. dry sherry
Toasted croutons
    OR 1/2 C. heavy cream, whipped

Dissolve bouillon cubes in water. Stir in soups and optional cream. Add curry powder and salt and pepper to taste. Simmer 10 minutes. Add sherry. To serve, float croutons on top, or serve topped with a dollop of whipped cream. Serves 4.

SEAFOOD BISQUE

10-1/2 oz. can tomato soup
10-1/2 oz. can green pea soup
2 C. heavy cream
Salt and pepper to taste
1 T. Worcestershire sauce
1/4 C. dry sherry
8 oz. crabmeat
8 oz. lobster

Combine soups, cream, salt and pepper, Worcestershire sauce and sherry until well blended. Add crabmeat and lobster; heat and serve. Serves 4.

CLAM BISQUE

10-1/2 oz. can cream of chicken soup
10-1/2 oz. can cream of celery soup
10-1/2 oz. light cream
2 8-oz. cans minced clams, with liquid
1/2 t. monosodium glutamate
3/4 t. salt
1/4 t. cayenne
1/4 C. vermouth
3 T. butter
Paprika

Blend soups and cream over low heat. Add clams, monosodium glutamate, salt and cayenne. Heat, but do not boil. Add vermouth and heat again. Garnish each mug of soup with a pat of butter and a sprinkle of paprika. Serves 8.

hearty soups

BOUILLABAISSE

5 fillets of sole OR turbot
6 frozen lobster tails
24 cherrystone clams
3/4 C. olive oil
3 C. onions, chopped
2 C. celery, diced
4 cloves garlic, minced
3/4 C. parsley, chopped
3 lbs. canned tomatoes, undrained
3 C. beef bouillon
1-1/2 C. sauterne
5 t. salt
1 t. thyme
1 t. paprika
1 t. saffron
1-1/2 t. monosodium glutamate
3/4 t. fennel
1/4 t. cayenne
2 lbs. shrimp, cleaned, shelled and deveined
2 lbs. scallops, well-rinsed

Cook fillets of sole or turbot in top of double boiler for 30 to 40 minutes, or until fish is white and firm. (Broth will accumulate.) Cool. Split lobster tails down back with kitchen shears. Scrub clam shells well and soak in water. Scrub again to remove any loose particles on shells. Heat olive oil in heavy kettle. Add onions, celery and garlic. Cook until lightly browned. Add parsley, tomatoes, bouillon and sauterne to kettle. Add seasonings and bring to boil. Add shrimp, scallops and lobster tails. Cover and simmer 4 to 6 minutes. Lift lobster out, and remove meat from shells. Return lobster to pan. Add fish fillets and broth that has accumulated. Add clams, and simmer entire mixture just until clam shells have opened. Discard any clam shells which do not open with the rest. Serves 12 to 14.

STEAK SOUP

3/4 C. butter
1 C. flour
1/2 gallon warm water
2 lbs. lean ground chuck
1 C. onions, diced
1 C. carrots, diced
1 C. celery , diced
10 oz. pkg. frozen mixed vegetables
10 oz. pkg. frozen corn
16 oz. canned tomatoes
1 T. monosodium glutamate
2 T. BV OR Bovril (broth and seasoning base)
1 to 1-1/2 t. salt
1 t. pepper

Melt butter and stir in flour to make a smooth paste. Gradually stir in 1/2 gallon warm water, stirring constantly. In large skillet, sauté ground chuck; drain and add meat to soup. Parboil onions, carrots and celery for 10 to 15 minutes. Drain and add to soup. Add frozen mixed vegetables, corn, tomatoes, monosodium glutamate, BV or Bovril, salt and pepper. Bring to boil, reduce to simmer and cook for 30 to 45 minutes, or until vegetables are tender. Makes 3 quarts.

OX TAIL SOUP

4-1/2 qts. water
4 lbs. ox tails
10-1/2 oz. can onion soup, undiluted
32 oz. canned tomatoes, with liquid
32 oz. tomato juice
1 bay leaf
Salt and pepper to taste
3 carrots, chopped
2 medium zucchini, diced
2 ears sweet corn OR 2 10-oz. pkgs. frozen corn
1/2 C. to 3/4 C. barley

In roasting pan, combine water, ox tails, onion soup, tomatoes, tomato juice, bay leaf, salt and pepper. Cook for 8 hours, covered, at 250°. Cool and refrigerate overnight. Skim off fat which has settled on top. Trim fat from ox tails, removing bones, cartilege, and any pieces which fall from top of bones. Add vegetables, cutting corn off the ears, and barley. Return to 250° oven and cook for 6 hours. Serves 10.

LENTIL BEAN SOUP

1 lb. pkg. dried lentil beans
Smoked ham hocks with 1 C. ham on bone
3 to 4 quarts water
1 C. celery, chopped fine
1 C. onion, chopped fine
2 to 3 carrots, chopped fine
10-1/2 oz. can tomato soup, undiluted
5 hot dogs, cut in chunks
4 oz. salami, chunk or sliced, diced
1 to 1-1/2 t. salt
2 slices Rye bread, toasted

Soak lentil beans with ham hocks in water overnight. The next morning add celery, onions and carrots and simmer slowly for 4 to 5 hours. Remove ham hocks and cut ham into bite-size pieces, discarding fat, skin and bones. Add ham, tomato soup, hot dogs and salami to soup. Salt to taste, and add bread. Cook slowly for 4 hours. Remove bread slices and throw away. Serves 10 to 12.

BLACK BEAN AND PORK SOUP

2 1-lb. pkgs. dried black beans
2 onions, coarsely chopped
2 large ham hocks
2 T. lemon juice
1 t. garlic powder
3 lbs. pork roast, cubed
4 10-1/2 oz. cans beef broth
4 10-1/2 oz. cans water
Salt and pepper to taste
1/2 C. dry sherry

Soak beans overnight in water; drain. Place beans, onions, ham hocks, lemon juice, garlic powder, pork roast, beef broth, water, salt and pepper in a large kettle. Bring to boil; cover and simmer slowly for 3 hours, adding more water from time to time, if necessary. Put half of bean mixture (no meat) in blender and puree. Return pureed mixture to soup and cook for 30 more minutes. Add sherry and heat. Serves 12.

CHICKEN SOUP AU GRATIN

2 chicken breasts, whole
1/4 t. to 1/2 t. salt
2 C. water
1/2 C. onion, chopped
1/2 C. carrot, chopped
1/2 C. celery, diced
10-1/2 oz. can cream of chicken soup
1/2 C. milk
Dash pepper
1 C. sharp cheese, grated

Simmer chicken in salted water, covered, until tender. Remove chicken, cool, remove skin and dice. Boil broth, uncovered, until reduced to 1 C. Add vegetables and simmer, covered, for 10 minutes, or until tender. Gradually stir in soup, milk and pepper. Reserve 3 T. cheese for garnish. Add remaining cheese and chicken. Heat and stir until cheese melts. Garnish with reserved cheese. Serves 4 to 6.

CHASEN'S CHILI

8 oz. dry pinto beans
5 C. canned tomatoes
1 C. green pepper, chopped
1-1/2 C. onion, chopped
2 cloves garlic, minced
1-1/2 T. oil
1/2 C. parsley, chopped
2-1/2 lb. lean ground beef
1 lb. lean ground pork
1/2 C. butter
1/4 C. chili powder
2 T. salt
1-1/2 t. pepper
1-1/2 t. cumin seed, crushed

In kettle, soak beans several hours or overnight in water to cover them by 2". Simmer until tender. Add tomatoes. Sauté green pepper, onions, and garlic in oil until soft. Add parsley. Brown beef and pork in butter and add to onion mixture. Add chili powder and cook for 15 minutes. Combine with beans and add remaining spices. Simmer for 1 hour, covered, and for 30 minutes more, uncovered. Skim fat from top and serve. Makes 4 quarts.

HEARTY CHICKEN GUMBO

4 whole chicken breasts
8 to 10 chicken thighs
6 C. water
2 stalks celery
2 carrots, diced
1 onion, quartered
Salt and pepper to taste
1 lb. ham, cubed
1/4 C. salad oil
2 large onions, minced
3 cloves garlic, minced
4 T. flour
2 T. tomato paste
1 green pepper, minced
5 green onions, sliced
2 T. parsley, chopped
1 t. thyme
1 bay leaf
Salt and pepper to taste
3 dozen oysters (optional)
2 C. rice, cooked

Cook chicken until just tender in 6 C. water seasoned with celery, carrots, onion, salt and pepper. Reserve stock and strain. Cool chicken; skin, bone and cut into bite-size pieces. Sauté chicken and ham in oil until browned. Transfer to deep kettle.

In same skillet, sauté onion and garlic, adding more oil if needed. Add to kettle. In skillet, stir flour into oil to make a roux, adding more oil if necessary. Add tomato paste and cook 3 minutes. Gradually stir in 2 to 3 C. reserved stock, stirring until thickened. Add green pepper and green onions to meat in kettle. Add parsley, thyme and bay leaf. Add thickened tomato sauce.

To mixture in kettle, add 3 to 4 C. reserved stock; salt and pepper to taste. Cook over low heat for 3 hours. Add oysters, if desired, and simmer 15 minutes more.

Cook rice according to package directions. To serve, place a mound of rice in each soup bowl, and serve gumbo over the rice. Serves 8.

salads

Salads may be simple greens to accent a hearty entrée or whole meals in themselves. In any case, they can be real scene stealers.

White salads, such as potato, tuna or chicken salad, need color added for zest. Line a salad bowl with dark green lettuce or spinach leaves, then mold the salad in the center. A rosette of parsley on the top finishes the presentation. Chicken salad is also attractive served on a ring of cantaloupe or pineapple, or mounded in a tomato shell. Again, accent with parsley.

Tossed salad often loses its character when it's mixed. A different approach is to arrange the various ingredients on a large platter lined with lettuce leaves and let guests choose what pleases them. (Some people really hate onions!) Place the salad dressing in a sauce dish for easy serving and follow the great Italian idea of offering a little Parmesan cheese to sprinkle on top.

green salads

GREEN GREEK SALAD

1 large head Romaine lettuce
8 oz. fresh spinach
10 cherry tomatoes, halved
1 avocado, peeled and sliced
10 fresh mushrooms, sliced

6 T. sesame seeds, toasted
1 C. croutons

Dressing:
1 t. salt
1/2 t. freshly-ground pepper
1 C. olive oil
1 t. dry mustard
6 T. red wine vinegar
2 T. honey
1 clove garlic

Combine Romaine lettuce, spinach, tomatoes, avocado and mushrooms in salad bowl. Chill. Blend salt, pepper, oil, dry mustard, vinegar and honey in blender. Add clove of garlic, if desired. Chill. Remove clove of garlic from dressing. To serve, toss salad with dressing. Garnish with sesame seeds and croutons; toss again lightly. Serves 12.

SPINACH SALAD

8 oz. bean sprouts, fresh or canned
3/4 lb. fresh spinach
1-1/2 T. sesame seeds
1/2 C. water chestnuts

Dressing:
1/2 C. peanut oil
1/4 C. soy sauce
2 T. lemon juice
1-1/2 T. onion, grated
1/2 t. pepper

Drain and wash bean sprouts. If using canned, soak in cold water for 2 hours. Drain thoroughly. Wash spinach and tear into bite-size pieces. Dry and chill. Toast sesame seeds in 350° oven until lightly-browned, watching carefully. Drain water chestnuts and slice very thin. In large salad bowl combine dressing ingredients and let stand 1 hour. Combine salad ingredients with dressing and serve immediately. Serves 4.

PRINCESS SALAD

1 T. butter
1/2 C. sesame seeds
1/4 C. Parmesan cheese, grated
10 oz. fresh spinach
1 head lettuce
1/2 C. mayonnaise
1 C. dairy sour cream

1 T. tarragon vinegar
1 T. sugar
1/4 C. green pepper, chopped
2 T. onion, minced
3/4 t. salt
1/4 t. garlic salt

Melt butter; add sesame seeds and cook over moderately-low heat, stirring, until seeds are lightly browned. Cool at room temperature. Add cheese to seeds and mix well. Tear spinach and lettuce into bite-size pieces. Combine remaining ingredients for dressing, mixing well. Toss greens with dressing and 3/4 of sesame seed mixture. Sprinkle remaining sesame seed mixture over top. Serves 6.

ROCKEFELLER SALAD

1 lb. fresh spinach
1 head leaf lettuce OR 1/2 head iceberg lettuce
1-1/2 C. large curd cottage cheese, drained
1/4 C. sugar
1 t. salt
1 t. dry mustard
1 T. onion juice
1/3 C. cider vinegar
1 C. salad oil
1 T. poppy seeds
1/2 lb. bacon, fried and crumbled

Tear spinach and lettuce into bite-size pieces. Add cottage cheese and toss. To make dressing, combine sugar, salt and dry mustard. Add onion juice, vinegar and oil gradually, mixing constantly. Add poppy seeds. To serve, add bacon to salad greens and toss with dressing. Serves 6.

WILTED SALAD

2 lbs. fresh spinach OR leaf lettuce
8 radishes, thinly sliced (optional)
1/2 lb. fresh mushrooms, thinly sliced (optional)
1/2 lb. bacon
1/2 C. green onions, sliced
3 eggs
1/4 C. sugar
1/4 C. red wine vinegar
Salt and pepper to taste

Wash, dry and tear spinach or leaf lettuce into bite-size pieces, and place in salad bowl. Add radishes and mushrooms, if desired. Cook bacon until crisp. Remove bacon, crumble and set aside. Sauté onions in bacon fat until golden. Drain onions on paper towel, reserving bacon grease. Combine eggs, sugar and vinegar, and pour into warm bacon grease, stirring constantly until slightly thickened. Add salt and pepper to taste. Add onions; stir and pour dressing over spinach, tossing lightly until coated. Sprinkle bacon over top of salad and serve immediately. Serves 8.

CATALINA SALAD

1/2 head endive	*Dressing:*
1 head iceberg lettuce	1/2 C. sugar
1/2 head Romaine lettuce	1 t. salt
8 oz. fresh spinach	1 t. dry mustard
1 C. mandarin orange sections, drained	1 t. paprika
1 tomato, peeled and cubed	1 t. celery salt
3 T. capers	1 t. grated onion
	1 C. salad oil
	1/4 C. vinegar

Tear greens into bite-size pieces; place in large salad bowl and chill. Meanwhile, prepare dressing: Combine sugar, salt, dry mustard, paprika, celery salt and grated onion. Alternate adding *first* some oil and then some vinegar to dry ingredients until all oil and vinegar is incorporated into dry ingredients, beating well. Chill. To serve, add mandarin orange sections, tomato and capers to greens. Toss salad ingredients with dressing. Serves 8.

MANDARIN TOSSED SALAD

1 head iceberg lettuce, torn into
   bite-size pieces
2 C. celery, chopped
2 T. fresh parsley, chopped fine
4 green onions, with tops, sliced
2 11-oz. cans mandarin oranges,
   drained
1/2 C. slivered almonds
1/4 C. butter

Dressing:
1 t. salt
Pinch pepper
1/2 t. Tabasco sauce
1/4 C. sugar
1/4 C. tarragon vinegar
1/2 C. salad oil

Combine lettuce, celery, parsley, green onions and mandarin oranges in salad bowl. Toast almonds in butter in 350° oven, just until golden, watching carefully. Combine dressing ingredients, mixing well, and combine with salad. Sprinkle toasted almonds over top, and serve at once. Serves 8 to 10.

CAESAR SALAD

2 eggs
1 clove garlic
3/4 C. olive oil
2 C. stale bread, cubed
2 large heads Romaine lettuce
1/2 t. salt
1/8 t. freshly-ground black pepper
Juice of 1 large lemon
5 to 6 anchovy fillets, chopped
1/2 C. Parmesan cheese, grated
Dash paprika (optional)

Drop eggs into boiling water for 1 minute. Drain and cool. Crush garlic in small bowl; pour in oil and let stand 3 to 4 hours. Brown the bread cubes in 1/4 of the garlic-oil mixture. Tear lettuce into a large salad bowl; season with salt and pepper. Pour remaining garlic-oil mixture over greens and toss. Combine eggs and lemon juice and add to greens. Toss again. Add chopped anchovies and grated cheese and toss again. Add croutons and serve, garnished with paprika, if desired. Serves 8 to 10.

fruit salads

CITRUS BRUNCH FRUIT

3 C. mandarin orange sections, drained
1-1/2 C. grapefruit sections, fresh or canned
1 C. sugar
1 C. water
1/4 t. to 1/2 t. cinnamon
1/2 t. nutmeg
1/2 C. fresh lemon juice
2 avocados
1 to 2 T. lemon juice

Combine orange and grapefruit sections. Make syrup from sugar, water, cinnamon and nutmeg. Bring to boil, stirring to dissolve sugar. Add 1/2 C. lemon juice and cool. Pour syrup over oranges and grapefruit and marinate overnight. Two hours before serving, slice avocados and brush with lemon juice. Add to fruit. To serve, drain fruit and avocados, reserving marinade. Serve on lettuce leaves, or in brandy snifter with some of the marinade poured over. Serves 10.

FROZEN FRUIT CUPS

12 oz. can frozen orange juice concentrate
12 oz. can water
16 oz. can pineapple tidbits, undrained
16 oz. can apricots, drained and diced
6 bananas, diced
1 C. miniature marshmallows (optional)
1 C. sugar
2 T. lemon juice

Fold all ingredients together gently. Place paper muffin liners in muffin pans. Fill liners with salad and freeze. When frozen, remove from muffin tin and store in freezer bag. Remove individual salads as needed a few minutes before serving. Remove paper liner and serve. Serves 32.

HOT CURRIED FRUIT

16 oz. can pear halves
16 oz. can pineapple tidbits
16 oz. can Elberta Freestone peaches
16 oz. can white cherries, pitted
2/3 C. brown sugar
1 t. to 3 t. curry powder
Juice of 1 lemon
1/2 C. butter, melted

Drain fruit on several thicknesses of paper toweling for 2 to 4 hours, replacing with dry paper towels as needed. Place fruit in 7" x 11" ungreased baking dish. Combine remaining ingredients and pour over fruit. Bake 1-1/2 hours, uncovered, in 350° oven. Serve warm. Serves 6.

CANTALOUPE RINGS

1 cantaloupe
1 pint fresh strawberries
1 pint fresh raspberries
1/2 C. sugar
Mint leaves for garnish

Cut cantaloupe into rings. Remove seeds and peel. Refrigerate. Marinate berries in sugar for at least 1 hour in refrigerator. Fill center of cantaloupe ring with berries. Garnish with mint leaves. Serves 4 to 6.

PINEAPPLE SHELL WITH FRUIT

1 large fresh pineapple

Spring Fruit:
1 C. fresh strawberries, halved
1 C. green seedless grapes, halved
1/4 C. kirsch
2 T. sugar

Winter Fruit:
2 oranges, sectioned
1 large banana, cut in chunks
1/4 C. maraschino cherries, halved
1/4 C. Grand Marnier

Ivy leaves for garnish

Slice pineapple with leaves, lengthwise. Remove fruit, leaving shell intact. Remove core, and cut pineapple into chunks. Add fruit, depending on season, liquor and sugar. Fill shells with fruit mixture, place on oval platter with leaves in opposite directions, and garnish platter with ivy leaves. Serves 2.

SUMMER SALAD

1 avocado
2 T. lemon juice
2 C. cantaloupe balls
1 C. fresh or frozen (defrosted)
   pineapple chunks, drained
1 C. fresh strawberries
1 pound cottage cheese
1/2 C. mayonnaise
1 T. honey
2 T. chopped toasted almonds
2 ripe cantaloupes

Peel and cube avocado; sprinkle with lemon juice. Combine the cantaloupe balls, pineapple and strawberries. Add cottage cheese and avocado, mixing lightly. Combine mayonnaise, honey and almonds. Cut melons in half, and heap fruit mixture lightly into each half. Spoon dressing over each half and serve. Serves 4.

NEW ENGLAND APPLESAUCE

20 Jonathan or Winesap apples, peeled and sliced
   OR enough to fill Crock-pot
1 C. sugar
1/2 C. water
Juice of 1/2 lemon
Cinnamon to taste
Nutmeg to taste

Place apples and sugar in Crock-pot in layers. Add water. Cover tightly and cook on low setting for 8 hours or overnight. Stir and gently mash apples. Add lemon juice, cinnamon and nutmeg. Refrigerate or freeze. Serves 8 to 12.

molded salads

LIME ICE CREAM SALAD

3 oz. lime jello
1 C. water
1 pint vanilla ice cream
1/2 C. mandarin oranges, drained and halved
1/2 C. banana, sliced
1/2 C. pecans, chopped
8 oz. can crushed pineapple, drained

Dissolve jello in boiling water. Add ice cream and stir until melted. Add remaining ingredients and refrigerate in 9" x 9" pan. Serves 9.

AVOCADO MOUSSE

1-2 T. unflavored gelatin
    OR 3 oz. lime jello
1 C. water
5 to 6 avocados, ripe
1 small white onion, grated fine
juice of 1 lemon
6 sprigs parsley, cut very fine
1/2 C. mayonnaise
1/2 t. salt
3/4 C. dairy sour cream

Dissolve gelatin in water. (If using plain gelatin, soften in cold water; if using lime jello, dissolve in boiling water.) Set aside and cool. Peel and mash avocado. Add onions, lemon juice, parsley, mayonnaise and salt. Stir in sour cream and add cooled gelatin. Mix well and pour into mold or clear glass bowl. Serves 6 to 8.

CITRUS AVOCADO MOLDED SALAD

2 T. unflavored gelatin
3/4 C. sugar
1/4 t. salt
2 C. boiling water
1-1/4 C. orange juice
1/4 C. lemon juice
1-1/2 C. fresh strawberries, sliced
1 avocado, diced
Mayonnaise to garnish

Combine gelatin, sugar and salt; add water. Stir until gelatin is dissolved. Add fruit juices and chill until partially set. Fold in strawberries and avocado. Chill in 7" x 11" glass dish or in individual molds. Garnish with mayonnaise. Serves 8.

GREEN GAGE PLUM SALAD

28 oz. canned green gage plums, pitted
3 oz. lemon jello
Few drops green food coloring
6 oz. cream cheese, diced
1/2 C. slivered almonds

Drain plums, reserving liquid. Add enough water to liquid to make 2 C. and heat to boiling. Add jello and stir until well-dissolved. Stir in food coloring, and chill until partially set. Meanwhile, put plums through a sieve. Add plum pulp, cream cheese and almonds to partially-set jello mixture. Chill until firm. Serves 8.

RED HOT JELLO SALAD

1/4 C. cinnamon red hots
1/2 C. water
3 oz. cherry jello
1 C. boiling water

2 C. apples, peeled and chopped
1/2 C. celery, chopped
1/2 C. pecans, chopped

Soak red hots in water overnight. Dissolve jello in boiling water. Add red hot liquid. Chill until partially set. Stir in apples, celery and chopped nuts. Chill until firm. Serves 6.

FROSTED BERRY MOLD

2 C. boiling water
6 oz. cherry jello
10 oz. pkg. frozen strawberries, undrained
16 oz. can cranberry sauce
1 C. pecans, chopped
3/4 C. mayonnaise
3/4 C. dairy sour cream

Combine water and jello, stirring until jello is dissolved. Add strawberries, cranberry sauce and pecans. Place in 7" x 11" glass dish and chill. Combine mayonnaise and sour cream and spread over top. Chill until set. Serves 12.

TOMATO ROQUEFORT ASPIC

1 bay leaf
2 cloves
1 C. water
3 oz. lemon jello
10-1/2 oz. can tomato soup
1 t. unflavored gelatin
1 small onion, chopped fine
1 t. sugar
1/2 t. salt
2 T. lemon juice
3 oz. Roquefort or blue cheese, crumbled

Boil bay leaf, cloves and water for 5 minutes. Combine remaining ingredients in large bowl. Strain water mixture into bowl and mix well. Pour into 8 individual molds or a 7" ring mold. Chill until set. Unmold by dipping briefly in hot water and inverting on serving plate. Serves 8.

SPICY ASPIC

6 C. tomato juice
2 onions, sliced
2 bay leaves
4 cloves
1/2 C. lemon juice
1/4 t. salt
Dash cayenne
1 T. Worcestershire sauce
4 T. unflavored gelatin
1 C. cold water
1 C. mayonnaise
3 T. capers, drained

Optional additions:
1/2 C. celery, diced
2 hard-boiled eggs, chopped
7 oz. can shrimp, drained
6 oz. jar marinated artichoke
  hearts, drained
16 oz. can hearts of palm, drained
1 avocado, diced

Cook tomato juice, onions, bay leaves and cloves for 5 to 7 minutes. Strain. Add lemon juice, seasonings and Worcestershire sauce. Soften gelatin in cold water and add to tomato mixture. Add any additions from optional list and chill in glass casserole or decorative ring mold. Serve with sauce made by combining mayonnaise and capers. Serves 12.

MOLDED ASPARAGUS SALAD

10-1/2 oz. can cream of asparagus soup, undiluted
8 oz. cream cheese
3 oz. pkg. lime jello
1/4 C. cold water
1/2 C. mayonnaise
3/4 C. celery, chopped
1/2 C. green pepper, diced
1 T. instant minced onions
1/2 C. pecans OR almonds, chopped
Lettuce leaves

Stir soup and cream cheese in top of double boiler until cheese melts. Add jello, stirring to dissolve. Remove from heat, add water and cool until mixture is syrupy. Add remaining ingredients and pour into individual oiled molds or 3-1/2 C. oiled mold. Serve on lettuce leaves. Serves 6 to 8.

vegetable salads

CURRIED GREEN BEAN SALAD

2 10-oz. pkgs. frozen French-style green beans
1/2 C. mayonnaise
2 t. Parmesan cheese, grated
2 t. pimiento, finely-chopped
1 t. salt
1/2 t. curry powder
1 T. onion, finely-minced
6 whole tomatoes, cut to fan out (optional)

Cook green beans according to package directions; drain and chill. Combine remaining ingredients except tomatoes and mix well. Toss beans with mayonnaise mixture. Spoon beans in center of each tomato or on lettuce leaves and serve. Serves 6.

TEXAS GREEN BEAN SALAD

2 20-oz. cans whole green beans, drained
1 T. vegetable oil
1 T. vinegar
1 small onion, grated
Salt and pepper to taste
1 C. dairy sour cream
1 t. horseradish
1 t. lemon juice
1/2 C. mayonnaise
1/4 t. dry mustard
1 small onion, sliced

Marinate green beans overnight in vegetable oil, vinegar, onion, salt and pepper. Add remaining ingredients the next day and let stand in refrigerator until ready to use. Serves 10.

BROCCOLI SALAD

1 C. onion, chopped fine
1 C. celery, chopped fine
1 small yellow summer squash, unpeeled, thinly-sliced
  OR 1/2 firm cucumber, unpeeled, thinly-sliced
1 C. fresh mushrooms, sliced
6 oz. jar marinated artichoke hearts,
  drained, cut into wedges
8 oz. can water chestnuts, drained and thinly-sliced
3/4 C. olive oil
2/3 C. wine vinegar
1/4 t. sugar
2 t. salt
2 10-oz. pkgs. frozen chopped broccoli
6 slices bacon, fried and crumbled

Combine onion, celery, squash or cucumber, mushrooms, artichoke hearts and water chestnuts in large bowl. Mix oil, vinegar, sugar and salt together. Toss with vegetables. Cook broccoli in 3 quarts water for 2 minutes. Remove immediately and blanch with cold water to stop cooking process. Drain thoroughly. Cut any larger pieces to bite size. Toss broccoli and bacon into salad. Add more salt if needed. Chill. Serves 10 to 12.

MIRIAM'S RELISH

16 oz. can lima beans
16 oz. can French-style green beans
12 oz. can Mexicorn
16 oz. can baby peas
1 green pepper, chopped fine
1 large onion, chopped fine
1 C. celery, chopped fine

1 C. vinegar
1 C. sugar
1 t. celery seed
1 T. salt
1/2 to 1 t. pepper
1/2 C. oil

Drain canned vegetables and combine with fresh vegetables. Stir vinegar and sugar together until sugar dissolves. Add celery seed, salt and pepper. Add oil and mix well. Pour over vegetables and marinate 2 hours. Chill. Makes 2-1/2 quarts.

CAPOÑATA

1 eggplant, diced
1/3 C. olive oil
1 onion, chopped
2 stalks celery, chopped
1/2 lb. mushrooms, sliced
4 oz. can ripe olives, drained and sliced
16 oz. can Italian plum tomatoes
3 T. capers
1/4 C. vinegar
1 t. basil
1 t. salt
1 T. vinegar
Lettuce leaves (optional)

In deep skillet, sauté eggplant in olive oil for 10 minutes. Add remaining ingredients and simmer, covered, for 15 minutes. Uncover and simmer until liquid is reduced, about 30 minutes. Chill. Serve on lettuce leaf as first course, or as relish in individual ramekins. Serves 6.

FRESH MUSHROOM SALAD

1/4 C. red wine vinegar OR tarragon vinegar
3/4 C. olive oil
Salt to taste
Freshly-ground pepper to taste
1 lb. fresh mushrooms, sliced
Lettuce leaves
1/2 C. green onion tops, sliced
   OR chopped chives
1/4 C. chopped fresh parsley

Combine vinegar, oil, salt and pepper for salad dressing. Toss mushrooms in dressing and let stand for at least 1 hour. To serve, place mushrooms on lettuce leaves and garnish with green onion tops (or chives) and parsley. Serves 10 to 12.

GREEN PEA SALAD

2 8-1/2 oz. cans early peas
4 hard-boiled eggs, chopped
4 green onions, sliced
4 stalks celery, chopped
2/3 C. mayonnaise
1 t. lemon juice
Salt and pepper to taste
Cayenne to taste
Lettuce leaves

Drain peas. Combine with remaining ingredients. Chill for at least 1 hour. Serve on lettuce leaves. Serves 8.

BENEDICTINE SALAD

1 ripe avocado
3 oz. cream cheese, at room temperature
1 T. lemon juice
Dash paprika
1 T. Worcestershire sauce
4 lettuce leaves
4 thick slices tomato
   OR 4 slices tomato aspic
4 deviled egg halves
1/2 C. mayonnaise
3 T. chili sauce

Combine avocado, cream cheese, lemon juice, paprika and Worcestershire sauce. On each lettuce leaf, place a slice of tomato (or aspic) and a deviled egg half, upside down. Cover with avocado mixture. Serve with dressing made by combining mayonnaise and chili sauce. Serves 4.

AVOCADO BOATS

3 ripe avocados
1 C. vinegar and oil salad dressing
6 lettuce leaves
10-1/2 oz. can beef consommé, chilled
1 C. dairy sour cream
2 T. small-grain black caviar

Peel, halve and pit avocados. Marinate 3 hours in salad dressing, turning occasionally. To serve, place avocado half on lettuce. Fill cavity with jellied consommé, generous dab of sour cream and 1 t. caviar. (Note: For a dinner salad, jellied consommé may be omitted.) Serves 6.

TOMATOES VINAIGRETTE

1/2 C. salad oil
3 T. red wine vinegar
1 t. Worcestershire sauce
1 scant t. salt
1 t. sugar
1 t. basil

1 T. chopped green onion
Dash thyme
Dash pepper
1 clove garlic, minced
4 tomatoes, peeled and sliced

Combine all ingredients except tomatoes. Refrigerate for 24 hours. The next morning, spoon vinaigrette over tomato slices and refrigerate until serving time. (Marinade may be reserved and used again.) Serves 6 to 8.

LAYERED VEGETABLE SALAD

2 to 3 C. fresh spinach, chopped
1 t. salt
1/4 t. pepper
1 T. sugar
1 lb. bacon, fried and crumbled
6 hard-boiled eggs, sliced
2 to 3 C. lettuce, shredded
8 oz. can water chestnuts, sliced
1 t. salt
1/4 t. pepper
1 T. sugar
10 oz. pkg. frozen peas, uncooked, thawed
1/2 C. Bermuda onions or scallions, sliced
1 C. mayonnaise
1 C. Miracle Whip
1 C. Swiss cheese, grated

Sprinkle raw spinach over bottom of 2-1/2 qt. flat casserole. Sprinkle salt, pepper and sugar over spinach. Top with bacon, sliced eggs, lettuce, water chestnuts, additional salt, pepper and sugar, peas and onions. Combine mayonnaise and Miracle Whip and spread over top. Sprinkle with grated cheese. Refrigerate for at least 12 hours before serving. Serves 8 to 12.

luncheon salads

APRICOT SOUFFLÉ RING WITH CHICKEN SALAD

Soufflé Ring:
1 C. apricot juice (from can of apricots)
1 C. apricot nectar
6 oz. lemon jello
2 C. heavy cream, whipped
Fresh mint leaves for garnish
Paprika

Chicken Salad:
1 large onion, sliced
4 stalks celery with leaves, sliced
Salt and pepper
4 whole chicken breasts
8 hard-boiled eggs, chopped
3 to 4 stalks celery, chopped
1/2 C. white grapes (optional)
1/4 C. chopped pecans (optional)
3/4 C. mayonnaise

Bring apricot juice and apricot nectar to a boil. Add jello and stir until dissolved. Chill until mixture is consistency of honey. (Check after 45 minutes.) Fold into whipped cream and chill in 6 C. ring mold.

Meanwhile, place onion, celery, salt and pepper in large kettle of water. Bring to boil and add chicken breasts. Simmer 1 hour, or until tender. Remove breasts and chill. Skin and bone chicken and cut into cubes. Add eggs, celery, grapes and nuts. Add only enough mayonnaise to mix thoroughly, but not to saturate.

Dip soufflé ring very quickly in hot water and unmold on round serving platter. Mound chicken salad in center of ring. Dust with paprika and garnish with fresh mint leaves. Serves 8 to 10.

SEA DREAM SALAD

7-1/2 oz. can crabmeat
1 C. rice, cooked
10 oz. pkg. frozen peas, cooked
3 stalks celery, chopped
1/3 C. green onions, sliced
1/2 C. dairy sour cream
1 C. mayonnaise
1 T. salad seasoning
1 T. lemon juice
Salt and pepper to taste
Leaf lettuce
Curry powder

Combine crabmeat, rice, peas, celery, green onions, sour cream, mayonnaise, salad seasoning, lemon juice and salt and pepper to taste. Chill 24 hours. Serve on bed of lettuce and garnish lightly with curry powder. Serves 4.

TACO SALAD

1 lb. lean ground beef
15 oz. can kidney beans, drained
1/4 t. salt
2 T. water
1 onion, chopped
4 tomatoes, peeled and quartered
1 head lettuce, torn
1-1/2 C. cheddar cheese, grated
1 C. Italian dressing
Hot sauce, to taste
1 large avocado, peeled and diced
10 oz. pkg. tortilla chips
1 large tomato, peeled and quartered
1 large avocado, peeled and sliced
Taco sauce (optional)

Brown beef and drain fat from pan. Add kidney beans, salt and water. Simmer 10 minutes and cool. Toss onion, tomatoes, lettuce and cheddar cheese with Italian dressing and hot sauce. Add avocado. Mix meat into salad mixture. Crush tortilla chips slightly and toss with salad just before serving. Garnish with tomato and avocado slices. Serve at once, and pass a bowl of taco sauce for those who like even more taco flavor. Serves 8 to 10.

PINEAPPLE TURKEY LUNCHEON SALAD

8 C. chicken OR turkey, cooked and diced
2 8-oz. cans water chestnuts, thinly-sliced
2 lbs. seedless green grapes
2 C. celery, thinly-sliced
2-1/2 C. toasted slivered almonds
2-1/2 C. mayonnaise
1 T. curry powder
2 T. soy sauce
Lettuce leaves
28 oz. can pineapple tidbits, well-drained

Combine chicken or turkey with water chestnuts, grapes, celery and half of the almonds. Mix mayonnaise with curry powder and soy sauce; toss with chicken mixture. Chill. Spoon onto lettuce leaves and garnish with remaining almonds and pineapple tidbits. Serves 16.

TURKEY SPINACH SALAD

1 bag fresh spinach, torn
1 head leaf lettuce, torn
1 head iceberg lettuce, torn
1/2 lb. fresh bean sprouts
    OR 16 oz. can bean sprouts, well-drained
8 oz. can or jar ripe olives, drained and sliced
4 oz. Roquefort or blue cheese, crumbled
2/3 lb. bacon, fried and crumbled
6 C. turkey, cooked and diced
8 oz. fresh mushrooms, sliced

Dressing:
1 quart mayonnaise
1/2 C. ketchup
1/2 C. pickle relish
4 hard-boiled eggs, chopped
2 T. grated onion and juice
1 t. curry powder

Combine salad ingredients; combine dressing ingredients. Toss and serve. Serves 12.

AVOCADO FROSTED SHRIMP MOLD

2 lbs. fresh shrimp
2 1/4-oz. envelopes seafood seasoning
1-1/2 C. rice, uncooked
1/3 C. Bermuda onion, chopped
Salt and pepper to taste
1 C. mayonnaise
1 T. Worcestershire sauce
2 dashes Tabasco sauce
1 T. lemon juice
Dash garlic powder
1 small green pepper, chopped
1/3 C. celery, chopped

Avocado Frosting:
3 avocados
Salt to taste
3 dashes Tabasco sauce
2 T. lemon juice
1/4 C. mayonnaise
1 T. onion juice

Cook shrimp in boiling water with seafood seasoning. Drain, cool, shell and devein shrimp. Set aside. Cook rice until firm in 2-1/4 C. salted water. Remove from heat and mix in onions. Add salt and pepper to taste. Combine mayonnaise, Worcestershire sauce, Tabasco sauce, lemon juice and garlic powder. In large bowl, combine rice mixture, mayonnaise mixture, shrimp, green pepper and celery. Press into 6 C. ring mold greased with mayonnaise. Chill. To prepare frosting, mash avocados; mix with remaining ingredients and blend until smooth. Just before serving, unmold rice ring. Cover with avocado frosting. Fill center and garnish platter with shrimp. Serves 6 to 8.

dressings & sauces

CAPER DRESSING

2 C. salad oil
2/3 C. white vinegar
2 cloves garlic, mashed
2 t. salt
Freshly-ground pepper
1/4 C. parsley, finely-chopped
10 T. capers, drained

Mix all ingredients well and refrigerate. Makes 2-2/3 C. dressing.

RAM DRESSING

1 pint mayonnaise
6 T. vinegar
2 t. horseradish
2 t. Worcestershire sauce
1 clove garlic, mashed fine
1/2 t. paprika

Place all ingredients in blender jar and mix well. Store in refrigerator. Makes 1 pint dressing.

ROQUEFORT DRESSING

Juice of 1 lemon
4 t. onion, grated
1 C. dairy sour cream
3 oz. pkg. Roquefort cheese
2 C. mayonnaise

Blend all ingredients and chill. Flavor improves with age. Makes 3 C. dressing.

VINAIGRETTE DRESSING

2 T. wine vinegar
Dash salt
Dash freshly-ground pepper
1 t. Dijon mustard
6 T. olive oil
Dash fines herbes (optional)

Combine vinegar, salt, pepper and mustard. Add olive oil 1 T. at a time, beating well after each addition. Add optional fines herbes. Store in refrigerator, but bring to room temperature before serving. Makes 1/2 C. dressing.

RÉMOULADE SAUCE

2 C. mayonnaise
2 eggs, hard-cooked and sieved
2 T. Dijon mustard
2 T. parsley, chopped
2 T. lemon juice
1 T. horseradish
1 clove garlic, crushed
1 t. anchovy paste (optional)

Combine all ingredients and chill for 1 hour. Serve on shrimp or crab salad (Also good as a cocktail dip.) Makes 2 C. sauce.

BLENDER MAYONNAISE

1 whole egg
2 egg yolks
1/2 t. salt
1/2 t. dry mustard
3 T. lemon juice
1/8 t. white pepper
1/4 C. salad oil
3/4 C. salad oil

Place egg, yolks, salt, mustard, lemon juice, pepper and 1/4 C. oil in blender jar. Cover and blend for 1 or 2 seconds on high. Remove lid and pour 3/4 C. oil very slowly into mixture while still blending. Store in refrigerator. Makes 1-1/4 pint.

RED FRENCH DRESSING

1/2 C. sugar
2/3 C. vinegar
2 t. Worcestershire sauce
2 t. dry mustard
1 t. salt
10-1/2 oz. can tomato soup, undiluted
Dash Tabasco sauce
1/2 clove garlic
1 C. vegetable oil

Blend all ingredients well. Store in refrigerator. Makes 2 C. dressing.

CREAMY FRENCH DRESSING

1/2 C. white wine vinegar
2 t. lemon juice
1 raw egg, slightly-beaten
3/4 C. heavy cream
1 C. salad oil
1 to 2 cloves garlic, mashed
2 t. Dijon mustard
1 t. Worcestershire sauce
2 t. salt
Freshly-ground pepper
1/2 t. white pepper
Dash sugar

Place all ingredients in blender jar and blend well. Chill. Makes 1 pint.

BLENDER HOLLANDAISE SAUCE

1 C. butter
4 egg yolks
2 T. lemon juice
1/8 t. to 1/4 t. salt
Pinch cayenne

Heat butter until bubbling. Place egg yolks, lemon juice, salt and cayenne into blender jar. Cover and blend on high speed briefly. Remove cover and add hot butter in steady stream while blender continues to run. Store in refrigerator, but serve at room temperature. Makes 1-1/4 C. sauce.

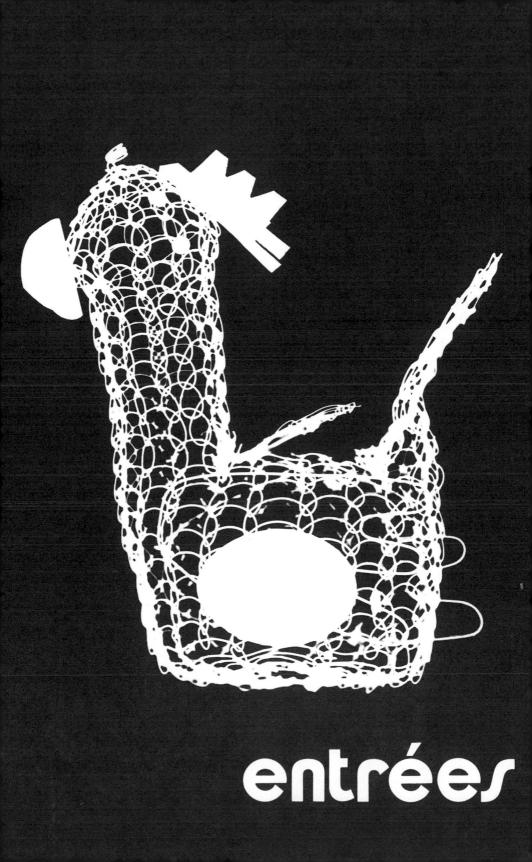

entrées

This is your big scene. Don't rush—play it to the hilt. If you've had a first course, guests are willing to wait. If you are inviting guests to the table from cocktails, don't announce dinner until you're completely satisfied with how everything looks. Present the food as something special, and everyone will think it is.

Parsley should be at the top of your shopping list before a party. It's an easy, inexpensive way to garnish any entrée, vegetable or salad. (For a parsley garnish with a different texture, deep-fry parsley bouquets, a few at a time, for 2 seconds in 380° oil, drain and salt lightly.)

If the meat is difficult to carve, you may want to do it in the kitchen and arrange the slices to make an attractive platter. The entrée, itself, can often give you an idea for an unusual garnish; think of what tastes compliment each other. Pitted prunes stuffed with large pecans look appetizing around a rolled roast of pork, thin, halved orange slices over the top of a roast chicken, or lemon twists with fish fillets, each on a base of parsley.

veal

VEAL IN WINE

3/4 lb. fresh mushrooms, sliced
1 onion, chopped fine
1/2 C. butter
1-3/4 lb. veal, pounded thin
1 C. parsley, chopped
1 C. white wine
Salt and pepper to taste
Garlic salt to taste

Sauté mushrooms and onion in butter until tender. Add veal and sauté quickly over moderately-high heat. Add parsley, wine and seasonings. Reduce heat and simmer 10 minutes. Serves 4.

VEAL PARMESAN

6 veal cutlets
1 C. flour
2 eggs, beaten
1 C. Italian bread crumbs
1 C. Parmesan cheese, grated
1/2 C. olive oil
1 clove garlic
3 C. Italian spaghetti sauce
6 slices mozzarella cheese
1/2 C. Parmesan cheese, grated

Dip each cutlet first into flour, then into eggs, and finally into bread crumbs combined with Parmesan cheese. Arrange cutlets on cookie sheet and place in refrigerator for 2 hours to set coating. Brown on each side in olive oil to which a clove of garlic has been added. Drain on absorbent paper. Arrange cutlets in 9" x 13" serving casserole and pour spaghetti sauce over top. Arrange one slice of mozzarella cheese on each cutlet and sprinkle with remaining 1/2 C. Parmesan cheese. Bake 30 minutes at 350°. Serves 6.

VEAL SUPREME

1/4 C. flour
1/2 t. salt
1/4 t. pepper
1-1/2 to 2 lbs. veal steak
   OR 4 veal chops
1/4 C. butter
10-1/2 oz. can cream of chicken soup
1/4 C. white wine
1 onion, sliced
1 green pepper, sliced

Combine flour, salt and pepper and coat veal. Sauté in butter until golden. Add soup, wine, onion and green pepper. Cook over medium heat 1 hour, or until veal is tender. Serve over rice. Serves 4.

VEAL STROGANOFF

6 slices bacon
2 lbs. veal
2 lg. yellow onions, chopped
3/4 lb. fresh mushrooms, sliced
2 C. dairy sour cream
1 C. white wine
1 C. white rice, uncooked

Cook bacon and set aside. Cut veal into large bite-size pieces and brown in bacon grease. Set aside. Brown onions and mushrooms. Return veal to pan. Combine sour cream and wine and stir into pan. Cover and simmer slowly for 2 hours, stirring occasionally. Cook rice according to package directions. Layer with veal in buttered baking dish. (May be prepared ahead to this point and refrigerated.) One hour before serving, crumble bacon on top and bake, uncovered, at 300° for 1 hour, or until piping hot. Serves 6.

ham

MISSOURI COUNTRY HAM

1 Missouri country-cured ham
1/2 C. vinegar
2 C. brown sugar
Whole cloves

Soak ham in cold water for 24 hours. Place in roaster half full of water with 1/2 C. vinegar. Bake at 375° 20 minutes per pound, or until the butt end of ham becomes loose. Remove skin and cover with brown sugar; score and decorate with cloves. Bake at 400° to 425° for 20 minutes. Serve sliced very thin, 24 hours after cooking.

VIRGINIA SUGAR-CURED HAM

1 Virginia sugar-cured ham
Whole cloves
1 C. brown sugar
3 oranges
1 C. dry sherry

Soak ham overnight in cool water. Pour off water and place in large boiler, skin side up; cover with cold water. Let come to boiling point and simmer, 20 minutes per pound, from the time it begins to simmer (or cook to 170° on meat thermometer). Add warm water as needed to keep ham covered. Lift from boiler and remove skin while warm. Place in uncovered baking pan. Stud with cloves 1" apart. Mix brown sugar with the juice and grated rind of 3 oranges. Spread over ham and bake in 400° oven for 20 to 30 minutes, or until well-glazed. Baste during glazing period with sherry.

129

HAM EN CROÛTE

10 to 12 lb. cooked smoked ham
1 C. orange marmalade
2 T. horseradish
2 T. cider vinegar
1 t. prepared mustard
6 C. flour
4 t. baking powder
1-3/4 t. salt
1 t. dry mustard
1/4 t. sage
1 C. shortening
1-1/2 to 1-3/4 C. cold milk

Trim rind and fat on ham to 1/4". Score fat and place ham in roasting pan. Combine marmalade, horseradish, vinegar and mustard to make glaze, and cover ham generously with half of glaze. Roast, uncovered, at 300° for 2 hours, basting frequently with glaze from pan.

Meanwhile prepare dough. Sift flour with baking powder, salt, mustard and sage. With pastry blender, cut in shortening until mixture resembles coarse meal. Gradually add enough milk to make a soft, but not sticky, dough. On lightly-floured board, knead dough 1 minute and shape into smooth ball.

Roll dough out to 1/4" thick rectangle. Place ham in center of dough. Spread ham with remaining glaze. Fold dough over ham, covering it completely. Reserve trimmings. Moisten edges to seal. Make hole in top to allow steam to escape. Decorate with leaves, flowers, etc., cut from pastry trimmings. Bake on large baking sheet in 450° oven for 10 minutes. Lower temperature to 350° and bake for 15 minutes more, brushing with cold milk 2 times during baking period. Serve hot or cold. (If served hot, make extra portion of glaze to spoon over ham and pastry slice as served.) Serves 20 to 24.

JAMAICAN HAM STEAK

2-1/2 lb. center slice cooked ham, 1-1/2" thick
1 cantaloupe
1 fresh pineapple
2 T. melted butter
3 T. honey
1/4 C. lime juice
Dash nutmeg
Parsley

To prepare ham slice, slash outer layer of fat at 2" intervals. Peel cantaloupe and cut into 6 rings, removing seeds. Cut each ring in half. Peel and core pineapple and slice into 6 rings. Cut each ring in half. Place butter, honey, lime juice and nutmeg in saucepan. Heat, stirring until blended. Brush both sides of ham with sauce. Grill ham 6" above medium-hot coals for 16 to 20 minutes, turning occasionally and basting frequently with sauce. Ten minutes before ham is done, baste melon and pineapple slices with sauce and place on grill. Cook fruit, turning and basting often until glazed and lightly-browned, about 10 minutes. Slice ham across the grain and arrange slices attractively in center of large platter. Place alternating slices of melon and pineapple around edge of platter, filling in with parsley. Pass remaining sauce. Serves 6.

HAM ROLLS

1-1/2 lbs. ground ham
3/4 lb. ground pork
3/4 lb. ground beef
2 eggs
1 C. oatmeal
1-1/2 C. milk
1 t. salt
Dash powdered cloves
Dash cayenne
3/4 C. red wine vinegar
1-1/2 C. water
2-1/4 C. brown sugar
1-1/2 C. raisins

Combine first 9 ingredients in a large bowl. Shape into rolls, using 1/2 C. mixture for each, and place in baking pan. Heat remaining ingredients for sauce and pour over ham rolls. Bake, uncovered, at 250° for 2-1/2 hours, turning and basting with sauce twice during baking period. Serves 10.

SURPRISE PACKAGE

10 oz. box frozen patty shells
1/2 C. onion, minced
3 T. butter
1/2 lb. fresh mushrooms, sliced
2 t. lemon juice
2 T. flour
2-1/2 C. cooked ham, diced
1/2 C. Swiss cheese, grated

Thaw patty shells. Sauté onion in butter for 2 minutes. Add mushrooms. Sprinkle with lemon juice and cook 2-1/2 minutes. Sprinkle with flour and cook 1 minute, stirring. Add ham and cheese. Make a big ball out of patty shell dough. Roll out and cut to a 13" square, reserving trimmings. Place on cookie sheet and mound filling in center. Fold corners of dough to center, over filling. Seal edges by placing strips made from dough trimmings over seams. Seal by brushing edges with small amount of water and pressing together. Bake 35 to 40 minutes at 375°. Serves 4 to 6.

CRÊPES FLORENTINE

12 Luncheon Crêpes, see pg. 223
1/2 lb. fresh mushrooms, finely-chopped
2 T. butter
10 oz. box chopped frozen spinach
1/3 C. dry onion soup mix
2 C. cooked ham, finely-chopped
6 T. flour
6 T. butter
2 C. milk
1 C. Swiss cheese, grated
1/2 t. Worcestershire sauce

Prepare crêpes. Sauté mushrooms in butter. Cook spinach and drain well. Add spinach, dry soup mix and ham to mushrooms. Set aside. Blend flour into melted butter in a saucepan. Gradually add milk, stirring constantly. Cook until thickened. Add cheese and Worcestershire sauce and heat until cheese is melted. Blend 1/2 C. of sauce into the ham mixture; fill crêpes with ham mixture and roll up, jelly-roll fashion. Place in 1 layer in greased baking dish, seam-side down. Spoon remaining sauce over top of filled crêpes. Cover and heat in 350° oven for 15 to 20 minutes. Serves 6.

pork

COLD BARBEQUED LOIN OF PORK

5 to 6 lb. pork loin roast, boned and tied
   OR equivalent amounts pork tenderloins
Dry mustard
Thyme
3/4 C. dry sherry
1/2 C. Japanese soy sauce
3 cloves garlic, chopped
2 T. fresh ginger, grated
8 oz. currant jelly
1 T. soy sauce
2 T. dry sherry
Parsley
Cherry tomatoes
2 C. applesauce
3 T. horseradish

Rub roast with dry mustard and thyme. Prepare marinade of sherry, 1/2 C. soy sauce, garlic and ginger; pour over roast and marinate for 2 hours at room temperature, turning frequently. Remove roast from marinade and roast, uncovered, 30 minutes per pound at 325°. Baste every 20 minutes with marinade. Remove from oven when meat reaches a temperature of 170°.

Melt the jelly in a heavy pan. When bubbly, add 1 T. soy sauce and 2 T. sherry. Cook for 2 minutes. Spoon over pork and cool in a chilly room. Do not refrigerate unless day is very hot. Garnish with parsley and cherry tomatoes. Combine applesauce and horseradish and serve with roast. Serves 10.

CROWN ROAST PORK

10 to 13 lb. crown roast of pork
OR full rib section of pork loin
4 t. salt
Freshly ground pepper
2 C. orange juice
1 C. brown sugar
2 T. ground ginger
1/2 t. ground cloves
1/2 C. dry sherry
1 T. flour
1 T. water
1 T. orange juice
Orange wedges for garnish

(If using pork loin roast, cut all ingredient amounts in half.) Season roast with salt and pepper. Place in 300° oven and roast, 35 minutes per pound. Combine orange juice, sugar, spices and sherry and pour over meat the last hour of baking, basting often. Prepare sauce by combining pan juices, flour, water and orange juice. Crown roast serves 10 to 14 people; pork loin serves 8 to 10 people. Garnish with orange wedges.

SWEET AND SOUR PORK

1-1/2 lbs. pork tenderloin
1/4 C. oil
1/2 C. water
20 oz. can pineapple chunks
1/2 C. brown sugar
1/4 C. cornstarch
3/4 C. pineapple juice
1/2 C. cider vinegar
1/4 C. soy sauce
1/2 t. salt
1 green pepper, cut into thin strips
1/2 onion, sliced thin

Cut pork into 2" x 1/2" strips. Brown slowly in hot oil. Add water; cover and simmer 1 hour. Drain pineapple, reserving syrup. Combine brown sugar and cornstarch; add reserved syrup, pineapple juice, vinegar, soy sauce and salt. Cook over low heat, stirring constantly, until thickened. Pour over hot cooked pork; let stand 10 minutes. Add pineapple, green pepper and onion. Cook 2 to 3 minutes. Serve over rice. Serves 6.

BAKED PORK CHOPS

6 loin pork chops, 1" thick
3 T. brown sugar
3/4 C. ketchup OR chili sauce
6 onion slices
6 lemon slices

Place chops in baking pan in single layer. Salt and pepper to taste. Spread 2 t. brown sugar and 2 T. ketchup on each chop. Top with slice of onion and slice of lemon. Add enough water to reach a level halfway up on chops. Bake, covered, at 350° for 2-1/2 to 3 hours. Uncover last half-hour of cooking. Serves 6.

BARBEQUED SPARERIBS

2-1/2 lbs. spareribs
1 to 2 T. oil
Seasoned salt and pepper
1 large onion, thinly-sliced
3/4 C. ketchup
1/2 C. vinegar
2 t. chili powder
1 t. salt
1/3 C. Worcestershire sauce
4 dashes Tabasco sauce
1 T. liquid smoke
1 t. barbeque spice

Cut through membranes of ribs in several places so that they will lie flat. Brown ribs in heavy skillet in oil. Place in roasting pan. Sprinkle with seasoned salt and pepper and scatter thinly-sliced onions on top. Combine remaining ingredients; heat and pour over ribs. Cover and bake 2 hours at 325°. During last hour, baste with sauce every 15 minutes. Serves 4.

MOCK DUCK

2 pork tenderloins, 1 lb. each
1-1/2 C. poultry stuffing mix
1 cooking apple, pared and chopped
2 T. butter
1 t. salt
1/2 t. pepper
3 T. onion, chopped
4 strips bacon
1 beef bouillon cube
1/2 C. water
1 T. melted butter
1 T. flour

Slice tenderloins almost to edge and open flat. Pound with rolling pin. Combine stuffing mix and apple and spread on one tenderloin. Place the other tenderloin on top and tie securely. Brown on all sides quickly in hot butter. Transfer to casserole longer and wider than tenderloins. Sprinkle with salt and pepper and cover with chopped onion. Place bacon over top. Cover and bake at 325° for 1-1/2 hours. Remove to hot platter. Skim fat and thicken sauce with 1 T. melted butter combined with 1 T. flour. Strain sauce and serve with sliced tenderloins. Serves 8.

PORK AND APPLE BAKE

8 pork chops, 1/2" thick
1/4 C. oil
Salt and pepper
4 C. bread crumbs, toasted
1-1/2 C. apples, unpeeled and chopped
3/4 C. celery, chopped
3/4 C. onion, chopped
1/2 C. raisins
1-1/2 t. sage
1-1/2 t. salt
1/4 t. pepper
1 beef bouillon cube
1 C. water
1 large apple, unpeeled, cut into wedges

Brown pork chops in oil. Season to taste with salt and pepper. Combine remaining ingredients except apple wedges and place in buttered 3-qt. casserole. Arrange pork chops and apple wedges on top. Cover and bake at 350° for 45 minutes. Serves 8.

SAUSAGE RING

2 lbs. medium-hot sausage
1-1/2 C. cracker crumbs
2 eggs
1/2 C. milk
1/4 C. onion, minced
1 C. apples, unpeeled and finely-chopped
Parsley sprigs

Grease 6 C. ring mold. Mix sausage, cracker crumbs, eggs, milk, onion and apples, and press into mold. Place ring mold on cookie sheet to catch any grease overflow, and bake at 350° for 1 hour. Let stand 10 minutes before unmolding. Garnish center of ring with parsley. Serves 8.

SAUSAGE-EGGS SUPREME

8 slices white bread
1-1/2 lbs. link sausage, cooked or smoked
1/4 lb. sharp cheddar cheese, grated
4 eggs
2-1/2 C. milk
1 t. prepared mustard
1/2 t. salt
10-1/2 oz. can cream of mushroom soup
1/2 C. milk

Remove crusts from bread and cube. Place in 7" x11" buttered casserole. Cut sausage into bite-size pieces and place on top of bread cubes. Add cheese. Combine eggs, milk, mustard and salt. Pour over cheese. Cover and refrigerate overnight. Combine mushroom soup and milk. Pour over top and bake, uncovered, for 1-1/2 hours at 300 °. Serves 6.

lamb

LAMB WELLINGTON

2 10-oz. or 11-oz. pkgs.
  pie crust mix
4 lb. (net) boned leg of lamb
Garlic salt
Salt and pepper
1/2 C. butter

2 t. rosemary, crushed
Garlic clove
1 egg white, unbeaten
6 oz. mint jelly
2 oz. bottled mint sauce

Prepare pie crust according to package directions and roll out so that it is double the size of the lamb. Season lamb with garlic salt. Rub inside and outside of lamb with salt and pepper. Stuff center with butter, rosemary and peeled garlic clove. Tie or sew opening closed. Place lamb on pastry and fold up, envelope-style. Pinch edges together after lamb is completely blanketed inside crust. Brush with egg white. Bake, uncovered, in 350° oven, 30 minutes per pound of lamb. Heat mint jelly and mint sauce together and serve with lamb. Serves 8.

LAMB SHANKS

4 lamb shanks, sawed in half
Seasoned salt
2 T. oil
2 chicken bouillon cubes

1 C. water
2 bay leaves
1/4 C. lemon juice
2 T. flour

Sprinkle each piece of lamb with seasoned salt and brown in oil in heavy skillet or Dutch oven. Dissolve bouillon cubes in water and add to meat, together with bay leaves and lemon juice. Bring to a boil; reduce heat and simmer, covered, until tender, about 2 hours. Lift shanks out and set aside. Remove bay leaves and grease from drippings. Thicken pan juices by stirring 2 T. of drippings into the 2 T. flour. Return to pan and stir until well blended and thickened. Spoon sauce over shanks. Serves 4.

CROWN ROAST OF LAMB WITH PILAF

Crown roast of lamb, with 20 chops
Garlic clove
Dash thyme OR oregano
Salt and pepper

1/2 C. dry white wine
1/2 C. water
Salt and pepper
3 T. butter
Parsley
20 paper frills for bone ends

Pilaf:
1/4 C. onion, minced
1 clove garlic, minced
1/4 C. butter
3 C. long-grain rice, uncooked
1/2 C. golden raisins
5 C. (or more) chicken broth
3 T. butter
2 T. Parmesan cheese, grated
1 C. thinly-sliced onions, halved
2 T. butter
1 T. oil
1/2 C. pine nuts
1 C. mushrooms, thinly-sliced
2 T. parsley, minced
Salt and pepper

Rub lamb well with garlic clove; sprinkle with thyme or oregano and salt and pepper. Put lamb in pan just large enough to hold it; remove top and bottom of tin can and place it in the center of the roast (to help the roast brown and keep its shape). Cover bone ends of chops with foil. Place in 400° oven for 20 minutes. Reduce heat to 325° and roast the lamb, basting several times, for 50 minutes more.

Meanwhile, prepare pilaf: Sauté onion and garlic in butter. Add rice, stirring until well coated. Add raisins and enough chicken broth to cover rice by 3/4". Bring to boil over high heat. Transfer to preheated 350° oven and bake, covered, for 20 to 25 minutes. Transfer to large bowl, add butter and Parmesan cheese and fluff with fork. Keep hot. Sauté sliced onions in butter and oil. Transfer onions with slotted spoon to a bowl. In same skillet, sauté pine nuts, tossing them until golden. Drain nuts on paper towel. In same skillet, sauté mushrooms, adding more butter if necessary. Combine all ingredients with rice and season pilaf with salt and pepper.

Transfer roast to platter; fill cavity with pilaf, mounding it, and keep hot. Pour off fat from roasting pan; add wine and water and combine with pan drippings. Reduce the liquid over high heat by half, and season with salt and pepper. Remove from heat and swirl in 3 T. butter. Strain juices around roast; garnish center of rice with sprig of parsley, and garnish platter with parsley bouquets. Replace foil on bone ends with paper frills. Serves 8.

BUTTERFLIED LEG OF LAMB

2 C. red wine
1 C. oil
1/4 C. red wine vinegar
1 t. monosodium glutamate
1 T. Worcestershire sauce
2 cloves garlic, mashed
2 t. rosemary
1 t. salt
Freshly-ground pepper
2 T. brown sugar
Chopped parsley (optional)
6 to 7 lb. leg of lamb,
  boned and butterflied
1 T. Schilling's Au Jus Mix
2 T. butter
Watercress

Make a marinade by combining wine, oil, vinegar, monosodium glutamate, Worcestershire sauce, garlic, rosemary, salt, pepper, brown sugar and parsley, if desired. Marinate lamb for 24 hours in refrigerator. Remove from marinade, reserving marinade for sauce. Grill over charcoal for 40 to 50 minutes, basting with marinade occasionally. (May also be baked in oven for 40 to 50 minutes at 450°, or until meat thermometer registers medium-rare.) Meat should be crisp on outside and pink on the inside.

Prepare sauce by combining marinade and au jus mix. Skim off oil and add butter. (Add any pan juices if meat has been roasted in oven). Correct seasoning. Slice lamb on the diagonal and garnish with watercress. Serve with warm sauce. Serves 6 to 8.

ROAST RACK OF LAMB

2 racks of lamb, shinbones removed
  and bones trimmed
2 cloves garlic, crushed
1 t. monosodium glutamate
1 T. Worcestershire sauce
1 t. rosemary
2 to 3 T. soft butter
Freshly ground pepper

Sauce:
6 oz. chili sauce
10 oz. currant jelly
1/4 C. butter
2 T. mint sauce OR mint jelly

Score fat side of the racks. Mix garlic, monosodium glutamate, Worcestershire sauce, rosemary and butter and spread over scoring. Grind pepper over top. (May be prepared day ahead to this point.) Bring lamb to room temperature before baking. Place lamb in an open pan and bake at 400° for 20 to 25 minutes. Place all sauce ingredients in saucepan and blend over medium heat. Serve sauce with lamb. Serves 6.

beef

FILLETS OF BEEF WITH ARTICHOKE SAUCE

14 oz. can artichoke hearts, drained
1/4 C. butter
1 T. lemon juice
1 T. lemon rind, grated
1/4 C. dry vermouth

4 1"-thick slices dark Russian Rye
  OR pumpernickel bread
1-1/2 to 2 T. butter
4 thick slices from tenderloin
  OR 4 fillets

Mash artichoke hearts with butter, lemon juice, lemon rind and vermouth. Set aside. Butter bread with 1-1/2 to 2 T. butter and warm in oven until butter is melted and bread is very hot. Broil meat to desired doneness. Place a piece of bread on plate, a piece of broiled meat on top of bread, and cover generously with hot artichoke sauce. Serves 4.

FILLETS OF TENDERLOIN FLAMBÉ

1/4 C. butter
1/4 C. shallots, finely chopped
Freshly-ground black pepper
6 fillets of tenderloin, 3/4" thick
Few drops olive oil
1-1/2 oz. brandy

In large flambé pan, melt butter. Add shallots and sauté until transparent. Remove from heat and let rest 30 minutes. Press pepper into both sides of fillets. Dribble a few drops of olive oil on each side of fillets. Return to heat and bring shallot butter to bubbling. Sizzle fillets for 2 minutes on one side and 1 minute on other side. Heat brandy, pour over fillets and ignite. Cover and when flame dies serve at once, spooning pan juices over each fillet. Serves 6.

TOURNEDOS - THREE WAYS

Sauté 4 1" - thick beef fillets in 2 T. butter and 2 T. oil, cooking 3 to 4 minutes per side. Salt lightly. Remove to warm platter.

Béarnaise Sauce:

1 T. tarragon wine vinegar	3 egg yolks
2 T. dry white wine	Pinch salt
2 T. shallots, chopped	3/4 C. butter
Dash freshly-ground pepper	Watercress

Combine tarragon vinegar, wine, shallots and pepper in saucepan and cook until almost all liquid is evaporated. Cool slightly. Place egg yolks, salt and tarragon mixture in blender. Melt butter and heat until bubbly, but not brown. Turn blender on and add butter in steady stream. Serve sauce with fillets and garnish with watercress. (Sauce may be prepared early in day.)

Mushroom-Madeira Sauce:

2 T. butter	8 to 10 fresh mushrooms, sliced
1/2 onion, chopped	2 T. butter
2 stalks celery, chopped	1/2 C. Madeira wine
1 bay leaf	2 t. tomato paste
2 sprigs parsley	2 t. cornstarch
4 peppercorns	2 T. water
2 C. canned beef broth	Salt to taste

Melt butter; sauté onion and celery. Add bay leaf, parsley, peppercorns and broth. Simmer 30 minutes; cool and strain. Sauté mushrooms in butter and set aside. Sauté fillets as directed; pour in cooled broth mixture. Add mushrooms and cook, scraping bottom and sides of pan. Add Madeira and tomato paste. Dissolve cornstarch in water and add, stirring until thickened. Taste, and add more salt and Madeira if necessary. Spoon over fillets.

Tournedos Henry IV:

4 slices white toasting bread	2 T. butter
1/4 C. butter	Dash fresh lemon juice
2 T. oil	Madeira Sauce
4 large fresh mushroom caps	Béarnaise Sauce

Trim crusts from bread, removing small triangles from each corner to make an attractive shape. Sauté in butter and oil until golden on both sides, adding more butter if needed. Remove and set aside. Sauté mushrooms in butter and add the lemon juice. Set aside. Prepare Madeira Sauce, omitting mushrooms; prepare Béarnaise Sauce. Place fillets on toast, spoon Madeira Sauce over and place a mushroom cap, cavity-side-up, on top. Fill mushroom caps with Béarnaise Sauce. Pass remaining Madeira Sauce. All versions serve 4.

BEEF TENDERLOIN

Whole or half beef tenderloin
Lemon pepper

Rub tenderloin all over with lemon pepper until it is well coated. Preheat oven to 450°. Place tenderloin in uncovered baking pan for 45 minutes. Serve immediately.

ROLLED RIB ROAST SUPREME

5 lb. rolled rib roast OR rolled sirloin roast
4 t. salt
1/2 t. pepper
1/4 C. butter
1 onion, grated
1 T. Worcestershire sauce
1 T. A-1 sauce
1/2 C. chili sauce
1 T. butter
3/4 lb. fresh mushrooms, whole or sliced
1/4 t. salt
3 T. butter
3 T. flour
Drippings from pan

Rub roast well with salt and pepper. In Dutch oven or heavy roasting pan, brown meat quickly on all sides in 1/4 C. butter. Cover with onion. Mix Worcestershire sauce, A-1 sauce and chili sauce. Pour over meat and dot with 1 T. butter. Bake 20 minutes per pound for rare in a 325° oven, basting frequently with drippings.

Place mushrooms in top of double boiler with salt and butter. Steam for 20 minutes. Mix meat drippings with flour. Add mushrooms and mushroom liquor; bring to boil and simmer slowly for 3 minutes. Pour over meat. Serves 8.

SAUERBRATEN

4 lb. bottom round roast
  OR chuck steak OR arm roast
Pepper
2 onions, sliced
2 stalks celery, chopped
4 bay leaves
6 peppercorns
1 clove garlic, crushed
2 T. sugar
1 T. salt
1 T. pickling spice
1 C. red wine vinegar
2 C. red wine
1 C. water
1/4 C. butter
2 T. flour
Salt and pepper
12 gingersnap cookies, finely-crushed
1 C. dairy sour cream
Fresh parsley, chopped

Rub meat with pepper. Combine onions, celery, bay leaves, peppercorns, garlic, sugar, salt, pickling spice, red wine vinegar, red wine and water for marinade. Place beef in a glass bowl and pour marinade over until beef is half covered. Refrigerate, and turn meat twice daily for 5 days.

Remove beef, reserving marinade, and dry beef well. Brown beef in butter. Remove beef and stir in flour. Add marinade and bring to boil. Replace beef, season with salt and pepper, cover and cook 3-1/2 hours on top of stove, or in 350° oven. Remove beef and keep warm in 200° oven. Strain marinade into saucepan. Add gingersnaps and beat with wire whisk until dissolved. Blend in sour cream. Slice beef into chafing dish and pour some of the gravy over it. Garnish with parsley and serve with remaining gravy and noodles. Serves 8.

STEAKS AU POIVRE

4 thin fillets OR cube steaks
Freshly ground pepper
2 English muffins, split and buttered
3 T. butter
3 T. cognac
1/2 C. white wine
2 T. butter
1 t. salt
2 T. fresh parsley, chopped

Press coarsely-ground pepper into steaks. Toast buttered English muffins. Sauté steaks in 3 T. butter in large skillet, quickly searing each side. Warm cognac, pour over steaks and ignite. When flame has died, blend in wine, butter and salt. Place steaks on muffin halves; pour pan juices over top and sprinkle with parsley. Serves 4.

FLANK STEAK PINWHEELS

2 2-lb. flank steaks
1/2 t. salt
1/4 t. pepper
1/3 C. Parmesan cheese, grated
2 T. fresh parsley, chopped
2 T. shortening
1 clove garlic, minced
10-1/2 oz. can tomato soup, undiluted
1 t. oregano
1 lemon, sliced
1 lb. spaghetti

Score both sides of steaks 1/8" deep. Rub in salt, pepper, Parmesan cheese and parsley. Roll from short sides and tie with strings. Heat shortening in Dutch oven. Add garlic and steaks and sauté on all sides. Add soup, oregano and lemon. Cover and simmer 1 to 1-1/2 hours, or until fork tender. Cook spaghetti according to package directions. Drain and put on platter. Slice steaks 1/2" thick and place on spaghetti. Remove lemon slices from sauce and pour sauce over meat. Serves 8.

CARPETBAG STEAK

3 lb. sirloin steak, 2" thick
18 fresh or frozen oysters, raw
Salt and pepper
1/2 C. butter
1 T. fresh parsley, chopped
Juice of 1/2 lemon
Salt and pepper to taste

Insert a sharp knife in the center of 1 side of steak. Slice horizontally to within 1" or 2" of the edges of the steak, making a pocket for the stuffing. Stuff the pocket with raw oysters. Sew the open edge together. Broil the steak in a preheated oven 12 to 15 minutes on each side. Meanwhile, combine the butter, parsley, lemon juice and salt and pepper. Combine butter mixture with pan juices and pour over steak. Serves 6.

TERIYAKI SHISH-KABOBS

32 1" cubes top sirloin
24 large fresh mushrooms, whole
3/4 C. vegetable oil
1/2 C. soy sauce
2 T. honey

1-1/2 t. ginger
2 T. vinegar
1 t. garlic powder
2 green onions, sliced

Marinate top sirloin cubes and mushrooms in remaining ingredients for 6 to 8 hours at room temperature. Allow 4 cubes of meat and 3 mushrooms per person and thread alternately on individual wooden skewers. Broil to desired doneness over charcoal. Serves 8.

TERIYAKI FLANK STEAKS

3 1-lb. flank steaks, tenderized
1 C. pineapple juice
1/4 C. soy sauce
1/4 C. dark corn syrup

1 clove garlic, minced
1 t. ginger, chopped
2 T. oil

Be certain that butcher runs steaks through tenderizing machine. Marinate steak for 36 hours in remaining ingredients, turning 3 or 4 times. Broil steaks over charcoal for 5 or 6 minutes on each side. Slice in very thin strips. Serves 6.

BEEF KABOBS

4 lb. sirloin tip roast, cut in 1" cubes
1/2 C. brandy
1/2 C. soy sauce
1/2 C. low-calorie Italian salad dressing
2 T. chives
1 t. garlic powder
1 t. salad herbs
8 small boiling onions
8 large fresh mushrooms
8 cherry tomatoes
1 green pepper, cut into 8 strips

Marinate beef cubes in mixture of brandy, soy sauce, salad dressing, chives, garlic and salad herbs overnight. Thread beef cubes, onions, mushrooms, cherry tomatoes and green pepper pieces on skewers. Broil over charcoal, brushing from time to time with marinade. Serves 8.

HICKORY-SMOKED BRISKET

1 whole brisket, 4 to 6 lbs.
Salt
Dampened hickory chips OR liquid smoke
1-1/2 C. ketchup
3/4 C. brown sugar
3/4 C. chili sauce
1/2 C. white wine vinegar
3/4 C. water
1/2 C. lemon juice
1/4 C. bottled steak sauce
1/4 C. prepared mustard
1 T. celery seed
2 T. Worcestershire sauce
1 clove garlic, minced
Dash Tabasco sauce
Freshly ground pepper to taste

Salt brisket and place on grill away from hot coals. Add dampened hickory chips, or brush meat with liquid smoke and close hood. Barbeque slowly for 4 hours, or until meat is tender. Cool and slice very thin across grain. Line up slices in shallow pan. Combine remaining ingredients and simmer 30 minutes; pour over meat. Heat 1 hour on grill or in 200° oven. Serves 8 to 12.

BAKED BRISKET OF BEEF

2 14-oz. bottles ketchup
14 oz. bottle water
1 large onion, sliced
3/4 C. brown sugar
1/4 C. granulated sugar
1/2 C. vinegar
1 T. celery seed

10 oz. bottled barbeque sauce
1 T. Worcestershire sauce
4 cloves garlic, minced
1 T. cinnamon
Salt to taste
6 lb. brisket
2 T. oil

Combine all ingredients except brisket and oil in saucepan and simmer for 30 minutes. Cool and strain. Brown brisket quickly in hot oil and place on rack of broiler pan. Pour 1/2 C. to 3/4 C. strained sauce over top. Add 1/2 C. to 1 C. water to bottom of broiler pan. Cover meat with foil, sealing edges tightly around pan. Bake 3 hours at 300°. Slice and serve with additional barbeque sauce. Serves 12. Makes 1-1/2 quarts sauce. (Sauce is also good on chicken.)

TENDERLOIN TIP STROGANOFF

8 lbs. tenderloin tips OR sirloin tip
1 lb. butter
3 lbs. fresh mushrooms
6 onions, sliced
5 T. tomato paste
1-1/2 t. paprika
Juice of 1 lemon
5 t. salt
1 t. pepper
7-1/2 C. dairy sour cream
Noodles, cooked
Poppy seeds

Cut meat into 3/4" x 2" or 3" strips. Sear in 1/2 lb. butter. Set aside. In another pan, sauté mushrooms and onions in remaining 1/2 lb. butter, until onions are clear. Add tomato paste, paprika, meat, lemon juice, salt and pepper. Cook *very* slowly for 45 minutes. Add sour cream 20 minutes before serving time and warm slowly, but do not boil. Serve with egg noodles tossed with poppy seeds. Serves 24.

148

CHINESE BEEF AND SNOW PEAS

1 lb. top sirloin, sliced into bite-size pieces
2 T. red wine
2 T. soy sauce
1 T. cornstarch
8 to 12 T. oil
1/2 lb. snow peas (Oriental pea pods)
2 cloves garlic, minced
1 t. sugar
1/4 C. soy sauce

Dry beef well and dredge with wine, soy sauce and cornstarch. In wok or large electric skillet, brown beef quickly in 1/4 C. oil, a little at a time, adding additional oil, 1 T. at a time, as needed. Remove beef to plate. Heat 4 T. more oil in same pan and quickly sauté snow peas until tender but still quite crisp. Return beef to pan, add garlic, sugar and additional 1/4 C. soy sauce. Mix well and serve hot. Good with Chinese fried rice or plain boiled rice. Serves 4.

CURRIED BEEF OR VEAL STEW

3 lbs. beef or veal stew meat
1/2 C. walnuts, chopped
1/2 C. coconut, grated
1/4 C. white corn syrup
10-1/2 oz. can cream of mushroom soup, undiluted
2 T. curry powder

Place meat, walnuts, coconut and corn syrup in deep casserole. Combine soup with curry powder and add. Bake 2-1/2 hours, uncovered, at 325°. Serves 6.

BENGAL CURRY

1/4 C. shortening
4 lbs. chuck roast, cut in 1" cubes
1 C. onion, sliced
2 T. curry powder
2 t. salt
1/2 t. pepper
1/4 t. cloves
1/4 C. crystallized ginger, chopped
1 t. dried mint leaves
1/4 C. flour
3 10-1/2 oz. cans beef bouillon, undiluted
1 C. coconut, shredded
1/4 C. lime juice
1 C. light cream

Pineapple Rice:
1 C. rice, uncooked
2-1/2 C. water
2-1/2 t. salt
1/2 C. water-2-1/2 T. butter
8-1/2 oz. can crushed pineapple, drained

Condiments:
Chopped cashews
Chopped cucumbers
Chutney, see pg. 214
Preserved kumquats

Heat shortening and sauté beef until brown. Remove meat and set aside. In 2 T. drippings, sauté onion, curry powder, salt, pepper, cloves, ginger and mint. Cook 5 minutes. Remove from heat. Add flour and stir until well blended. Gradually stir in bouillon. Add beef, bring mixture to boil, then reduce heat and simmer, covered, for 1-1/2 hours. Cool; cover and refrigerate overnight. When ready to serve, let stand at room temperature 15 minutes then reheat slowly. Stir in coconut, lime juice and cream. Cook 5 minutes.

Cook rice in salted water according to package directions. Cover and refrigerate. Forty minutes before serving, preheat oven to 300°. Turn rice into pan, fluffing with a fork. Sprinkle with 1/2 C. water and heat, covered, for 30 minutes, stirring several times with fork. Add butter and pineapple and mix well. Serve curry over rice with suggested condiments or other condiments of your choice. Serves 8.

BOEUF BOURGUIGNON

1 onion, chopped
2 T. bacon grease or shortening
2 lbs. rump pot roast OR round steak, cut in 1" cubes
2 T. flour
1 t. bouquet garni
1 C. red wine
1 C. beef bouillon
1/2 lb. fresh mushrooms, sliced

Brown onion in bacon fat or shortening, then brown meat. Sprinkle meat with flour and bouquet garni. Add wine and bouillon. Cover tightly and cook 2-1/2 to 3 hours in 300° oven (or on top of stove, adding more liquid if needed). Thirty minutes before serving, add mushrooms. Serve over buttered noodles. Serves 4.

RAGOUT FRANÇAIS

2 lbs. stewing beef, cut in 1-1/2" cubes
2 T. butter
1 T. flour
Salt and pepper
3/4 C. red wine
3/4 C. water
1/2 lb. small white onions
1 large carrot, sliced
1 C. firm white mushrooms
1 clove garlic
1 t. bouquet garni
2 to 3 C. beef bouillon
1 jigger brandy (optional)

Brown beef in melted butter; remove. Add flour to pan juices to make a roux. Season with salt and pepper; add wine and water, stirring. Add onions, carrot, mushrooms and garlic. Return meat to pan and add bouquet garni. Add just enough beef bouillon to cover meat. Cover tightly and simmer 3 to 4 hours over low heat. Add brandy just before serving, if desired. Good served over long grain and wild rice mixture. Serves 6.

FIVE-HOUR STEW

3 lbs. beef stew meat, cubed
1 T. lemon pepper
1 C. dry red wine
2 C. carrots, diced
1 C. celery, diced
1/2 lb. fresh small mushroom caps
20 small boiling onions, parboiled and peeled
20 oz. can tomatoes, with liquid
5 T. minute tapioca
2 slices stale bread
1 T. sugar

Spray a 5-qt. Dutch oven and close-fitting lid with non-stick vegetable coating. Place stew meat, seasoned with lemon pepper, in bottom. Add red wine, carrots, celery, mushrooms, onions and tomatoes. Stir in tapioca. Crumble bread over and add sugar last. Cover and place in 250° oven. Stir *once* after 1-1/2 hours. Allow to cook 5 hours in all. (May be prepared the day ahead and reheated.) Serves 10.

IRISH STEW

4 lb. chuck roast, cubed
Salt and pepper
1 T. Worcestershire sauce
2 T. pickling spice, wrapped in cheesecloth
3 bay leaves
12 oz. bottled chili sauce
2 10-oz. cans Snap-E-Tom
2 garlic cloves, minced
7 oz. ketchup
3 T. sugar
3 potatoes, cubed
3 carrots, diced
6 boiling onions

Brown meat with salt, pepper and Worcestershire sauce. Cover with water and add pickling spice, bay leaves, chili sauce, Snap-E-Tom, garlic, ketchup and sugar. Boil potatoes and carrots just until tender. Drain and add. Boil onions until tender and add with the boiling liquid. Refrigerate for 1 day. To serve, reheat in a 250° oven for 1 hour, or until heated through. Serves 10.

CROCK-POT OLD ENGLISH SHORTRIBS

8 to 14 Old English shortribs
Liquid smoke
Onion powder
Salt
Pepper
Barbeque sauce

Trim excess fat from ribs and cover each rib with liquid smoke. Sprinkle with onion powder, salt and pepper. Place in Crock-pot standing on end. Turn on high setting and cover. Cook for 5 hours. Remove ribs and skim fat from top of meat juices. Return ribs to Crock-pot. Pour barbeque sauce over ribs and turn to low setting for 1 hour to blend sauce with meat juices. Serves 6 to 8.

CHIPPED BEEF À LA RUSSE

2 T. butter
1 heaping T. flour
2 C. dairy sour cream
14 oz. can artichoke hearts, drained and halved
    OR 10 oz. box frozen artichoke hearts, cooked and halved
1/2 lb. dried chipped beef
1/2 C. dry white wine
Dash cayenne
4 slices bread, crusts removed
1/4 C. Parmesan cheese, grated

Make white sauce with butter, flour and sour cream. Add artichoke hearts, beef, wine and cayenne. Cut bread slices in half diagonally and toast. Spoon mixture on toast points and sprinkle Parmesan cheese on top. Serves 4.

CANNELLONI

Pasta:
3 C. flour
1/4 t. salt
3 eggs
1/4 C. water
2 T. olive oil
6 qts. water
1 T. salt

Filling:
1 lb. Italian sausage, cooked
2 C. chicken, cooked and chopped
2 10-oz. pkgs. frozen chopped
   spinach, cooked and drained
1/2 C. Parmesan cheese, grated
1/2 t. thyme
1/4 t. black pepper

Béchamel Sauce:
1/4 C. butter
1/4 C. flour
3 C. milk, heated
3/4 t. salt
3/4 C. Parmesan cheese, grated
3/4 C. Parmesan cheese, grated (opt.)

Red Sauce: (optional)
3/4 C. onion, chopped fine
1/4 C. olive oil
16 oz. can tomato sauce
2 T. tomato paste
1/2 t. Italian seasoning
1/2 t. sugar
1 t. salt
1/2 t. black pepper
3/4 C. Parmesan cheese, grated

To prepare pasta, mix flour and salt in large bowl. Add eggs, water and olive oil. Mix. Knead dough on floured board until smooth. Let rest 20 minutes, covered with towel. Roll out half of dough at a time, as thinly as possible, and cut into 4" squares. Bring water to a boil and add salt. Drop pasta pieces, 3 at a time, into water and cook 2 to 3 minutes. Remove with slotted spoon to bowl of cold water. Remove from cold water and place on damp towels until ready to fill.

Combine filling ingredients, squeezing together with hands to blend well. Place 1 to 2 T. filling along one edge of each piece of pasta and roll up. Place, seam-side down, in greased 7" x 11" baking dish in 1 layer. (Two baking dishes will be needed.)

Make béchamel sauce by melting butter and stirring in flour; cook 1 minute. Add milk, stirring until thickened; mix in salt and Parmesan cheese and spread over cannelloni. If red sauce is not used, sprinkle 3/4 C. Parmesan cheese over béchamel sauce and bake for 30 minutes at 350°.

To make red sauce, sauté onion in oil. Add remaining ingredients (except Parmesan cheese) and simmer until sauce is slightly thickened, about 10 minutes. Spoon red sauce over top of béchamel sauce. Sprinkle with 3/4 C. Parmesan cheese and bake for 30 minutes at 350°. (May be prepared ahead and frozen. Bring to room temperature before final heating.) Serves 8.

ITALIAN SPAGHETTI SAUCE

1 lb. ground beef
1 lb. bulk Italian sausage
1 onion, finely-chopped
1/2 lb. fresh mushrooms, sliced
2 T. Italian seasoning
1 t. paprika
2 12-oz. cans tomato paste
2 15-oz. cans tomato sauce
3/4 C. red wine
1/2 bunch parsley, finely-chopped
1 T. caraway seeds
Salt and pepper to taste

Brown beef and sausage in Dutch oven; drain. Add chopped onion and mushrooms. Cook 5 minutes and add remaining ingredients. Cover and simmer for 1-1/2 hours. (Freezes well.) Serves 6.

BEEF NEOPOLITAN

2 lbs. sirloin tip, cut in 1" cubes
2 T. olive oil
1 t. salt
1/8 t. pepper
6 oz. can sliced mushrooms
1/3 C. dry sherry
16 oz. can stewed tomatoes
10 oz. pkg. frozen chopped spinach, thawed
5-1/2 oz. box Noodles Romanoff
1/2 C. cheddar cheese, grated
1/4 C. Parmesan cheese, grated

Sauté meat in oil until lightly browned. Add salt, pepper, mushrooms, sherry, tomatoes and spinach and heat to boiling. Reduce heat and simmer, covered, for 10 minutes. Add uncooked noodles with seasonings and cheese from package. Mix well. Place in a greased 2-qt. casserole. Top with grated cheddar cheese and bake for 30 minutes, or until noodles are tender. Sprinkle Parmesan cheese over top and serve. Serves 6.

MOCK RAVIOLI

1 large onion, chopped
2 T. oil
2 lbs. ground beef
1 clove garlic, minced
3 oz. tomato paste
1/2 t. thyme
1/2 t. rosemary
8 oz. can tomato sauce
2 10-1/2-oz. cans beef consommé
1/4 lb. fresh mushrooms, sliced
Salt and pepper
3 10-oz. pkgs. frozen chopped spinach, cooked and drained
3 eggs, beaten
1/3 C. oil
3/4 C. fresh bread crumbs
1/3 C. parsley, chopped
3/4 C. sharp cheese, grated
1 clove garlic, minced
3/4 lb. shell macaroni, cooked

Sauté onion in oil. Add beef, garlic, tomato paste, thyme, rosemary, tomato sauce, consommé, mushrooms, salt and pepper. Simmer 10 to 15 minutes. Combine spinach, eggs, oil, bread crumbs, parsley, cheese and garlic. In a greased 9" x 13" baking dish make 2 layers each of macaroni, spinach mixture and meat mixture. Bake 30 to 40 minutes at 325°. Serves 12.

HAMBURGER QUICHE

1/2 lb. ground beef
1/3 C. green onions, sliced
1/2 C. mayonnaise
1/2 C. milk
2 eggs
1 T. cornstarch
1/2 lb. cheddar OR Swiss cheese, grated
Dash pepper
1 t. Worcestershire sauce
9" unbaked deep pie shell

Brown meat and onions; drain. Combine mayonnaise, milk, eggs and cornstarch. Stir in meat, cheese, pepper and Worcestershire sauce. Place in unbaked pie shell and bake at 350° for 35 minutes, or until brown and set. Serves 6.

LASAGNA

1 lb. Italian bulk sausage
1 lb. ground beef
1 clove garlic, minced
1 T. dried parsley flakes
1 T. basil
1-1/2 t. salt
1/2 t. pepper
16 oz. can tomatoes
6 oz. can tomato paste
6 oz. can tomato sauce
8 oz. Lasagna noodles
2 t. olive oil
3 C. small-curd cottage cheese
2 eggs, beaten
2 t. salt
1/2 t. pepper
2 T. parsley flakes
1/2 C. Parmesan cheese, grated
1 lb. mozzarella cheese, sliced

Brown meat; spoon off excess fat. Add garlic, parsley flakes, basil, salt, pepper, tomatoes, tomato paste and tomato sauce. Simmer, uncovered, for 30 minutes, stirring frequently. Cook noodles until tender in boiling salted water, to which 2 t. olive oil has been added. Drain and rinse in cold water. Combine cottage cheese, eggs, seasonings and Parmesan cheese.

In a 9" x 13" baking dish, layer half of the noodles, half of the cottage cheese mixture, half of the mozzarella cheese and half of the meat mixture. Repeat layers. Bake, uncovered, for 30 minutes at 375°. Let stand for 15 minutes before cutting. Serves 12.

PIZZA LOAVES

1-1/2 lbs. ground beef
1/2 t. salt
1/4 t. pepper
3/4 t. oregano
1/2 t. basil
2 T. ripe olives, chopped
2 T. green onion tops, chopped
6 oz. can tomato paste
1 loaf French bread
1 tomato, thinly-sliced
6 slices American cheese
4 oz. mozzarella cheese, grated
1 C. Parmesan cheese, grated

Brown beef lightly and drain. Add salt, pepper, oregano, basil, olives, onion tops and tomato paste. Mix. Split loaf of bread in half horizontally and vertically, making 4 sections. Spread meat mixture on bread. Arrange sliced tomato on top of meat mixture, then American and mozzarella cheese. Sprinkle with Parmesan cheese. Place on cookie sheet and bake for 20 minutes at 350°. Serves 4 to 6.

ITALIAN MEAT LOAF

1-1/2 lbs. hamburger
1 egg
3/4 C. cracker crumbs
1/2 C. onion, chopped
1/3 C. tomato sauce
1 t. salt
1/2 t. oregano
1/8 t. pepper
2 C. mozzarella cheese, grated
2/3 C. tomato sauce

Combine hamburger, egg, cracker crumbs, chopped onion, 1/3 C. tomato sauce, salt, oregano and pepper. Shape into 10" x 12" rectangle on wax paper. Sprinkle mozzarella cheese on top. Roll up, jelly-roll fashion, and press ends to seal. Place in shallow baking dish. Bake at 350° for 1 hour. Drain fat. Pour 2/3 C. tomato sauce over top and bake 15 minutes longer. Serves 6.

GOLDBERG'S PIZZA

1 envelope dry yeast
1/3 C. + 2 T. warm water
1-1/2 C. flour
1/4 C. olive oil
1/2 t. salt
14 oz. can Italian plum tomatoes
1-1/2 oz. tomato paste
1-1/2 oz. water
1/2 t. salt
1/4 t. pepper
1/4 t. basil
1 t. sugar
1 t. oregano
12 oz. mozzarella cheese, grated
1 lb. bulk Italian sausage
   OR hamburger
1/2 C. Parmesan cheese, grated

Dissolve yeast in warm water. Mix flour, olive oil, salt and yeast in large bowl. Knead well; cover and let rise 1 hour. Grease 14" pizza pan with olive oil. Pat dough into pan. Squeeze drained tomatoes to make 1 C. tomato pulp. Combine pulp with tomato paste, water, salt, pepper, basil, sugar and oregano. Spread on crust. Sprinkle mozzarella cheese on top of tomato sauce. Sauté sausage or hamburger lightly; drain and distribute evenly on top of cheese. Top with 1/2 C. Parmesan cheese. Bake for 15 minutes at 500°. Serves 6 to 8.

poultry and game

HOLLANDAISE CHICKEN

1 C. flour
1 t. salt
1/4 t. pepper
1 t. paprika
8 chicken breasts, boned
1/2 C. butter
1 lb. fresh mushrooms, sliced
1/3 C. flour
1/4 t. salt
2 T. light cream
13-3/4 oz. can chicken broth
2 T. dry sherry

Sauce:
2 egg yolks
1 T. lemon juice
1/8 t. salt
Pinch cayenne
1/2 C. butter

Combine flour, salt, pepper and paprika. Cut chicken into bite-size pieces and coat with flour mixture. Brown chicken in butter and set aside. Sauté mushrooms, adding more butter if necessary. Remove mushrooms. To drippings, add 1/3 C. flour, 1/4 t. salt and light cream; simmer until thickened. Gradually add chicken broth. Return chicken to pan and simmer 20 minutes. Remove from heat and stir in sherry and mushrooms. (May be prepared ahead to this point.)

Just before serving, prepare sauce by combining in blender egg yolks, lemon juice, salt and cayenne. Melt butter and add slowly in steady stream while blender continues to run. Cover chicken with sauce and broil for 10 minutes. Serves 8.

160

SUPRÊMES À LA MARSALA

1 carrot, chopped
1/2 onion, chopped
1 stalk celery, chopped
2 T. butter
1/2 t. tarragon
1/2 C. beef broth
2 slices toasting white bread
3 T. butter
2 ham slices, 1/4" thick, 4" x 4"
2 chicken breasts, split, boned and skinned
Salt
Few drops lemon juice
1/4 C. butter
1 shallot OR green onion, finely-chopped
1/4 lb. fresh mushrooms
2 T. butter
1/4 C. Marsala wine
1 rounded t. cornstarch
2 T. water
Parsley

Sauté carrot, onion and celery in butter until vegetables are brown. Add tarragon and beef broth. Simmer 15 to 20 minutes; cool and strain, pressing juices from vegetables. Set aside.

Trim crusts from bread and sauté bread briefly in 3 T. butter. Place ham on each slice of toast and place in 350° oven for 10 minutes.

Meanwhile, salt chicken breasts and sprinkle with drops of lemon juice. Sauté over high heat in 1/4 C. butter, smooth side down first, until lightly browned, about 4 minutes per side. Remove from skillet. Add shallot or green onion to pan juices; sauté 1 minute and add reserved beef stock to deglaze pan. In another pan, sauté mushrooms in 2 T. butter. Add mushrooms and Marsala to broth and thicken slightly with cornstarch dissolved in water. Place chicken breasts on toast and ham and pour some sauce over each. Garnish with parsley and serve with remaining sauce. Serves 2.

CHICKEN AND HAM MORNAY EN BRIOCHE

5 whole chicken breasts
1 onion
3 stalks celery
1 carrot, chopped
6 chicken bouillon cubes
1/2 C. butter
3/4 C. flour
2 C. light cream
1/2 C. sherry
4 to 5 C. chicken stock

1 C. Swiss cheese, grated
1 t. salt
Juice of 1/2 lemon
1/4 t. grated nutmeg
3 lbs. canned ham, cut in 3/4" cubes
1 lb. fresh mushrooms
1/4 C. butter
2 large brioche
1 bunch parsley

In large kettle, cover chicken breasts with water and add onion, celery, carrot and bouillon cubes. Cook for 20 minutes, or until tender. Reserve stock and strain for sauce. Cool chicken; skin, bone and cut into large bite-size pieces. Set aside.

To prepare Mornay sauce, melt butter in 3 or 4-qt. saucepan. Stir in flour and cook 2 minutes without browning. Add cream, sherry and 4 C. of reserved stock. Cook, stirring constantly, until thickened. Add another cup of stock if sauce is too thick. Add Swiss cheese; stir until melted. Mix in salt, lemon juice, nutmeg, chicken and ham. Sauté mushrooms in 1/4 C. butter and add. Correct seasonings—it may need more salt, lemon juice or sherry. Cover pan with foil. (May be frozen at this point and will keep 2 to 3 weeks in freezer.)

Remove Mornay from freezer at noon the day of party. Three and one-half hours before serving time, place pan in larger pan filled with 2" hot water. Bake, covered loosely with foil, at 375°, stirring several times during cooking period.

Make, or order, 2 large brioche. Remove top knob with sharp knife and hollow out brioche, leaving a 3/4" shell. Replace knob, wrap brioche in foil and heat in 375° oven for 1/2 hour.

To serve, place brioche shells on large platter and remove knobs. With a cup, ladle Mornay into shells, letting some spill over sides. Replace knobs. Surround brioche with parsley and serve remaining Mornay in side dish. Serve the knob as one portion and spoon Mornay from side dish over it. (It's a large serving, so give it to a man.) Then cut 5 pie-shaped servings from each brioche. Serves 12.

COQ AU VIN

6 slices bacon, diced
2 T. butter
4 lbs. chicken parts
10 whole fresh mushrooms
12 tiny white onions
2/3 C. green onions, chopped
1 clove garlic, minced
3 T. flour

Salt and freshly-ground pepper
1/4 t. thyme
2 C. Burgundy
1 C. condensed chicken broth
2 T. brandy
Fines herbes (optional)
6 slices French bread, sautéed
    in butter (optional)

Fry bacon in Dutch oven until crisp; set aside. Add butter to drippings and sauté chicken parts. Remove chicken. Pour off all but 3 T. fat; add mushrooms and white onions and brown slightly. Remove and set aside. Sauté green onions and garlic. Stir in flour, salt, pepper and thyme. Stirring constantly, add Burgundy and chicken broth and bring to boil. Remove from heat and blend in brandy. Add bacon, chicken, onion and mushrooms. Cool and refrigerate overnight. One hour before serving, bake, covered, in 350° oven for 1 hour, or until chicken is tender. Sprinkle lightly with fines herbes, if desired. May be served as is, or on a slice of sautéed French bread. Serves 6.

CHICKEN AU GRATIN

20 pieces chicken
Paprika
8 green onions, sliced
4 C. cheddar cheese, grated
10-1/2 oz. can cream of celery soup, undiluted
10-1/2 oz. can cream of chicken soup, undiluted
1/4 C. vermouth
1-1/2 C. dairy sour cream
8 oz. box chicken-flavored rice

Use two 7" x 11" casseroles. Place chicken in casseroles and sprinkle generously with paprika. Sprinkle green onions over chicken, then cheese. Combine soups, vermouth and sour cream. Pour over chicken and cheese in casseroles. Bake, uncovered, at 325° for 1 hour and 15 minutes. Prepare rice according to package directions and serve with chicken, spooning sauce from chicken over rice. Serves 12 to 14.

CURRIED CHICKEN

4 chicken breasts, skinned and boned
1/2 t. salt
1/4 t. pepper
Dash garlic powder
1/4 t. seasoned salt
1 T. curry powder
2 T. butter

1 T. oil
2 T. shallots OR scallions, chopped
1 C. chicken broth
3 T. slivered almonds, chopped
1 t. cornstarch
1/4 C. heavy cream
Chopped parsley

Cut chicken into 1" strips. Coat with mixture of salt, pepper, garlic powder, seasoned salt and curry powder. In a heavy skillet, melt butter and oil until hot. Add chicken and shallots or scallions and sauté until lightly browned. Stir in chicken broth and almonds. Bring to a boil, reduce heat and simmer 25 minutes. Combine cornstarch and cream. Stir into chicken and bring to boil again. Garnish with chopped parsley. Serve with rice and curry condiments. Serves 4.

CASHEW CHICKEN

1 lb. cubed raw chicken
1 T. cornstarch
2 T. dry sherry
1 t. salt
2 T. water
1/2 C. chopped onion
2 T. fresh ginger, chopped

1 C. dried Chinese mushrooms
1/4 C. oil
1 C. small sprigs fresh broccoli
1/2 C. raw cashews
1/4 C. oil
1/4 C. soy sauce
1 C. water chestnuts, sliced

Dredge raw chicken cubes (skinned and boned) with mixture of cornstarch, sherry, salt, water, onion and ginger. Sauté dried mushrooms (which have been reconstituted in water and drained well) in 1/4 C. oil. Remove from pan. Quickly sauté broccoli in same pan until tender, but still quite crisp. Remove from pan. Quickly sauté cashews until golden, adding 1 to 2 T. more oil if necessary. Add 1/4 C. oil to pan, or as much as is needed to make 1/4 C. in pan, and sauté the chicken until it is just tender and color has turned. Add mushrooms, broccoli, cashews, soy sauce and water chestnuts. Heat thoroughly and serve hot. Good with rice and other Chinese entrées. Serves 4.

CHICKEN BOLOGNESE

4 chicken breasts, halved and boned
1 egg
1 T. water
8 thin slices cooked ham
8 slices mozzarella cheese

1/3 lb. fresh mushrooms, sliced
1/4 C. butter, melted
1 T. parsley, chopped
1/4 t. garlic powder
1/3 C. to 1/2 C. dry sherry

Pound each piece of chicken thin, being careful not to tear meat. Brush 1 side of each breast with egg and water mixture. Place a slice of ham and a slice of cheese on each breast, leaving a 1/4" margin. Roll, jelly-roll fashion. Brush seam edge with egg and water mixture again and press together. Place, seam side down, in 7" x 11" baking pan. Sauté mushrooms in butter for 2 minutes. Add parsley, garlic powder and sherry. Simmer 3 minutes and pour over chicken.(May be prepared ahead to this point and refrigerated until baking time.) Bake at 350° for 25 minutes, or slightly longer if taken directly from refrigerator. Allow 2 rolls per person. Serves 4.

CHICKEN ROCKEFELLER

8 oz. can chopped spinach
1 C. small-curd cottage cheese
1 egg
1/4 C. Parmesan cheese, grated
1/2 t. garlic salt
Pinch black pepper
2-1/2 lb. whole frying chicken
2 T. olive oil
1/8 t. thyme
1/8 t. oregano
1/8 t. rosemary

Drain spinach well and squeeze dry. Drain cottage cheese well, lightly pressing all moisture out. Combine spinach, egg, cottage cheese, Parmesan cheese, garlic salt and pepper. Cut through breast of whole chicken. Place chicken with back facing you and press down on back until it is flat. (Break the back.) Now place chicken so neck is facing you. In order to create a pocket for the stuffing, begin to pull up on the skin at neck with fingers. Work hand back through chicken, using a knife to cut when necessary. When pocket is complete, work fingers into legs, too. Stuff all pockets with spinach mixture.

Season olive oil with thyme, oregano and rosemary. Place chicken in shallow baking pan and brush with olive oil. Bake for 1 hour at 375°. Divide into fourths to serve. Serves 4.

CASSOULET

4 slices bacon
8 chicken thighs
8 chicken breast halves
2 lbs. smoked sausage
1 onion, chopped
1 green pepper, chopped
1/2 lb. fresh mushrooms, sliced
8 oz. tomato sauce
1 C. vermouth

1/8 t. ground cloves
1/4 C. parsley
1/4 t. thyme
1 bay leaf
1 t. dried garlic flakes.
Salt and pepper to taste
1 t. basil
2 15-oz. cans navy beans, drained

Fry bacon; drain and set aside. Brown chicken in bacon fat and set aside. Cut sausage in chunks and brown with onion, green pepper and mushrooms. Combine all ingredients except beans in large skillet. Simmer slowly for 40 minutes, uncovered. Add beans. Transfer to serving casserole. (May be prepared ahead to this point.) Bake, covered, for 1 hour at 325°. Serves 8.

CHICKEN LIVERS IN WINE

1-1/2 lbs. chicken livers
1/2 C. flour
1/2 C. butter
1 t. paprika
1 t. thyme
2 t. salt
1/2 t. pepper
1/2 C. green onions, sliced
1/4 C. green pepper, chopped
1 C. red wine
2 chicken bouillon cubes
1 C. water

Coat livers with flour. Brown in butter. Add paprika, thyme, salt, pepper, green onions, green pepper and wine. Dissolve bouillon cubes in water and add. Cook slowly until liquid is almost absorbed. Serve with rice. Serves 6.

BAKED CHICKEN SANDWICH

16 slices textured white bread, crusts removed
1/2 C. butter
1/4 lb. fresh mushrooms
2 T. butter
2 C. cooked chicken, cubed
3 hard-cooked eggs, chopped
1/3 C. ripe olives, sliced
3/4 C. mayonnaise
2 T. onions, chopped
10-1/2 oz. can cream of chicken soup, undiluted
1 C. dairy sour cream
2 T. sherry
Paprika

Butter both sides of bread. Place 8 slices of bread in buttered 9" x 13" pan. Sauté mushrooms in 2 T. butter. Cover bread with mixture of chicken, eggs, mushrooms, olives, mayonnaise and onions. Arrange remaining 8 slices of buttered bread on top of mixture. Combine soup, sour cream and sherry and pour over top. Sprinkle with paprika. Bake for 30 minutes at 325°. Serves 8.

SMOKED TURKEY

10 to 15 lb. turkey
2 C. dry white wine
Hickory chips
1-1/2 C. butter
1/2 C. lemon juice
3/4 C. Worcestershire sauce
1-1/2 t. salt
1 t. seasoned salt
1/2 t. garlic salt
Tabasco sauce to taste

Remove turkey giblets; rinse cavity. Place turkey on rack in oven roasting pan and fill cavity with 1 C. of the wine. Prepare charcoal and add dampened hickory chips. Combine butter, lemon juice, Worcestershire sauce, salt, seasoned salt, garlic salt and Tabasco sauce and bring to slow boil. Add remaining 1 C. wine and heat. Place turkey in open roaster on grill 12" to 15" above coals. Cook 6 to 8 hours with hood closed. During first 1-1/2 hours, baste every 15 to 20 minutes with sauce. Replenish charcoal and hickory chips as needed.

QUAIL BITS

6 strips bacon
6 quail
Salt
10-1/2 oz. can beef consommé
10-1/2 oz. water

Place a strip of bacon across breast of quail. Sprinkle lightly with salt and place in baking pan. Add equal parts of consommé and water until liquid reaches 1/2" in baking pan. Cover and bake at 275° for 4 hours. For last half hour, turn temperature to 325° and remove cover. Serve with bacon on breast. Serves 4 to 6.

DOVES OR QUAIL IN WINE SAUCE

4 to 6 whole quail
   OR 8 to 12 dove breasts
1 t. salt
3/4 C. flour

1/2 C. butter
1/4 C. fresh mushrooms, sliced
1/4 C. onion, chopped
1/2 C. white wine

Wash birds and coat with mixture of salt and flour. Sauté in butter until brown. Set aside. In same pan, sauté onions and mushrooms. Return birds to pan and add wine. Simmer for 30 minutes, basting frequently. Serves 2 to 4.

MICROWAVE QUAIL

2 quail
Salt and pepper
2 T. butter, melted
1-1/2 t. Kitchen Bouquet
1/2 t. honey

3 T. Madeira wine
3 oz. can sliced mushrooms,
   with liquid
1 T. flour
10" x 16" cellophane cooking bag

Salt and pepper quail. Marinate for 6 to 12 hours in mixture of butter, Kitchen Bouquet, honey and wine. Combine mushrooms and their liquid with flour. Blend in marinade. Place in oven bag in 1-1/2 qt. casserole. Place quail on top of mushroom mixture. Close bag with piece of string. Make six 1/2" slits in top of bag. Cook 5 minutes in microwave range. Use sauce in oven bag for spooning over quail when served. Allow 2 quail per person. Serves 1.

TUSCANY QUAIL

6 quail
Salt and pepper
1/2 C. cognac
1/2 C. dry white wine
2 T. lemon juice
2 bay leaves, crushed
5 peppercorns, bruised
6 T. olive oil

3 T. tomato paste
1/2 C. chicken broth
2 cloves garlic, crushed
12 whole black olives, pitted
12 anchovy fillets
3/4 C. strained marinade
1/4 C. dry white wine
1 jigger Marsala wine

Rub inside of quail with salt and pepper. Marinate in mixture of cognac, 1/2 C. white wine, lemon juice, bay leaves and peppercorns for 6 hours. Remove birds from marinade. Dry thoroughly, sprinkle with salt and pepper and brown well on all sides in hot olive oil. Remove birds. Add tomato paste, chicken broth, garlic, olives and anchovies to drippings. Blend in strained marinade and 1/4 C. white wine. Cover and simmer 10 minutes. Return birds to pan. Cover and cook slowly for 1 hour. Add jigger of Marsala to sauce and pour over birds. Serves 4.

ROAST DUCK WITH CUMBERLAND SAUCE

2 ducks (Teal, Gadwall, Widjeon or Mallard)
1 white onion, cut in cubes
1 apple, unpeeled, cut in cubes
1 orange, unpeeled, cut in cubes
1/4 C. butter, melted
1/4 C. orange juice
6 T. currant jelly
3 T. sugar
2 T. lemon juice
2 T. dry sherry
Pinch salt

Stuff ducks with pieces of raw onion, apple and orange. Baste with melted butter and orange juice. Roast, uncovered, at 450° to 500° until breast meat is pink and juice from knife insertion runs clear. (20 to 30 minutes for Teal; 30 to 40 minutes for Gadwall or Widjeon; 40 to 50 minutes for big Mallards.)

Heat together currant jelly, sugar, lemon juice, sherry and salt to blend. Sauce may be served warm or chilled. Serves 4.

ROAST WILD DUCK

2 Mallards (OR 4 Teal OR 3 Gadwalls,
   Redheads, Wood Ducks, Pintails, etc.)
Salt
3 oranges, quartered
3 onions, quartered
1-1/2 C. orange juice

3 T. butter, melted
1/2 C. honey
1 T. Worcestershire sauce
1/4 C. dry sherry
1 to 3 T. butter, melted
1 to 3 T. flour

Parboil ducks in salted water for 45 minutes. Salt cavity and fill with quartered oranges and onions. Place, breast down, in a tight-fitting pan. Combine orange juice, butter, honey, Worcestershire sauce and sherry. Baste duck with sauce and place in 375° oven for 45 minutes. Baste again after 1/2 hour, and check to see if pan needs a little water to prevent duck from sticking. Reduce heat to 275° and roast for an additional 2-1/2 to 3-1/2 hours, depending on size of ducks, basting every 30 minutes. To make gravy, thicken pan juices with mixture of 1 T. butter and 1 T. flour per cup of juice. Serves 4.

WILD GOOSE WITH ORANGE SAUCE

1 wild goose
Salt
2 to 3 apples, quartered
2 to 3 onions, quartered
1 C. butter
6 T. orange juice concentrate, undiluted
1/4 C. dry sherry

Parboil goose for 20 minutes in salted water. Salt cavity and stuff with apples and onions. Bake at 350° for 1 hour. Combine remaining ingredients for orange sauce. Reduce oven temperature to 225° to 250°. Cover pan with foil or lid and bake 2 more hours, removing lid for last 30 minutes to brown. Baste throughout cooking with orange sauce. Serve remaining sauce with goose.

PAELLA VALENCIANA

3 lb. chicken, cut into pieces	5 chorizos (Spanish sausages)
5 C. water	1 medium onion, chopped
1 onion	2 cloves garlic, minced
1-1/2 t. salt	1 pimiento, cut into strips
1/2 t. saffron	2 tomatoes, peeled and chopped
1 T. flour	2 C. rice, uncooked
1/2 t. salt	4-1/2 C. chicken broth
1/2 C. olive oil	7 oz. can minced clams, undrained
1-1/2 lbs. raw shrimp, shelled	3/4 C. frozen peas, defrosted
1 C. cooked ham, diced	Salt and pepper to taste

Set aside chicken breasts, drumsticks, thighs and wings. To make chicken broth, cover remaining pieces with 5 C. water, adding onion and 1-1/2 t. salt. Boil 30 minutes; strain and measure broth to make 4-1/2 C. Add saffron to broth. Dust remaining chicken pieces with flour and 1/2 t. salt; cook in olive oil in heavy skillet until crispy, brown and tender. Remove chicken to large casserole or Paella pan. Place shrimp, ham and chorizos in skillet. Cook in oil until lightly browned. Add to chicken. Sauté onion, garlic, pimiento and tomatoes in skillet until tender. Add rice and stir to glaze. Bring chicken broth to boil and add. Add clams and liquid; bring to boil again and cook 5 minutes. Add peas and cook 5 minutes longer, uncovered. Combine with chicken. Rearrange some chicken and shrimp over top of rice. Cover and place over low heat (or in 300° oven) for 20 minutes or until all liquid is absorbed. Serves 5 to 6.

WINE POACHED SALMON

2 quarts water
2 sprigs parsley
5 peppercorns
2 bay leaves
Pinch thyme OR tarragon
Slice of lemon
1 medium onion, sliced
8 cloves
3 T. butter
1 t. salt
2 bottles dry white wine
6 to 7 lb. whole salmon
1 or 2 recipes Blender Mayonnaise, see pg. 122

Garnish:
Lettuce leaves
Parsley
Lemon slices
Olives
Pimiento
Cherry tomatoes
Radish flowers
Cucumber slices
Carrot curls

Place large fish poacher across 2 surface units on range. Add water. Tie parsley, peppercorns, bay leaves, thyme, lemon slice, onion and cloves in piece of cheesecloth. Add to poacher. Add butter and salt. Bring to boil, lower heat and simmer for 20 to 25 minutes. Turn off heat, leaving spices in water. Add wine. Return to simmer and add salmon. (Salmon should be just covered by liquid. If not, add only enough water to accomplish this. Bring to simmer again.) Cook 6 to 8 minutes per pound, until fork tender. Remove salmon and cool. When cool, gently remove skin. (May be prepared the day ahead to this point.)

One-half hour before serving, place salmon on serving tray. Surround with lettuce leaves. Ice salmon with mayonnaise and stuff mouth with parsley. Decorate salmon with sliced lemons, olives, pimiento and sliced cherry tomatoes. (Guest of honor's name or initials may be put on.) Decorate lettuce leaves with radish flowers, cucumber slices, carrot curls and lemon flowers with cherry tomatoes as centers. Serve as main course, first course or as hors d'oeuvre with Melba toast.

FILLETS OF SOLE WITH SCALLOPS MORNAY

9 fillets of sole OR baby flounder
3/4 lbs. scallops
1 to 1-1/2 C. white wine
Salt and pepper

Bouquet Garni:
1/2 stalk celery
1 piece carrot
1 sprig parsley
1 bay leaf
1/2 t. thyme

Mornay Sauce:
3 T. flour
3 T. butter, melted
1-1/2 C. fish stock (wine broth)
Salt and pepper to taste
1/2 C. Gruyère cheese, grated
1/2 C. light cream
Dash cayenne
Paprika

Cut fillets in half. Wrap each half around one large or two small scallops and place, seam-side-down, in large buttered casserole. (Do not crowd—use 2 casseroles if necessary.) Pour remaining scallops over top. Add enough wine to just cover fish. Tie bouquet garni ingredients in a small piece of cheesecloth and add. Salt and pepper to taste. Poach fish for 20 minutes at 350°, or just until fish flakes. Reserve poaching liquid for sauce. Discard bouquet garni.

Remove fish to heated platter, and make sauce: combine flour and butter in saucepan and cook until yellowish in color. Gradually stir in fish stock, stirring until thickened. Cook 10 minutes; salt and pepper to taste. Add Gruyère cheese and stir until melted. Dilute with cream. Add cayenne and taste for salt. Pour sauce over fish and broil just to glaze. Sprinkle with paprika and serve. Allow 3 wrapped fillets per person, and spoon remaining scallops over each serving. Serves 6.

FILLETS OF SOLE WITH MUSHROOM STUFFING

4 fillets of sole (2 lbs.)
1/4 lb. mushrooms, finely-chopped
3 T. butter
1-1/2 C. bread crumbs, toasted
1 T. parsley, chopped
1/2 t. salt
Dash pepper
2 T. lemon juice
2 egg yolks, slightly-beaten

1 T. lemon juice
Salt and pepper
1 T. butter
1/4 C. dry white wine
1 recipe Blender Hollandaise
   Sauce, see pg. 123
Chopped parsley
Lemon wedges

Rinse fillets under cold water; pat dry. To prepare stuffing, sauté mushrooms in 3 T. butter. Stir in bread crumbs, parsley, salt, pepper and 1/2 t. lemon juice until well blended. Mix in egg yolks. Brush fillets with remaining lemon juice; sprinkle with salt and pepper. Spoon stuffing onto half of each fillet, dividing evenly. Fold over other half. Place in buttered 2-qt. shallow baking dish, dot with butter, pour in wine and cover with foil. Bake at 350° for 20 to 30 minutes, or until fish flakes easily when tested with a fork. Meanwhile prepare hollandaise sauce. Sprinkle fillets with chopped parsley, garnish with lemon wedges and serve with hollandaise sauce. Serves 4.

SEAFOOD CHEDDAR

3 qts. water
1 C. lemon juice
4 bay leaves
4 cloves
2 t. salt
2 pinches tarragon leaves
1 lb. fresh scallops
2 frozen lobster tails
   OR 1 lb. frozen lobster meat
1-1/2 lb. shrimp, shelled and deveined

2 10-1/2-oz. cans cream of
   mushroom soup, undiluted
1 lb. sharp cheddar cheese, grated
1 T. hot mustard
1 clove garlic, crushed
1 C. dry sherry
1-1/2 C. rice, uncooked
1 C. almonds, slivered
2 T. butter
1/2 C. currants

Fill a 6-qt. kettle half full of water. Add lemon juice, bay leaves, cloves, salt and tarragon. Bring to boil. Add scallops, lobster and shrimp. Stir until heated. Bring to boil and boil vigorously for 1 minute. Remove from heat. Heat mushroom soup in top of double boiler. Add cheese, mustard and garlic and stir until cheese is melted. Slowly stir in sherry. Drain fish and cut into bite-size pieces. Combine with cheese sauce. Cook rice according to package directions. Sauté almonds in butter and add to rice together with currants. Serve rice with Seafood Cheddar. Serves 8.

HALIBUT LOAF WITH ALMOND SAUCE

1-1/4 lb. halibut
2 C. stale bread crumbs
2 C. light cream
2 t. onion, grated
1 t. lemon juice
1 t. salt
Dash pepper
Dash celery salt
4 egg whites

Sauce:
4 oz. blanched almonds, chopped
1 T. butter
2 C. light cream
2 T. butter
1-1/2 T. flour
1/2 t. salt

Skin and bone halibut and put through food grinder, raw. Combine halibut, bread crumbs and cream and cook to smooth paste. Add onion, lemon juice, salt, pepper and celery salt. Beat egg whites until stiff and gently fold in. Place in buttered loaf pan or other casserole. Set in pan of hot water and bake for 1 hour at 350°. Meanwhile sauté almonds in butter. In double boiler, heat cream. Blend butter and flour together. Add to cream stirring to blend. Add salt and almonds. Serve over Halibut Loaf. Serves 4 to 6.

SEAFOOD RING WITH SHRIMP

2 lbs. fresh or frozen halibut
  OR haddock
2 T. butter
2 T. flour
1/2 C. light cream
1 t. salt

4 eggs, separated
2 C. heavy cream, whipped
1 T. green pepper, chopped
1 recipe Blender Hollandaise
  Sauce, see pg. 123
3 lbs. shrimp, cooked

Poach fish until tender, removing skin and bones if whole, and grind very fine. Set aside. Make white sauce of butter, flour and cream. Add salt and gradually stir in beaten egg yolks, then the fish. When cool, fold in beaten egg whites and whipped cream. Place in well-greased ring mold which has been dotted on the bottom with chopped green pepper. Place in pan of water and bake at 325° for 30 minutes, or until set. Prepare hollandaise sauce. Remove fish mold to platter and fill center with cooked shrimp. Cover with hollandaise sauce and serve. Serves 8.

SHRIMP CURRY

1/2 C. onion, chopped	1/4 t. pepper
5 T. butter	1 bouillon cube
5 T. flour	1 C. water
2 t. curry powder	2 t. ketchup
1 t. dry mustard	1-1/2 C. milk, warmed
1/4 t. salt	1 lb. shrimp, cooked

Sauté onion in butter until tender. Combine dry ingredients and add to onion. Combine bouillon, water and ketchup and add gradually, stirring over low heat. Add milk, stirring until thickened. Add shrimp and heat through. Serve with rice and curry condiments, such as coconut, raisins, nuts and pineapple. Serves 4.

SHRIMP CREOLE

3 stalks celery
1 large onion, sliced
3 T. olive oil
1 T. chili powder
2 T. flour
16 oz. can tomatoes
2 t. sugar
7 drops Tabasco sauce
Salt to taste
1 C. sauterne or white wine
2 lbs. shrimp, cooked
6 C. wild rice
 OR 2 6-oz. boxes Long Grain and Wild Rice

Chop celery and sauté with onion in olive oil. Add chili powder and flour. Add tomatoes. Mix and bring to simmer. Add sugar, Tabasco sauce and salt. Add sauterne and simmer until consistency of thin gravy is reached, approximately 15 to 20 minutes. Meanwhile, prepare rice according to package directions. Set aside. Add shrimp to wine sauce. Heat through and serve on bed of wild rice. Serves 6.

SHRIMP FRIED RICE

3 green onions, tops included, chopped
1 onion, chopped
1/2 C. butter
3 C. cold cooked rice
2 eggs, beaten
4 oz. water chestnuts, drained and sliced
Soy sauce to taste
7-3/4 oz. can tiny shrimp, drained and rinsed

Sauté onions in butter in wok or large frying pan over moderately-high heat. Stir in rice, mixing until heated and coated with butter. (Add more butter if necessary.) With wooden spoon, make a path to bottom of pan; pour in eggs and gently scramble. Mix throughout rice. Add water chestnuts and sprinkle liberally with soy sauce to taste. Gently fold in shrimp and heat. Serves 4.

SHRIMP V.I.P.

1 lb. shrimp, cooked, shelled and deveined
3 T. oil
1 T. lemon juice
3/4 C. rice, uncooked
1/4 C. green pepper, minced
1/4 C. onion, minced
2 T. butter
1 C. heavy cream
1 t. salt
1/8 t. pepper
1/8 t. mace
Dash cayenne
1 C. condensed cream of tomato soup
1/2 C. sherry
1/2 C. slivered almonds
Paprika

Place shrimp in 2-qt. buttered casserole, and sprinkle with oil and lemon juice. Cook rice according to package directions. Sauté minced peppers and onions in butter. Add to casserole. Add rice. Combine cream, salt, pepper, mace, cayenne, tomato soup and sherry; add to casserole. Top with slivered almonds and paprika. Bake at 350° until bubbly, about 55 minutes. (May be prepared ahead and refrigerated several hours before baking.) Serves 6.

CRABMEAT QUICHE

2 C. crabmeat
1 T. celery, chopped
1 T. onion, chopped
2 T. parsley, chopped
2 T. dry sherry
Pastry for single-crust pie

4 eggs, slightly-beaten
2 C. light cream
1/4 t. nutmeg
1/2 t. salt
1/4 t. white pepper

Flake crabmeat; combine with celery, onion, parsley and sherry. Refrigerate at least 1 hour. Line china quiche pan or glass pie pan with pastry. Prick with fork and bake for 5 minutes at 450°. Sprinkle inside of pastry shell with crab mixture. Combine eggs, cream, nutmeg, salt and pepper and pour over mixture in pie shell. Bake 15 minutes at 450°. Reduce temperature to 350° and bake 15 to 20 minutes longer, or until silver knife inserted 1" from edge comes out clean. Serves 8.

CRABMEAT BROCCOLI PIE

1-1/4 C. flour
2 t. baking powder
1/2 t. salt
1/2 C. butter
1/4 C. milk
1 T. chives, chopped
10 oz. pkg. frozen chopped broccoli
7-1/2 oz. can crabmeat
3 hard-cooked eggs, diced
1/2 C. celery, diced
2 T. green onion, sliced
1 C. mild cheddar cheese, grated
1 C. mayonnaise
Paprika

Sift together flour, baking powder and salt. Cut in butter and add milk and chives. Stir and mix until dough forms a ball. Pat into 9" pie pan, covering bottom and sides. Cook broccoli and drain well. Place broccoli on pie crust. Combine crabmeat, eggs, celery, green onion, cheese and mayonnaise and spread over broccoli. Dust with paprika. Bake at 375° (or 350° if using a glass pan) for 30 minutes, or until brown. Serves 6.

SEAFOOD QUICHE

3/4 C. crabmeat
3/4 C. shrimp, cooked
3/4 C. Swiss cheese, grated
1/4 C. celery, cooked
1/4 C. green onions, sliced
1 unbaked 9" pastry shell
1/2 C. mayonnaise
2 T. flour
1/2 C. dry white wine
2 eggs, slightly beaten

Combine crab, shrimp, cheese, celery and onions. Place in pie shell. Combine mayonnaise, flour, wine and eggs. Pour over crab mixture and bake for 50 minutes at 350°. Serves 6.

CRAB CHEESE SOUFFLÉ

1/4 C. sweet butter
1/4 C. flour
1-1/2 C. milk, scalded
1 C. sharp cheddar cheese, grated
1-1/2 C. mild cheddar cheese, grated
1 t. salt
Pinch nutmeg
6 eggs, separated
7-1/2 oz. can crabmeat

Melt butter in saucepan. Stir in flour; blend well and add hot milk, stirring constantly. Bring to boil, add cheeses and stir until cheese is melted. Add salt and nutmeg and remove from heat. Add egg yolks, 1 at a time, stirring well after each addition. Add crabmeat. Beat egg whites until stiff and fold carefully into cheese sauce. Pour into buttered soufflé dish. Bake for 30 minutes at 375°. Serve immediately. Serves 6.

LUNCHEON CRÊPES WITH CRABMEAT FILLING

1 recipe Luncheon Crêpes, see pg. 223
3 T. butter
3 T. flour
1-1/2 C. milk
Salt and pepper
1-1/2 C. crabmeat
1/4 C. dry sherry
1/4 t. lemon rind, grated
1/4 t. nutmeg
1/2 to 1 t. curry powder
2 T. fresh parsley, minced
3/4 C. Blender Hollandaise Sauce, see pg.123
1/2 C. dairy sour cream
1/4 C. slivered almonds, toasted

Prepare crêpes and set aside. Melt butter and stir in flour until well blended. Gradually add milk, stirring until thickened and smooth. Salt and pepper to taste. Stir in crabmeat, sherry, lemon rind, nutmeg, curry and parsley.Place approximately 1/4 C. filling on each crêpe and roll as for a jelly roll. Place crêpes in buttered 7" x 11" casserole, seam side down. Blend hollandaise sauce and sour cream and pour over top of crêpes. Top with almonds and bake for 10 to 15 minutes at 400°. Serves 6.

SEASIDE SANDWICH

2 7-1/2-oz. cans crabmeat
1/2 C. green onions, sliced
2 T. lemon juice
1 T. mayonnaise
1/4 C. chili sauce
4 English muffins, split
1/3 C. butter
1/4 C. mayonnaise
1 T. lemon juice
2 eggs, separated
1/3 C. cheddar cheese, grated

Combine crabmeat, onions, lemon juice, 1 T. mayonnaise and chili sauce. Butter muffins and spread with crabmeat mixture. Bake at 400° for 4 minutes. Meanwhile, blend remaining mayonnaise, 1 T. lemon juice, egg yolks and cheese. Beat egg whites until stiff and fold into mayonnaise mixture. Spread over crabmeat and broil for 3 to 4 minutes. Serves 4 to 6.

TUNA NEWBURG STRATA

8 slices bread, buttered
7 oz. can tuna
1/4 lb. Swiss cheese, grated
2 T. parsley, chopped
1 t. onion, grated
1 C. milk
10-1/2 oz. can cream of shrimp soup
3 eggs

Arrange 4 slices buttered bread to cover bottom of buttered baking dish. Drain and flake tuna and combine with Swiss cheese, parsley and grated onion. Spread over bread. Top with remaining 4 slices buttered bread. Heat milk and soup, stirring just until soup is melted. Remove from heat. Beat eggs and combine slowly with soup mixture. Pour over sandwiches; cover and chill. One hour before serving time, uncover and place in cold oven. Bake at 350°, uncovered, for 1 hour, or until top is puffed and golden. Serve at once. Serves 4.

TUNA ROCKEFELLER

7 oz. can tuna, packed in water
1/3 C. bread crumbs
10 oz. pkg. frozen chopped spinach,
  cooked and drained
1 T. lemon juice
1/2 C. mayonnaise
2 T. Parmesan cheese, grated
1 C. Swiss cheese, grated
4 whole fresh mushroom caps
1 t. butter
Paprika

Combine tuna, bread crumbs and spinach. Add lemon juice, mayonnaise and Parmesan cheese. Put equal amounts of mixture in 4 seafood shells or ramekins.Sprinkle top with Swiss cheese and bake at 350° for 20 minutes. Top each serving with a large, buttered mushroom cap. Sprinkle with paprika and broil for 2 or 3 minutes. Serves 4.

TUNA ROSCOE

7 oz. can white tuna
1 C. celery, chopped
10 oz. pkg. frozen Italian green beans
8 oz. can water chestnuts,
    drained and sliced
1 T. lemon juice
1/2 C. mayonnaise
1-1/2 t. soy sauce
Dash garlic powder
1 C. Chinese chow mein noodles

Combine tuna and celery. Blanch beans for 2 minutes in boiling, salted water and plunge into ice water. Drain. Add beans and water chestnuts to tuna, cutting large beans in half. Prepare dressing by combining lemon juice, mayonnaise, soy sauce and garlic powder. Toss with tuna mixture. Immediately before serving, add chow mein noodles and toss again. Serves 6.

ITALIAN PIES

1 C. flour
1 T. sugar
1/2 t. salt
6 T. butter
1 egg yolk
1-1/2 T. lemon juice
1 T. water
1 small clove garlic, minced
1 onion, minced
3 to 4 large slices Swiss cheese
6 to 8 thick slices tomato
1/2 C. flour
6 to 8 anchovies, minced
1 C. heavy cream
Fresh parsley, chopped

Mix flour, sugar and salt. Cut in butter. Mix egg yolk, lemon juice and water and blend into dry ingredients. Chill dough until firm enough to handle. Roll out on floured board. Cut to fit 6 to 8 individual ramekins or custard cups, just even with top edges. Mix garlic and onion and sprinkle over pastry. Break 1/2 slice of cheese over garlic and onion. Dip tomato slices in flour and place on cheese. Top with anchovies. Pour 2 to 3 T. heavy cream over each pie. Bake at 400° for 25 to 30 minutes. Garnish with parsley. Serves 6 to 8.

SCALLOPS ORIENTAL

1 lb. fresh scallops
1 T. butter
3 large, whole Chinese mushrooms
  (available in dried form)
1-1/2 T. butter
1 C. snow peas (Oriental pea pods)
1-1/2 C. celery, sliced diagonally
2 T. oil
1 C. clam juice
1-1/2 t. cornstarch
1/4 t. salt
1 T. lemon juice
1 clove garlic, minced

In wok or large skillet, sauté scallops in 1 T. butter. Drain on towel. Reconstitute mushrooms according to package directions. Dry and sauté in 1-1/2 T. butter. Set aside. Sauté snow peas quickly and remove from pan while they still maintain crispness. Sauté celery in oil for 4 minutes. Add mushrooms, clam juice, cornstarch, salt, lemon juice and garlic. Stir over high heat until sauce thickens. Add snow peas and scallops and heat through. Serves 4.

LENTEN SPAGHETTI

8 oz. spaghetti
3-3/4 oz. jar smoked oysters
2 T. butter
1 C. celery with leaves, sliced
1/4 C. water
2 T. vinegar
1 T. instant minced onion
1/2 t. salt
2 medium avocados, peeled and diced
1/4 C. fresh parsley, chopped

Cook spaghetti as directed on package. Drain oil from oysters into large saucepan. Add butter and celery and cook slowly for 10 minutes, stirring occasionally. Add water, vinegar, onions and salt. Fold in spaghetti and oysters. Add avocado and parsley. Toss lightly. Serves 6.

EGGS COPENHAGEN

1/4 C. butter
2 T. onions, finely-chopped
4 green onions, tops included, sliced
12 eggs
2/3 C. heavy cream
8 oz. cream cheese, diced
1/2 t. lemon juice
1 t. salt

Melt butter in double boiler. Add chopped onions and green onions. Combine eggs, cream, cream cheese, lemon juice and salt. Add to mixture in double boiler. Cook slowly, stirring often, until set but still soft. Serves 8.

WOODCOCK

1 lb. whole fresh mushrooms
1/2 C. butter
2 T. flour
2 C. milk
8 hard-cooked eggs, finely-chopped
4 oz. can pimiento, drained and finely-chopped
1/4 lb. New York sharp cheese, grated
3 English muffins

Sauté whole mushrooms in butter. Stir in flour and gradually add milk, stirring constantly until thickened. Add eggs and pimiento. Place in baking dish and cover with grated cheese. Bake 30 minutes at 350°. Split muffins, butter and toast halves. Serve Woodcock over muffin halves. Serves 6.

DEVILED EGGS IN CURRY SAUCE

6 eggs, hard-cooked
1/2 t. Worcestershire sauce
2 T. mayonnaise
1 t. dry mustard
1/2 t. salt
Dash pepper

2 T. butter
3 T. flour
1-1/2 C. milk
1/2 t. salt
1/2 t. curry powder
1/2 C. cheddar cheese, grated

Split eggs, lengthwise. Remove yolks to small bowl and mash. Add Worcestershire sauce, mayonnaise, mustard, salt and pepper and beat until smooth. Spoon into egg whites. Place eggs in buttered casserole, just large enough to accommodate them in a single layer. (May be done ahead to this point and refrigerated.) To make sauce, melt butter in small saucepan; add flour and cook 3 minutes. Add milk and stir until smooth and thickened. Add salt and curry. Taste and adjust seasonings. Pour over eggs. Top with cheese. Bake at 350° for 30 minutes. Serves 6.

BRUNCH EGGS WITH SPANISH SAUCE

1 loaf toasting white bread
1/2 C. butter
6 eggs
3 C. milk
3/4 t. dry mustard
3/4 t. white pepper
1 lb. cheddar cheese, grated

Sauce:
1/3 C. onion, chopped
1/4 C. green pepper, chopped (opt.)
3/4 C. fresh mushrooms, sliced
3 T. oil
1 T. cornstarch
16 oz. can tomatoes, with liquid
1 t. salt
Dash pepper
2 t. sugar
Dash cayenne

Butter both sides of bread and cut in cubes. Set aside. Combine eggs, milk, mustard and pepper. Layer cheese and bread cubes in buttered 9" x 13" casserole. Pour egg mixture over; cover and refrigerate 8 to 12 hours, or overnight. Bake, uncovered, at 350° for 30 to 45 minutes, or until eggs are set.

Meanwhile make sauce by browning onion, green pepper, if desired, and mushrooms in oil. Combine cornstarch with 2 T. liquid from canned tomatoes and add to vegetable mixture. Add tomatoes and remaining liquid from can, salt, pepper, sugar and cayenne. Cook over low heat, stirring often, until vegetables are tender and sauce is slightly thickened, 15 to 20 minutes. Serve with Brunch Eggs. Serves 8.

MOUNT MELLARY EGGS

1/4 C. butter
14 oz. can artichoke hearts, drained and sliced
Salt and pepper
8 eggs, hard-cooked and chopped
3 tomatoes, peeled and sliced
3 oz. cheddar cheese, grated

Melt 2 T. of the butter in 8" x 8" casserole. Make one layer of the following ingredients in the following order: artichoke hearts, salt and pepper, chopped eggs, salt and pepper, remaining 2 T. butter, tomatoes, salt and pepper and grated cheese. Bake 30 minutes at 375°. Serves 6.

CURRIED EGGS IN SHRIMP SAUCE

8 eggs, hard-cooked
1/3 C. mayonnaise
1/4 t. dry mustard
1/2 t. paprika
1/2 t. salt
Dash pepper
1/4 to 1/2 t. curry powder
2 T. butter
2 T. flour
10-1/2 oz. can cream of shrimp soup
10-1/2 oz. milk
1/2 C. cheddar cheese, grated
1 C. soft bread crumbs
1 T. butter, melted
Toast points or patty shells

Cut eggs in half. Mash yolks with mayonnaise, mustard, paprika, salt, pepper and curry powder. Fill eggs and place in 9" x 9" casserole dish. Melt butter, add flour and stir until smooth. Add soup and milk, and cook over medium heat to thicken slightly. Add cheese, and stir to melt cheese. Pour over eggs. Combine bread crumbs with butter and sprinkle over top. Bake for 15 to 20 minutes at 350°. Serve over toast points or patty shells. Serves 8.

EGGS À LA BENEDICTINE

2 T. butter
2 T. flour
1 C. milk
1/2 C. American cheese, grated
2 egg yolks, beaten
1/4 C. dry sherry
1/4 t. dry mustard
1/4 t. salt
1/8 t. pepper
4 eggs
Dash vinegar
2 English muffins
4 slices ham, broiled
4 large slices tomato, broiled

Make a white sauce in double boiler with butter, flour and milk. Add cheese, beaten egg yolks, sherry, mustard, salt and pepper. Stir until thickened. Reduce heat to low until ready to serve. Poach eggs in water to which a dash of vinegar has been added. Remove eggs to small dish and pour sauce over eggs. Split and toast English muffins. Place 1 piece of ham on each muffin half, then a large slice of broiled tomato. Lift one poached egg from the sauce and place on each muffin half. Pour 1/3 C. sauce over each poached egg. Serves 4.

ANNA'S NEVER-FAIL SOUFFLÉ

1/4 C. butter
5 T. flour
1 t. salt
1/2 t. paprika
Dash cayenne
1-1/2 C. milk
1 C. cheddar cheese, grated
6 eggs, separated

Melt butter in saucepan. Add flour, salt, paprika and cayenne and blend well. Add milk gradually and cook until thickened, stirring constantly. Add cheese and stir over low heat until cheese is melted. Remove from heat. Beat egg yolks until thick and lemon-colored and blend into cheese mixture. Beat egg whites until stiff and fold in. Pour into a 2-qt. greased soufflé dish. Place dish in pan of warm water. Bake 40 to 50 minutes at 350°. (Soufflé will have a golden-brown crust when done.) Serves 6.

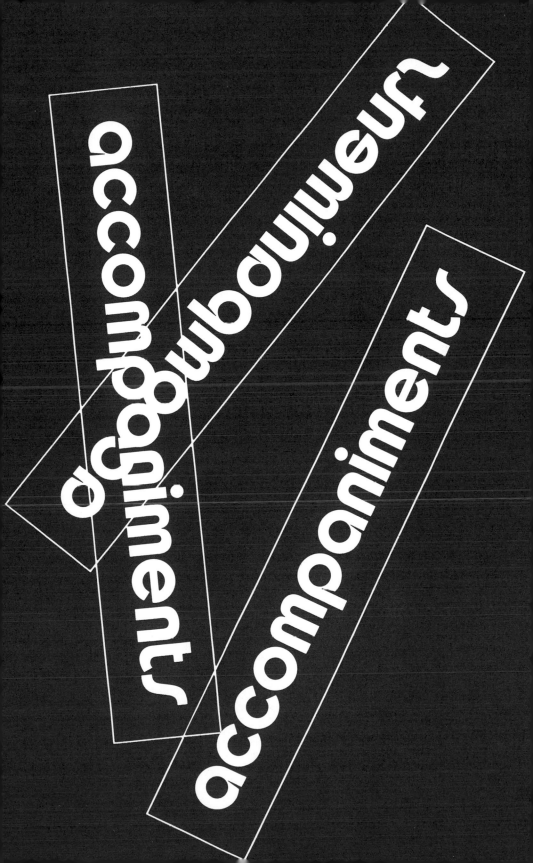

Side dishes play a supporting but important part in the production. An unusual serving dish can help give emphasis. For instance, soufflé dishes are quite versatile and useful, even if you have no luck at all making a soufflé. They're terrific for casserole, potato or cheese dishes. Bake in them, then put them on a platter surrounded with grilled tomatoes or parsley clusters.

Serving two vegetables on one platter is a great look if the tastes and colors complement each other. Peas are attractive surrounded by glazed carrot sticks; little new potatoes drizzled with parsley butter may be bordered with French-cut green beans; or spinach is lovely with a mound of sautéed or creamed mushrooms in the center.

Cold vegetables make a striking summer accompaniment. Using large pieces of lettuce as a base, place cold asparagus or whole green beans (cooked only until tender) down the center of a long platter and outline with tomato wedges or alternating slices of tomatoes and onions. Top it all with a vinaigrette dressing, and sprinkle hard-cooked egg pressed through a sieve down the center of the green vegetable.

vegetables

ARTICHOKE HOLLANDAISE WITH ASPARAGUS TIPS

8 large artichokes
1 lemon
2 T. salt
2 T. oil
Juice of half lemon
  OR 1 T. white vinegar
56 to 64 2" asparagus tips
1/4 C. butter, softened
Salt and pepper to taste
1 recipe Blender Hollandaise Sauce, see pg. 123

Discard stems and outer leaves of artichokes. Cut through artichokes 1-1/2" above base. Rub cut surfaces with 1/2 lemon. Trim base and sides of each artichoke and drop into a bowl of cold water with juice of 1/2 lemon. Fill a stainless steel or enamel kettle two-thirds full with cold water. Add salt, oil and juice of 1/2 lemon. Bring to boil and add drained artichokes. Boil for 30 minutes.

Meanwhile steam the asparagus tips for 6 to 8 minutes, or just until tender. Drain and toss gently with 3 T. of the butter. Season with salt and pepper and keep warm.

Drain artichokes upside-down until cool enough to handle. Pull out centers and scrape out the chokes. Rub surfaces with 1/2 lemon. Rub artichokes with remaining 1 T. softened butter, leaving a bit of butter in center of each. Sprinkle with salt and pepper. Fill artichokes with hollandaise sauce. Arrange asparagus tips in hollandaise sauce, tips up, using 7 or 8 in each artichoke. Serves 8.

191

CREAMED ARTICHOKES

2 T. butter
2 T. flour
1/4 t. salt
1/8 t. pepper
1 C. milk
1/2 C. dry sherry
2 14-oz. cans artichoke hearts, drained and halved
8 oz. can water chestnuts, drained and sliced
4-1/2 oz. jar sliced mushrooms, drained
1/2 C. cheddar cheese, grated
1 T. pimiento, chopped
English muffins or patty shells

Make a white sauce with butter, flour, salt, pepper and milk. Add sherry and stir until smooth. Add artichoke hearts, water chestnuts, mushrooms, cheese and pimiento. Heat and stir to melt cheese. Serve over toasted English muffins or patty shells. Serves 8.

ASPARAGUS AU CHABLIS

3 lbs. fresh asparagus
1 C. green onions, sliced
1 C. butter
1/2 t. thyme
1/2 t. rosemary
2 t. chopped pimiento
1/2 t. salt
1 C. Chablis wine
2 T. Parmesan cheese

Steam fresh asparagus until tender but still crisp. Place in flat, buttered 7" x 11" casserole. Sauté onions in butter; stir in thyme, rosemary, pimiento and salt. Spoon over asparagus. Pour in Chablis. Sprinkle with Parmesan cheese and bake at 350° for 10 minutes. Serves 8.

ASPARAGUS FOLDOVERS

24 spears asparagus, fresh
   OR 2 10-oz. boxes frozen asparagus spears
1 loaf soft sandwich bread
1/2 C. butter, softened
1 to 1-1/2 C. Parmesan cheese, grated

Trim asparagus spears to length of a slice of bread. Steam asparagus spears until just tender but still crisp. Drain well. Remove crusts from bread. Roll each slice flat between wax paper. (Use as many pieces of bread as you have asparagus spears.) Spread each slice with butter and sprinkle heavily with Parmesan cheese. Place one asparagus spear on each bread slice and roll up, diagonally. Place seam-side-down on ungreased baking sheet, brush with remaining butter, melted, and sprinkle with remaining Parmesan cheese. Bake for 10 to 12 minutes at 400°. Makes approximately 24 foldovers.

BARBEQUED GREEN BEANS

4 slices bacon, diced
1 medium onion, chopped
2 16-oz. cans whole green beans, drained
10-1/2 oz. can tomato soup, undiluted
2 T. brown sugar
2 t. barbeque sauce
Salt and pepper to taste

Fry bacon in skillet. Add onion and cook until lightly browned. Add remaining ingredients. Mix thoroughly and pour into greased 1-1/2 qt. casserole. Bake at 350° for 30 to 45 minutes, or until heated through. Serves 6.

CALICO BEANS

1/2 lb. bacon
1 onion, chopped
10 oz. pkg. frozen baby lima beans
16 oz. can pork and beans, undrained
16 oz. can cut green beans, drained
16 oz. can red kidney beans, drained
1/2 C. ketchup
1/2 C. brown sugar
1/4 C. wine (OR 2 T. vinegar)
1 T. prepared mustard
1/2 t. salt

Fry bacon. Drain and crumble. Sauté onion in 2 T. of bacon grease until golden. Cook limas according to package directions. Drain and combine all ingredients. Bake in 2-qt. casserole or bean pot at 300° for 1 to 2 hours. Serves 12. (To reheat, add additional wine.)

HERBED GREEN BEANS

1 lb. fresh green beans
   OR 2 10-oz. pkgs. frozen green beans
1/4 C. butter
1/2 C. onion, chopped
1/2 clove garlic, minced
1/4 C. celery, chopped
1/2 C. parsley, minced
1/4 t. rosemary
1/4 t. basil
3/4 t. salt

Cook green beans and drain. Melt butter and sauté onion, garlic and celery. Add parsley, rosemary, basil and salt; cover and simmer 10 minutes. Just before serving, toss the herb-flavored butter with green beans. Serves 12.

194

SWISS CHEESE GREEN BEANS

2 T. flour
2 T. butter
1-1/2 C. dairy sour cream
1/2 t. onion, grated
1 t. salt
1/4 t. sugar
2 16-oz. cans whole green beans, drained
1/2 lb. Swiss cheese, grated
1/2 C. bread crumbs
2 T. melted butter

Make a white sauce with flour, butter and sour cream. Add onion, salt and sugar. Place a layer of beans, a layer of cheese and repeat layers in a 7" x 11" buttered casserole. Pour white sauce over. Sauté bread crumbs in butter and sprinkle over top of white sauce. Bake at 400° for 20 minutes. Serves 8.

GREEN BEAN BAKE

1/4 C. onions, chopped
3/4 lb. mushrooms, sliced
1/4 C. butter
2 T. flour
1-1/2 C. milk
Dash of Tabasco sauce
1 t. soy sauce
1/2 t. monosodium glutamate
1/2 t. salt
1/4 t. pepper
1/4 lb. cheddar cheese, grated
2 lbs. fresh whole green beans, cooked and drained
8 oz. can water chestnuts, drained and sliced
4 oz. slivered almonds

Brown onions and mushrooms in butter. Stir in flour, then milk. Add Tabasco sauce, soy sauce, monosodium glutamate, salt, pepper and cheese. Add beans. Stir all ingredients lightly and place in 1-qt. buttered casserole. Place sliced water chestnuts on top and cover with almonds. Bake at 375° for 35 to 40 minutes. Serves 8.

BROCCOLI RING

1-1/2 C. coarse soda cracker crumbs
3 C. chopped broccoli
3 eggs
1-1/2 C. canned tomatoes
1 medium onion, sliced
1-1/2 C. diced celery, parboiled
4-1/2 T. butter
3/4 t. salt
1/2 t. pepper

Horseradish-Hollandaise Sauce:
3 egg yolks
Juice of 1 lemon
3/4 C. butter
1/4 C. horseradish

Crush cracker crumbs well. Cook fresh or frozen broccoli. Place remaining ingredients in blender jar and combine. Mix together with broccoli and cracker crumbs. Place in greased 6-cup ring mold. Set in pan of water and bake at 350° for 1 hour.

Meanwhile prepare sauce: Place 3 egg yolks in top of double boiler. Add lemon juice and stir in pieces of butter, 1 T. at a time, pulling pan away from water occasionally as the butter blends into the mixture. (May be made early in the day and left at room temperature.) Stir in horseradish just before serving. Spoon over broccoli ring. Serves 6 to 8.

BROCCOLI FRITTERS

1-1/4 lbs. fresh broccoli
  OR 2 10-oz. boxes frozen chopped
  broccoli
1/2 onion, minced
1/4 C. butter
1/4 C. flour
3 T. butter
2 egg yolks

1/2 C. flour
1 egg
1/2 T. oil
1/2 C. herb stuffing mix, crushed
Shortening or oil for
  deep fat frying

Cook broccoli in boiling salted water until tender but crisp. Drain well. Dry on absorbent paper and chop very fine. In large skillet, sauté onion in 1/4 C. butter. Add broccoli and cook over low heat 3 minutes. Combine 1/4 C. flour and 3 T. butter and stir into broccoli mixture. Stir in egg yolks. Spread mixture in flat buttered dish. Chill 4 hours or overnight. Shape into balls, using 1/4 C. measure for uniform size. Roll each ball first in flour, then in egg beaten with salad oil, then in stuffing crumbs. Heat shortening to 375°; fry broccoli balls, a few at a time until golden, about 3 minutes. Serve immediately, or keep warm in 200° oven. Serves 8.

BROCCOLI WITH PINE NUTS

1 bunch fresh broccoli
1/2 C. butter
1/2 C. golden raisins
1/2 C. pine nuts
2 T. lemon juice

Steam broccoli until tender but still crisp. Melt butter; stir in raisins and pine nuts. Sauté until nuts are golden, approximately 3 minutes. Stir in lemon juice and pour over broccoli. Serves 6.

HERBED BRUSSELS SPROUTS

2 lbs. brussels sprouts
3/4 C. chicken broth
1/4 C. white wine
1/4 t. sage
3 T. Dijon mustard
1 C. heavy cream
1/4 C. slivered almonds, toasted

Simmer brussels sprouts in chicken broth and wine until barely tender. Drain. Stir in sage, mustard and cream. Shake pan so that sprouts are coated. Sprinkle with toasted almonds. Serves 8.

MINTED CARROTS

1 lb. carrots
1/2 C. chicken broth
1/2 t. salt
1/3 C. butter

Pepper to taste
2 T. sugar
1 T. brown sugar
6 sprigs fresh mint

Wash, scrape, rinse and cut carrots diagonally into 1/4" slices. Place in saucepan with chicken broth and salt. Cover tightly; bring to boil and cook until carrots are tender, 6 to 10 minutes. Add butter, pepper and sugars. Continue cooking until liquid is reduced to 1 T. Chop mint leaves, sprinkle over carrots and toss. Serves 4.

SWEET AND SOUR CARROTS

2 lbs. fresh carrots
1 red onion, thinly-sliced
1 green pepper, sliced in thin 1" strips
4 oz. can or jar pimiento, chopped
1 C. fresh parsley, chopped
1/2 C. butter
1 C. sugar
1/2 C. vinegar
10-1/2 oz. can tomato soup, undiluted
1/4 t. salt
1 t. dry mustard

Clean carrots and cut into 1/2" pieces. Cook until tender but still crisp. Drain and place half of carrots in a large, deep, buttered casserole. Top with onion slices, green pepper, pimiento and parsley. Add remaining carrots. Melt butter in saucepan; add sugar, vinegar, soup, salt and dry mustard. Bring to boil and cook 2 to 3 minutes. Pour sauce over carrots. Refrigerate 24 hours. To serve, heat in oven for 40 minutes at 350°. Serves 8. (Also good served cold.)

CORN RING WITH MUSHROOM SAUCE

1/4 C. butter, melted
1/4 C. flour
2 C. hot milk
1 t. salt
1/8 t. pepper
Dash cayenne
1-1/2 C. corn, canned or fresh
4 eggs, separated

Mushroom sauce:
1 C. fresh mushrooms, sliced
1/4 C. butter
2 T. flour
Dash salt
Dash pepper
1 C. chicken broth
    OR 1 C. water and
    1 chicken bouillon cube
Chopped pimiento or parsley (opt.)

Blend butter and flour in saucepan. Add hot milk gradually, stirring until smooth. Season with salt, pepper and cayenne. Add corn and cook 2 minutes. Remove from heat and add beaten egg yolks. Beat egg whites until stiff and fold into corn mixture. Pour into greased 6 C. ring mold and set in pan of water. Bake for 1 hour at 300°.

To make sauce, lightly brown mushrooms in butter. Blend in flour, salt and pepper. Gradually add chicken broth, stirring until mixture comes to a boil. Add pimiento or parsley, if desired, and simmer 1 to 2 minutes longer. Spoon over corn ring. Serves 8.

SCALLOPED EGGPLANT

1 large eggplant (4 C. diced)
1/3 C. milk
10-1/2 oz. can cream of mushroom soup, undiluted
1 egg, slightly-beaten
1/2 C. onion, chopped
3/4 C. packaged herb-seasoned stuffing

Cheese Topping:
1/2 C. packaged herb-seasoned stuffing
2 T. butter, melted
1 C. sharp cheese, grated

Peel eggplant and dice. Cook in boiling, salted water until tender, 6 to 7 minutes. Drain. Meanwhile, gradually stir milk into soup; blend in egg. Add drained eggplant, onion and stuffing. Toss lightly and turn into 6" x 10" baking dish.

For cheese topping, finely crush stuffing and toss with melted butter. Sprinkle over casserole. Top with grated cheese and bake at 350° for 20 minutes. Serves 6 to 8.

CREAMED MUSHROOMS

1 lb. fresh mushrooms, sliced
1/4 lb. crackers, crushed
1-1/4 C. light cream
1 t. salt
Pepper to taste
2 T. butter

Combine mushrooms, crackers, cream and seasonings. Place in 1-qt. buttered casserole and dot with butter. Bake at 350° for 45 minutes to 1 hour. Serves 6.

STUFFED ONIONS

8 white onions
1 C. mayonnaise
1/4 C. fresh lemon juice
1/2 C. dairy sour cream
1/3 C. milk
1/8 t. nutmeg
Salt and pepper to taste
10 oz. box frozen chopped spinach

Cook onions in boiling water until tender, about 1 hour. Cool. Remove top stem of onions with straight slice across. Cut off root area carefully, leaving as much of the bottom intact as possible so that filling will stay in. Remove and reserve center of onions, leaving 2 or 3 layers of the outside for shell. Chop reserved onion. Combine mayonnaise, lemon juice, sour cream, milk, nutmeg, salt and pepper, and mix half of this with the chopped onions. Cook spinach half as long as package directs and drain very well. Combine with creamed onion mixture. Mound spinach mixture in onion shells and cover with remaining half of sauce mixture. Bake for 20 minutes at 350°. (Delicious with beef.) Serves 8.

PEAS AUBERGE

2 T. butter
1/4 head iceberg lettuce, torn
2 green onions, sliced
1 t. sugar
1 t. monosodium glutamate
1/8 t. freshly-ground pepper
1 bay leaf
2 10-oz. pkgs. frozen peas
1/4 lb. fresh snow peas (Oriental pea pods)
2 T. chives, chopped
2 T. parsley, chopped
1/4 C. butter

Melt 2 T. butter in large skillet. Add lettuce, onions, sugar, monosodium glutamate, pepper and bay leaf. Crumble frozen peas into same pan. Add snow peas. Cover and bring to a quick boil. Cook for 3 to 5 minutes. Turn heat off, leave pan covered and let steam 1 minute. Add chives, parsley and remaining butter. Toss well. Serves 8.

PEAS ORIENTAL

1 lb. fresh mushrooms, thickly-sliced
1/4 C. butter
3 10-oz. pkgs. frozen peas
2 8-oz. cans water chestnuts, drained and sliced
2 16-oz. cans bean sprouts, drained and rinsed
2 10-1/2 oz. cans cream of mushroom soup, undiluted
2 3-oz. cans French fried onion rings

Sauté mushrooms in butter. Parboil peas. Mix mushrooms, peas and remaining ingredients (except onion rings) in a large casserole. Bake 30 minutes at 350°. Crumble onion rings on top of casserole and bake at 350° for 5 to 10 minutes. Serves 12.

CHEESE POTATOES

2 10-oz. boxes frozen hash brown potatoes
1 t. salt
1/2 t. pepper
2 T. onion, minced
10-1/2 oz. can cream of chicken soup, undiluted
1 C. dairy sour cream
1/2 C. cheddar cheese, grated
2 T. butter

Thaw potatoes. Mix with salt, pepper, onion, soup and sour cream.Sprinkle cheese on top and dot with butter. Bake 1 hour, or until brown and bubbly in a 350° oven. Serves 10.

RATATOUILLE

2 large onions, chopped
2 large green peppers, chopped
2 cloves garlic, mashed
1/4 C. olive oil
1 lb. zucchini squash, sliced
1/4 C. butter
1 eggplant, unpeeled and diced
1/2 lb. fresh mushrooms, quartered
4 tomatoes, peeled and chopped
8 oz. can tomato sauce
1-1/2 t. fines herbes
1/8 t. thyme
Salt and pepper to taste
8 oz. pkg. herb-seasoned stuffing
1/2 C. Parmesan cheese, grated
1 C. Swiss cheese, grated

Sauté onion, peppers and garlic in oil until onions are transparent. Lift from pan with slotted spoon and place in buttered casserole. Sauté zucchini in butter for 5 to 10 minutes. Lift out and place in casserole. Sauté eggplant, adding more butter if necessary. Lift out and place in casserole. Sauté mushrooms; lift out and place in casserole. Add tomatoes, tomato sauce, fines herbes, thyme, salt and pepper and stuffing to casserole. Mix lightly with fork and top with Parmesan cheese and Swiss cheese. Bake at 350° for 30 minutes, or until just heated through. (May be made ahead and refrigerated.) Serves 12.

SPINACH INTRIGUE

2 10-oz. pkgs. frozen chopped spinach
1/2 lb. fresh mushrooms, sliced
2 T. onions, chopped
1/2 C. butter
6 oz. can tomato paste
1 C. dairy sour cream
Paprika

Cook spinach according to package directions. Drain thoroughly and set aside. Sauté mushrooms and onions in butter. Place spinach in 6" x 10" buttered casserole. Add onions, mushrooms and butter. Mix. Spread tomato paste on top of casserole, completely covering spinach. Cover tomato paste completely with sour cream. Sprinkle with paprika, and bake at 350° for 20 minutes, or until thoroughly heated. Serves 8.

SPINACH QUICHE

Pastry for 9" pie pan
1 C. dried beans
1 egg yolk
2 T. green onions, sliced
2 T. butter
1-1/4 C. chopped spinach, cooked and well-drained
4 eggs
1-1/2 C. heavy cream
Salt and pepper to taste
Dash freshly-grated nutmeg
1/2 C. Swiss cheese, grated
1 T. butter, cut in small pieces

Line pie pan with pastry. Place a piece of aluminum foil, shiny side down, in pastry shell and cover with dried beans. Bake in 425° oven for 15 to 20 minutes. Remove from oven, discard foil and beans and brush shell with slightly-beaten egg yolk to seal crust. Return to oven for 3 to 4 minutes. Cool shell. Sauté onions in butter. Combine spinach and onions. Beat eggs, cream, salt, pepper and nutmeg. Stir in spinach mixture and pour filling into pastry shell. Sprinkle with cheese, dot with butter and bake at 375° for 30 to 45 minutes, or until set. Serves 6.

SPINACH BROCCOLI CASSEROLE

10 oz. pkg. frozen chopped spinach
10 oz. pkg. frozen chopped broccoli
5 oz. cream of mushroom soup, undiluted
8 oz. jar Cheese Whiz
1/4 lb. fresh mushrooms, sliced
2 T. butter
1/4 t. nutmeg
1/4 t. salt
1/8 t. pepper
2 T. Parmesan cheese, grated

Cook broccoli and spinach until barely tender. Drain well. In double boiler, combine soup and cheese, stirring until smooth. Sauté mushrooms in butter. Combine all ingredients except Parmesan cheese and place in buttered 1-1/2 qt. casserole. Top with Parmesan cheese. Bake at 325° for 25 minutes. Serves 6.

SPINACH ON ARTICHOKE BOTTOMS

6 oz. jar marinated artichoke bottoms, drained
   OR 6 oz. jar marinated artichoke hearts, drained
2 10-oz. pkgs. frozen chopped spinach, defrosted
3 T. butter, softened
6 oz. cream cheese, softened
1/4 C. milk
Freshly-ground pepper
1/2 C. Romano cheese, grated

Place artichoke bottoms or hearts in bottom of 1-qt. buttered casserole. Squeeze spinach dry and sprinkle over artichokes. Blend butter and cream cheese; add milk. Spread to cover spinach. Grind pepper over top, and sprinkle Romano cheese over surface. (May be prepared ahead to this point.) Bake, covered, for 40 minutes at 350°. Remove cover after first 30 minutes. Serves 4.

STUFFED CROOKNECK SQUASH

40 whole crookneck squash   1 t. salt
   (about size of an egg)   1/4 t. pepper
1/2 C. onion, chopped   Chopped fresh parsley
1/2 C. butter

Cook whole squash in boiling water for 20 to 30 minutes, until almost tender. Drain and run cold water over squash. Cut top 1/3 off squash and scoop out pulp. (Some will break, but 24 are needed whole.) Drain pulp. Sauté onion in butter. Mash pulp, remaining broken squash, onions, salt and pepper. Stuff squash with mixture. (May be prepared ahead to this point.) Bake at 350° for 15 minutes. Sprinkle with chopped parsley. Serves 12.

YELLOW SQUASH SOUFFLÉ

4 lbs. yellow squash   1 t. salt
8 oz. cream cheese   12 Ritz crackers, crushed
1/2 C. butter   2 T. butter

Wash squash, brushing skins. Slice and boil in salted water until tender. Drain very well, pressing water out of squash. Blend squash, cream cheese, 1/2 C. butter and salt. Place in buttered 1-qt. soufflé dish, top with cracker crumbs and dot with remaining 2 T. butter. Bake for 30 minutes, uncovered, at 350°. Serves 4 to 6.

CHEESE SOUFFLÉ TOMATOES

8 large firm tomatoes
1/4 C. butter
1/2 C. flour
1-1/4 t. salt
1/8 t. pepper
Dash nutmeg
1/8 t. seasoned salt
1 C. milk
1/4 C. heavy cream
1-1/2 C. Swiss cheese, grated
1-1/2 C. rice, cooked
1/4 C. parsley, snipped
4 egg yolks

Wash tomatoes; cut off tops and scoop out pulp. Drain, upside down. Melt butter; stir in flour, salt, pepper, nutmeg and seasoned salt. Slowly add milk and cream. Cook until smooth and thick. Reserve 2 T. Swiss cheese and add remaining cheese to sauce. Remove from heat. Stir in rice, parsley and egg yolks, one at a time. Cut foil pieces to fit around each tomato extending 1" above top of tomato. Fill tomatoes with cheese mixture and place in shallow baking dish. Sprinkle with reserved 2 T. cheese. Bake at 350° for 30 minutes. Remove foil and serve immediately. Serves 8.

TOMATOES PROVENÇALE

1/4 C. butter
2 T. oil
2 pints cherry tomatoes
2 cloves garlic, crushed
2 shallots OR green onions, chopped
Salt and freshly-ground pepper to taste
2 T. parsley, chopped
1/4 C. coarse bread crumbs

Heat butter and oil in skillet; add tomatoes and sauté quickly, about 2 minutes. Add garlic, shallots, salt, pepper and sauté for an additional 3 to 4 minutes. Remove tomatoes and place in a warm serving dish. Sprinkle with chopped parsley. Brown crumbs in skillet until golden. Sprinkle over tomatoes. Serves 6 to 8.

TOMATO STACK-UPS

3 large tomatoes
Salt
4 oz. Swiss cheese, shredded
10 oz. pkg. frozen chopped broccoli, cooked and drained
1/4 C. onion, chopped

Cut tomatoes into 3/4" slices. Sprinkle lightly with salt. Set aside 2 T. of the shredded cheese. Combine remaining cheese, broccoli and onion. Place tomato slices on baking sheet. Spoon broccoli mixture onto tomatoes. Sprinkle with reserved cheese. Broil 7 to 8" from heat, until cheese is bubbly and browned. Serves 6.

STUFFED TOMATOES

8 firm tomatoes
1-1/2 lbs. fresh mushrooms, sliced
1/2 C. butter
1/4 C. flour
3/4 C. dairy sour cream
4 oz. blue cheese
1/4 t. salad seasoning
2 t. fresh parsley, chopped
2 T. dry sherry
Salt and pepper to taste
4 oz. pkg. almonds, slivered and blanched

Remove core and pulp of tomatoes with melon scoop or teaspoon. Sauté mushrooms in butter; combine flour and sour cream and add to mushrooms. Add remaining ingredients except almonds and simmer until sauce is smooth and thick. Stuff the tomatoes with sauce and place in 2-qt. buttered casserole. Refrigerate overnight, or until 20 minutes before serving time. Bake 15 minutes in 375° oven. Sprinkle almonds on top and return to oven for 5 minutes. Serve immediately. Serves 8.

ZUCCHINI WITH SPINACH PUREE

6 small zucchini squash
2 T. butter, melted
2 10-oz. pkgs. frozen spinach
3 T. onion, chopped
2 T. butter
2 T. flour
3/4 C. milk, warmed
2 t. lemon juice
1/4 t. nutmeg
10 to 12 Ritz crackers, crushed
2 T. butter, melted
Parsley
1 large carrot

Wash and trim ends from zucchini. Cook in salted water for 10 minutes. Cut in half lengthwise, and scoop out seeds to make a shell. Rub entire surface with butter. Cook spinach in small amount of salted water, just until entirely thawed. Drain spinach well. Sauté onion in butter until soft but not brown. Add flour and cook 2 minutes, stirring. Add warm milk, stirring constantly until thickened. Blend in spinach, lemon juice and nutmeg. Season to taste. Place spinach mixture in blender jar and blend until smooth. (Mixture should be thick enough to mound on spoon.) Fill zucchini with puree. Toss Ritz crackers with butter. Sprinkle over spinach puree in zucchini. (May be prepared ahead to this point.) When ready to serve, heat for 20 to 30 minutes, uncovered, on cookie sheet in 375° oven. To serve, arrange zucchini spoke-fashion on large round platter. Decorate with parsley and make carrot curls by peeling long, thin pieces from center of carrot with vegetable peeler. Roll up, secure with toothpick and chill in bowl of water for several hours. Remove toothpicks, drain and garnish platter with carrot curls. Serves 12.

ZUCCHINI TOMATO CASSEROLE

1/2 onion, chopped
2 T. butter
3 C. sliced zucchini
3 small tomatoes, peeled and chopped
Salt and pepper to taste

1/3 C. Italian bread crumbs
1/2 lb. mozzarella cheese, grated
1/3 C. Parmesan cheese, grated
4 T. butter

Sauté onion in butter. In a buttered 1-1/2 qt. casserole, layer half of zucchini, onion, tomatoes, salt and pepper, bread crumbs, mozzarella cheese, Parmesan cheese and dots of butter. Repeat layers. Bake at 350°, uncovered, for 45 minutes. Check after 30 minutes and add 2 T. water if dry. Serves 6.

potpourri

RICE WITH CHIVES

1-1/2 C. chicken bouillon
3/4 C. rice, uncooked
1/2 t. chives
Salt to taste

Bring bouillon to a simmer; add rice, chives and salt. Cover; reduce heat to low and cook for 25 minutes, or until liquid is absorbed. Serves 4.

RIZ VERT

1/2 C. olive oil
2 stalks celery, sliced
6 green onions, sliced
2 cloves garlic, minced
1/2 lb. spinach, chopped
2 carrots, grated
2 C. rice, uncooked
4 C. chicken broth
    OR canned chicken consommé
2 t. salt
1/2 t. pepper
3 T. butter
3 T. parsley, chopped
1/2 C. Parmesan cheese, grated

Heat oil in saucepan. Add celery, green onions, garlic, spinach and carrots. Cook over low heat for 20 minutes. Add rice; cook 5 minutes, stirring frequently. Add chicken broth, salt and pepper. Stir, cover and cook over low heat until rice is tender, approximately 25 minutes. Add butter, parsley and cheese. Place in 7" x 11" buttered casserole and bake in 350° oven for 20 minutes. Serves 10.

WILD RICE

1 C. wild rice, uncooked
1 onion, diced
1 lb. fresh mushrooms, sliced
6 T. butter
2 beef bouillon cubes
1/4 C. light cream
Salt and pepper to taste

Cook rice in double boiler according to package directions. Drain and rinse well until water is completely free of green tint. Sauté onion and mushrooms in butter. Add bouillon cubes and stir until dissolved. Add cream and salt and pepper to taste. Pour sauce over cooked rice and bake in 350° oven for 45 minutes, covered. Serves 8.

WILD RICE CASSEROLE

1/2 C. butter
10-1/2 oz. can beef consommé, undiluted
10-1/2 oz. can onion soup, undiluted
8 oz. can water chestnuts, sliced and drained
8 oz. can sliced mushrooms, drained
6 oz. box Long-Grain and Wild Rice

Place butter and soups in 1-1/2 qt. casserole and place in 350° oven until butter is melted. Add water chestnuts, mushrooms and rice with seasonings. Stir to mix and return to 350° oven for 1 hour, uncovered. Serves 8.

CHINESE FRIED RICE

2 C. onions, chopped
2 T. oil
2 C. cooked rice, cold
2 eggs, stirred slightly
1 T. soy sauce
1/2 t. salt
1/2 C. frozen peas, defrosted
2 C. cooked meat (bacon, ham, shrimp, pork, etc.) Optional

Sauté onions in oil until brown. Add rice and sauté. Blend in mixture of eggs, soy sauce and salt. Add peas and cooked meat, if desired. Stir until eggs have set and mixture is thoroughly heated. Serves 4.

209

BAKED SOUR CREAM ENCHILADAS

12 corn tortillas
1/3 to 1/2 C. oil
1 onion, chopped
2 T. oil
28 oz. solid-pack tomatoes, chopped
1 t. oregano
Dash salt
2 to 3 T. salsa jalapeño
1 lb. Monterrey jack cheese
2 C. dairy sour cream
Salt to taste

Soften tortillas in hot oil briefly; remove and drain on paper towels. Sauté onion in oil. Add tomatoes. Crush oregano and add; add salt and salsa jalapeño. Cook slowly for 15 to 20 minutes. Set aside. Cut 12 cubes from part of cheese. Place a cube of cheese and some sauce in each tortilla; roll up and place in greased casserole, seam-side-down. Do not crowd. Spoon salted sour cream on top and add remaining sauce. Grate remaining cheese and sprinkle over top. Bake 30 minutes at 350°. Serves 6 to 8.

GREEN CHILIES AND CHEESE

3 4-oz. cans whole green chilies
1 lb. sharp cheese, grated
4 eggs
2 C. milk
1 C. flour
2 t. salt
1 t. pepper

Butter a 1-1/2 to 2-qt. casserole. Drain chilies, reserving liquid. Rinse chilies and remove seeds. Layer cheese and chilies in casserole. Combine eggs, milk, flour, salt, pepper and reserved liquid. Pour over chilies and cheese and bake 1 hour at 325°. Serves 8.

UNCLE HENRY'S PIE

4 oz. can whole green chilies
10 oz. sharp cheese, grated
4 eggs

Drain chilies. Split, remove seeds and rinse chilies. Grease 8" pie pan lightly or spray with non-stick vegetable coating. Line with chilies. Put cheese over chilies. Beat eggs with wire whisk and pour over cheese. Bake at 325° for 30 minutes, or until knife comes out clean. Serves 6.

CALIFORNIA CASSEROLE

1/4 C. butter
1 C. onion, chopped
1 C. + 2 T. rice, uncooked
2 C. dairy sour cream
1 C. small-curd cottage cheese
1 t. basil
1/2 t. salt
1/8 t. pepper
3 4-oz. cans whole green chilies
2 C. sharp cheddar cheese, grated
Chopped fresh parsley

Grease 9" x 13" casserole. Sauté onion in butter until soft. Cook rice according to package directions. Add to onion, sour cream, cottage cheese, and seasonings. Toss to blend all ingredients well. Drain chilies; rinse and remove seeds. Layer half of rice mixture in casserole, half of chilies and half of cheese. Repeat layers. Bake 25 minutes at 375°. Sprinkle with parsley. Serves 12.

SPAGHETTI AL BURRO

1 C. parsley, chopped
I T. basil
1 t. salt
1/8 t. white pepper
1 clove garlic, minced
1/2 C. olive oil
2 T. melted butter
3/4 C. Parmesan cheese, grated
1/4 C. English walnuts, chopped
2 T. boiling water
1 lb. spaghetti, cooked

Combine parsley, basil, salt, white pepper, garlic, olive oil, butter, Parmesan cheese and walnuts. Add 2 T. boiling water, and stir mixture into drained spaghetti. Serves 8.

SWISS NOODLES

8 oz. medium-wide egg noodles
1 t. oil
5 T. butter
1/2 lb. Swiss cheese, grated
Salt and pepper to taste
4 C. milk
Paprika

Cook noodles until barely tender in boiling, salted water, to which 1 t. oil has been added. Drain and rinse in cold water. In deep 2-1/2 to 3-qt. buttered casserole, make 2 layers each of noodles, butter, cheese, salt and pepper, ending with cheese on top. Pour milk into casserole to within 1" from top of noodles. Sprinkle generously with paprika. Cover and bake 1 hour, or until bubbly, at 350°. Uncover and continue baking for 30 minutes, or until top is crusty. Serves 8.

YORKSHIRE PUDDING

1-1/4 C. milk
1/4 C. water
1 C. flour
1 t. salt
4 eggs
2 T. beef drippings from roast

Beat milk, water, flour, salt and eggs until smooth and bubbly. Set aside for 30 minutes. Beat 1 minute more. Put 1/2 t. of hot fat into each of 12 sections of muffin tin. Heat in 500° oven for 1 to 2 minutes. Place 3 T. batter in each section and bake at 500° for 8 to 12 minutes, or until browned. Serve with beef au jus or gravy. Makes 12.

CHEESE GRITS

1-1/2 C. grits
6 C. water
1 lb. New York sharp cheese, grated
3/4 C. butter
3 eggs, beaten
1 T. seasoned salt
1 t. paprika
2 t. salt
Several drops Tabasco sauce

Cook grits in 6 C. water according to package directions. While still warm, add remaining ingredients. (May be prepared ahead to this point.) Bake in 2-1/2 qt. buttered soufflé dish for 1 to 1-1/2 hours at 350°. Serves 12.

SPOON BREAD

1/2 C. butter
5 eggs, separated
1/2 C. yellow cornmeal
2 C. milk
1 t. salt

Melt butter in top of double boiler. Add beaten egg yolks, cornmeal, milk and salt. Continue cooking over boiling water, stirring constantly to avoid lumps, until mixture is very thick. Remove from heat, cool slightly and fold in stiffly-beaten egg whites. Bake in buttered 2-qt. casserole in middle of 325° oven for 45 to 60 minutes. Serve immediately. Serves 6 to 8.

PINEAPPLE DATE CHUTNEY

1 fresh pineapple, cored and cubed
3 C. light brown sugar
3 C. cider vinegar
1 C. raisins
1 C. currants
1 C. pitted dates, chopped
1/4 C. lemon juice
3 T. fresh ginger, minced
2-1/2 T. green peppercorns
1 red pepper, halved and seeded
1 t. salt
1/2 t. ground allspice

Bring all ingredients to a boil and cook over high heat until thick, about 30 minutes. Spoon mixture into sterilized jars and seal. Makes 2 quarts. (A nice complement to any curry entrée.)

APPLE CHUTNEY

3 red peppers
3 green peppers
12 tart apples
12 ripe tomatoes
6 onions
1 C. celery, diced
2 oz. crystallized ginger
1 lb. raisins
2 qts. cider vinegar
3 C. sugar

Cut peppers in half and remove seeds. Pare and core apples. Chop peppers, apples, tomatoes, onions and celery coarsely. Place in large kettle with ginger, raisins, vinegar and sugar. Cook until chutney is thick and clear, about 1 hour. Fill sterilized jars and seal at once. Makes 4 quarts.

BROWN RICE DRESSING

2-1/2 C. brown rice
OR half wild rice and half
brown rice
chicken broth
1 C. onion, diced
1 C. celery, diced
1/2 C. butter
1/4 to 1/2 C. minced fresh parsley

2 C. pecans, chopped
Turkey giblets, cooked and chopped
1 pint fresh oysters, sautéed (opt.)
1-1/2 t. salt
1 t. thyme
1/2 t. poultry seasoning
Pepper to taste

Cook rice according to package directions substituting chicken broth for water called for in directions. Sauté onion and celery in butter. Add remaining ingredients and combine. Stuff turkey and place remaining dressing in casserole. Heat in 350° oven for 15 to 20 minutes, or until thoroughly heated. Serves 14 to 16.

CORNBREAD STUFFING

2 8-1/2 oz. boxes cornbread mix
1 large onion, chopped
1 large stalk celery, chopped
1/2 C. butter, melted
1 lb. sausage, mild

1 T. poultry seasoning
1 t. salt
1/4 t. pepper
1 to 1-1/2 C. hot water
OR turkey broth

Bake cornbread as directed on package. Cook onion and celery in butter until tender. Brown sausage and drain. Crumble cornbread, add poultry seasoning, and salt and pepper. Dampen cornbread with water or broth until moist. Add celery, onion and sausage. Mix well. Stuff an 18 to 20-lb. turkey lightly.

SAUSAGE RICE STUFFING

1 lb. bulk sausage
1 onion, chopped
1 green pepper, chopped
2-3/4 oz. dry chicken noodle soup
(2 packets)

1 C. wild or plain rice, uncooked
1 C. celery, diced
1 C. almonds, sliced and toasted
5 C. water

Brown sausage lightly in skillet. Drain. In same skillet, sauté onion and green pepper. Combine these ingredients with noodle soup mix, rice, celery, almonds and water. Stuff a 15-lb. turkey lightly. (To make a sausage casserole, double amount of sausage. Bake in 4-qt. casserole for 1-1/2 hours at 375°.) Serves 6.

215

breads

There aren't enough good words to say about homemade bread. It tastes good, looks good, smells good, feels good, and it makes you feel good to bake bread. No other cooking endeavor can satisfy so many of the senses.

The things you can do with bread are almost limitless. Bread may be baked in any kind of ovenproof container, even a flowerpot. You may add things to any basic recipe—chopped nuts, slightly sautéed onions, grated cheese or wheat germ. You may roll things up in it—cinnamon and sugar; mustard and onions; or thickened spaghetti sauce. A small round loaf, hollowed, makes a nice vessel for seafood salad or thick shrimp dip; fill a large brioche with chicken and ham mornay or fresh strawberries in sweetened whipped cream. For a different twist, try a braided ring with colored Easter eggs baked right in it. Most bread recipes make two loaves, and there's no nicer or more welcome gift for a friend.

Because of its qualities, bread in a loaf shape should be served whole in an earthy-type container. A wicker basket or rough, well-worn bread board is ideal. The board should suit the shape of the loaf, and a napkin tied on the handle adds a colorful note. Butter, mounded in a crock, may be placed on the board and passed with the bread. If the bread lends itself to being torn rather than sliced, the hostess should act as the guide. On the other end of the scale, lovely light rolls may be presented delightfully in a silver bread basket wrapped in Belgian linen.

quick breads

SUGAR-COATED BREAKFAST MUFFINS

5 T. butter
1/2 C. sugar
1 egg yolk
1-1/2 C. flour
1-1/8 t. baking powder
1/4 t. salt
1/4 t. nutmeg
1/2 C. milk
2 egg whites

Topping:
6 T. butter, melted
1/2 C. sugar
1 t. cinnamon

Cream butter and sugar; add egg yolk. Sift dry ingredients and add to creamed mixture alternately with milk. Beat egg whites until stiff and fold in. Grease muffin tins and fill half full with batter. Bake at 350° for 20 to 25 minutes. Remove from oven and quickly dip top of muffins in melted butter, then in mixture of sugar and cinnamon. Serve warm. Makes 1 dozen.

APPLESAUCE MUFFINS

1-3/4 C. flour
1 t. soda
1/2 t. cinnamon
1 t. allspice
1/2 t. salt
1/2 C. butter
3/4 C. sugar
1 egg
1 C. applesauce
1 C. raisins

Sift flour. Measure and resift 3 times with soda, spices and salt. Cream butter and sugar. Add egg. Beat well; add applesauce and flour mixture. Gently fold in raisins. Fill muffin cups two-thirds full and bake at 350° for 20 to 25 minutes. Makes 14 muffins.

REFRIGERATOR GINGERBREAD MUFFINS

2/3 C. shortening
1 C. sugar
2 eggs, beaten
4 C. flour, sifted
2 t. soda
1 t. ginger
1/4 t. allspice
1/4 t. nutmeg
1 C. sour milk OR buttermilk
1 C. light molasses
1 t. vanilla
1 C. raisins (optional)
1 C. walnuts or pecans, chopped (optional)

Cream shortening and sugar; add eggs and mix well. Sift dry ingredients and add alternately with sour milk and molasses. Add vanilla and optional raisins and nuts. Refrigerate overnight. As needed, fill muffin tins half full and bake at 350° for 20 to 25 minutes. (Batter will keep in refrigerator for 4 to 5 weeks.) Makes 5 dozen muffins.

REFRIGERATOR BRAN MUFFINS

1 C. boiling water
1 C. 100% Bran
1-3/4 C. sugar
1/2 C. vegetable shortening
2 eggs
2-1/2 C. flour
2-1/2 t. soda
1/2 t. salt
1-3/4 C. buttermilk
2 C. All Bran
3/4 C. raisins (dark or golden)

Pour boiling water over 100% Bran. Let stand until cool. Cream sugar and shortening. Add eggs, one at a time. Sift dry ingredients and add alternately with buttermilk. Beat until smooth. Add cooled 100% Bran, All Bran and raisins. Refrigerate overnight. Do not stir. As needed, dip spoon in batter to fill muffin tins half full. Bake for 20 minutes at 400°. (Batter keeps 4 to 5 weeks in refrigerator.) Makes 3 dozen muffins.

CRANBERRY MUFFINS

1/4 C. sugar
2 C. flour
3/4 t. baking soda
1/4 t. salt
1 egg
1/4 C. shortening, melted and cooled
3/4 C. sour milk OR buttermilk
1 C. cranberries, chopped
1/2 C. sugar

Sift 1/4 C. sugar, flour, baking soda and salt into 3-qt. bowl. Beat egg; add shortening and sour milk. With fork, gently combine dry ingredients with liquid mixture, just until moistened. Do not beat. Combine cranberries and 1/2 C. sugar and fold in. (Mixture will not be smooth.) Fill greased muffin tins three-quarters full. Bake at 375° for 25 minutes. Makes 1 dozen.

QUICK COFFEE CRISPS

8 slices white bread
2 T. butter, softened
2 T. orange marmalade
   OR 1 t. cinnamon mixed with
   1/4 C. sugar

With cookie cutter, cut 2 rounds from each slice of bread. Spread rounds with butter, then marmalade; OR sprinkle with cinnamon-sugar mixture. Place rounds on cookie sheet and bake at 350° for 20 minutes. Serves 4 to 6.

PENNSYLVANIA DUTCH FUNNEL CAKES

2 eggs
2 C. milk
2 C. flour
1/4 C. sugar
1 t. baking powder
1/2 t. salt
Powdered sugar
Oil for deep frying

Beat eggs and add milk. Sift flour, sugar, baking powder and salt. Add to milk mixture and stir until smooth. Holding your finger over the bottom of a funnel, pour some batter into the funnel. Remove finger and swirl batter into 375° deep fat, forming rings around rings. Fry briefly until golden brown. Drain and sprinkle with powdered sugar while hot. (These are good with ice cream or with syrup poured over them.) Makes 3 dozen.

SPICED APPLE PANCAKES

2 C. biscuit mix
1/2 t. cinnamon
1 egg
1-1/3 C. milk
3/4 C. apple, peeled and grated

Cider Sauce:
1 C. sugar
2 T. cornstarch
1/2 t. pumpkin pie spice
2 C. apple cider
2 T. lemon juice
1/4 C. butter

Combine biscuit mix, cinnamon, egg and milk until smooth. Add apples. Pour batter from 1/4 C. measure onto hot griddle. Bake until bubbles appear; turn and cook other side until golden. Makes 18 pancakes. Serve with Cider Sauce.

To make Cider Sauce, mix sugar, cornstarch and pumpkin pie spice in saucepan. Stir in cider and lemon juice. Cook, stirring constantly, until mixture thickens and boils. Boil and stir 1 minute. Remove from heat and blend in butter.

IDA BELLE WAFFLES

4 eggs
2 C. milk
2-1/2 C. flour, sifted
2 T. sugar
1 T. baking powder
1 t. salt
1/2 C. butter, melted

Separate eggs; beat yolks and add milk. Sift dry ingredients and add slowly, beating well. Add melted butter. Fold in stiffly-beaten egg whites. Grill on hot waffle iron. Makes 14 small waffles.

ADIRONDACKS

2 C. flour
1 t. baking soda
1/4 t. baking powder
3 T. sugar
1 t. salt
2 C. buttermilk
4 eggs, separated
2 T. butter, melted

1 C. heavy cream
1 T. sugar
1 t. vanilla

1/2 C. butter, melted
1 C. brown sugar
Warm syrup

Sift dry ingredients into large bowl. Add the following, one at a time, mixing after each addition: buttermilk, egg yolks and melted butter. Beat egg whites until stiff, but not dry, and gently fold into batter. Cook on a hot griddle.

Whip cream with sugar and vanilla. Serve Adirondacks with pitcher of melted butter, bowl of brown sugar, warm syrup and sweetened whipped cream. Put melted butter and brown sugar between each pancake and on top. Pour syrup over stack and top with a dollop of whipped cream. Serves 6.

LUNCHEON CRÊPES

2/3 C. flour
1/2 t. salt
3 eggs
1 C. milk
3 T. butter, melted
Vegetable oil·

Combine flour and salt. Lightly beat eggs, and sift flour mixture over top of eggs. Beat until smooth, and stir in milk and melted butter. Let batter stand for 1 hour. Lightly oil 6" skillet and heat until a drop of water sizzles in skillet. Spoon approximately 3 T. batter into pan; rotate pan quickly so that batter covers bottom of pan. Cook 1 minute; turn and cook 30 seconds on other side. Remove from skillet and repeat procedure until all batter is used. Brush pan with oil between each crêpe. (Crêpes may be prepared ahead and refrigerated; reheat in slow oven before filling.) Makes 12 crêpes.

KRINGLER

1 C. flour	1 C. water	3/4 C. powdered sugar
1 C. sugar	1/2 C. butter	1 T. milk
1/2 C. butter, softened	1 C. flour	1/2 t. almond extract
1 T. water	3 eggs	2 oz. sliced almonds
	1/2 t. almond extract	

Mix flour and sugar; cut in butter. Add 1 T. water and stir. Pat onto cookie sheet with sides. Bring 1 C. water to boiling; add butter, stirring to melt. Remove from heat and add flour, eggs, and almond extract, blending well. Spread this mixture on top of first layer. Bake for 45 minutes at 350°. Remove from oven and spread with mixture of powdered sugar, milk and almond extract. Sprinkle with sliced almonds. Cool and cut into bars. Serves 12.

SWEDISH APPLE COFFEE CAKE

1-1/2 C. sugar	Glaze:
1/2 C. shortening	3 T. butter
2 eggs	3 T. brown sugar
1 t. vanilla	2 T. milk
1-1/2 C. flour	
1 t. cinnamon	
1 t. soda	
Dash salt	
Dash ground cloves	
3 C. apples, peeled and diced	
1/2 C. nuts, chopped	

Cream sugar, shortening, eggs and vanilla. Sift dry ingredients and add to creamed mixture. Fold in apples and nuts. Bake in a greased 9" x 9" pan at 375° for 35 to 40 minutes. Heat butter, brown sugar and milk together, stirring to dissolve brown sugar. Drizzle over top of cake. Serves 9.

BLUEBERRY COFFEECAKE

1 C. butter
2 C. sugar
2 eggs
1 C. dairy sour cream
1/2 t. vanilla
2 C. cake flour
   OR 1-5/8 C. all-purpose flour
1 t. baking powder
1/4 t. salt
1/2 C. blueberries, fresh
   OR canned and well-drained

Filling:
1/2 C. brown sugar
1 t. cinnamon
1/2 C. nuts, chopped
Powdered sugar

Cream butter and sugar; add eggs. Fold in sour cream and vanilla. Add dry ingredients. Fold in blueberries. Grease and flour a tube pan or bundt pan. Pour 1/3 of batter in pan. Combine brown sugar, cinnamon and nuts for filling. Sprinkle first third of batter with half of filling, then add 1/3 more batter, remaining filling and remaining batter. Swirl gently with spatula. Bake at 350° for 55 to 60 minutes. Cool in pan. Remove from pan and sift powdered sugar over top. Serves 12 to 16.

CINNAMON BISCUIT RING

3/4 C. sugar
1 T. cinnamon
1/2 C. butter, melted
2 cans refrigerator biscuits (not flaky)
   containing 10 biscuits each
1/4 C. raisins
1/4 C. nuts, chopped

Combine sugar and cinnamon. Melt butter. Dip each biscuit in butter, then in sugar-cinnamon mixture, covering all sides well. In 8" or 9" pie pan, overlap biscuits, standing on end in ring pattern. Place raisins and nuts between each biscuit. Bake 20 to 30 minutes at 375°. Slide out of pan while warm. Biscuits will separate easily for serving. Serves 10.

PEAR BRAN BREAD

3 fresh Bartlett pears, cored, peeled and chopped
   OR 6 canned pear halves, drained
2 eggs, beaten
1 C. Bran Buds
1-1/2 C. flour
1/2 C. sugar
1 t. baking powder
1/2 t. salt
1/2 t. soda
1/4 C. vegetable shortening
3/4 C. pecans, chopped

Combine pears, eggs and Bran Buds and let stand. Combine flour with sugar, baking powder, salt and soda. Add shortening and pear mixture, and mix only until flour is moistened. Stir in pecans. Bake in greased 8" x 4" loaf pan on lower rack of oven at 350° for 1 hour, or until tester comes out clean. Makes 1 loaf.

CHERRY NUT BREAD

3/4 C. sugar
1/2 C. butter
2 eggs
2 C. flour
1 t. baking soda
1/2 t. salt
1 C. buttermilk
1 C. walnuts, chopped
10 oz. jar maraschino cherries, drained and chopped
1 t. vanilla

Cream sugar, butter and eggs. Sift dry ingredients together and add to creamed mixture with buttermilk. Beat until blended. Stir in nuts, cherries and vanilla. Pour batter into greased 9" x 5" loaf pan and bake at 350° for 55 to 60 minutes. Makes 1 loaf.

ZUCCHINI PECAN BREAD

4 eggs
2 C. sugar
1 C. oil
3-1/2 C. flour
3/4 t. baking powder
1 t. cinnamon
2 C. zucchini squash, unpeeled and grated
1 C. raisins
1 C. pecans, chopped
1-1/2 t. vanilla

Beat eggs. Gradually add sugar and oil. Combine dry ingredients and add to creamed mixture alternately with zucchini. Stir in raisins, pecans and vanilla. Turn into 2 greased and floured 9" x 5" loaf pans. Bake on lowest rack of oven at 350° for 1 hour, or until tester comes out clean.

OLD-FASHIONED BISCUITS

1 C. flour
2 t. baking powder
1/2 t. salt
2 rounded T. lard
1/3 C. milk

Sift together flour, baking powder and salt. Add lard; work into flour with fingers until no lumps are left. Add milk and mix with fork. Knead for 30 seconds on lightly-floured board. Roll out 1/2" thick and cut into 2" rounds. Bake at 475° for 10 to 12 minutes. Makes 8.

MILLIE'S POPOVERS

1 T. shortening
2 eggs
1 C. milk
1 C. flour
1/2 t. salt

Grease 6 custard cups heavily inside and around edges with shortening, and place cups inside muffins tins. Place in 450° oven to heat while preparing batter. Place eggs, milk, flour and salt in blender jar and blend to incorporate all particles. Fill heated cups half full and bake for 20 minutes at 450°. Reduce heat to 350° and bake 10 minutes longer. Makes 6.

RIO-GRANDE CORNBREAD

1-1/2 C. cornmeal, sifted
1 C. flour, sifted
2 t. sugar
1 t. salt
1 T. baking powder
1/4 t. soda
1-1/2 C. buttermilk
2 eggs, beaten
1/2 C. salad oil

Optional:
1/4 C. onion, chopped
1/3 C. longhorn cheese, grated
4 oz. green chilies, drained
    rinsed, seeded and chopped

Combine cornmeal, flour, sugar, salt and baking powder. Dissolve soda in buttermilk and add to dry ingredients with eggs. Add oil and optional ingredients, if desired, and pour into hot, well-oiled iron cornstick pans or large iron skillet. Bake at 425° for 15 minutes. Serves 8 to 10.

JUNIOR LEAGUE TOAST

1 loaf VERY THIN sliced bread
1 T. Schilling's Salad Supreme
1/2 C. butter, softened

Cut bread slices in half diagonally, forming a triangle. Dry out in 250° oven for 30 minutes. Cool. Mix Salad Supreme with softened butter and spread on dry toast. Heat to serve. Serves 12 to 16.

CHEESE STRAWS

1 scant C. flour
1/2 t. baking powder
1 t. salt
Dash cayenne
1/3 C. butter
1 C. New York sharp cheese, grated
2 to 3 t. water

Mix flour, baking powder, salt, cayenne and butter. Add cheese and enough water to make a stiff dough. Roll out and cut in 3" x 1/4" strips. Bake on cookie sheet at 400° for 10 minutes, or until slightly brown. Makes 5 dozen.

yeast breads

OLD-FASHIONED CINNAMON ROLLS

Dough:

2 pkgs. dry yeast	1/2 C. butter, melted	*Glaze: (for each pan)*
1/2 C. warm water	1 C. sugar	1-1/2 T. warm water
1-1/2 C. milk	1 T. cinnamon	1 C. powdered sugar
1/4 C. sugar		1/4 t. vanilla
1-1/2 C. butter		
1/2 t. salt		
4 eggs, beaten		
8 C. flour		

Soften yeast in warm water. Heat milk, sugar and butter; stir until butter melts. Cool to lukewarm; add salt and softened yeast. Add eggs and blend well. Place 8 C. flour in large mixing bowl. Add egg and milk mixture, stirring until mixture forms a ball. Knead 5 minutes, adding about 1/4 C. more flour as necessary, until dough is smooth and elastic. Place dough in greased bowl, cover and let rise until doubled, about 1 hour. Punch down and chill for 3 hours or overnight. (Dough will keep in refrigerator up to 3 days.)

To assemble, divide dough into 8 pieces. Work with one piece at a time and keep the rest refrigerated. Roll each piece out on a floured board to a 9" by 12" rectangle. Brush with 1 T. melted butter. Combine sugar and cinnamon; spread 2 T. of this mixture over butter. Roll dough tightly, as for a jelly roll, starting with the longer side. Seal edge. Cut roll into 8 slices, 1-1/2" thick. Place 16 slices, cut sides up, in a greased 8" pan, 1/2 " apart. (Two pieces of dough, or 1/4 of entire dough will be needed to fill each pan.) Let rise until nearly doubled in size, about 45 minutes. Bake at 375° for 20 to 25 minutes, or until golden brown.

Prepare glaze by combining warm water, powdered sugar and vanilla. Pour glaze over each pan of rolls. (May be baked, glazed and frozen.) Makes 5 dozen rolls.

GREEK REFRIGERATOR ROLLS

1/2 C. milk
1/4 C. sugar
1 t. salt
1/2 C. butter
1 pkg. yeast
1 egg
1/3 C. orange juice, fresh
1/4 t. orange rind, grated (optional)
1 stick cinnamon
1/2 C. warm water
4 C. flour

Scald milk; stir in sugar, salt and butter. Cool to lukewarm. Combine yeast, egg, orange juice and orange peel, if desired. Boil cinnamon stick in water for 3 minutes. Discard stick. Combine yeast, milk mixture and water mixture in large bowl; blend in flour. Mix well and place in greased bowl. Cover and allow to double in size in warm place for 2 hours. Punch down, turn out on floured surface and shape into rolls. Place on greased baking sheet, cover and let rise 1-1/2 hours or more. Bake for 20 minutes at 350°. Makes 2 dozen rolls. (Dough may be prepared and refrigerated for 3 to 4 days.)

HUNGARIAN SWEET ROLLS

1 C. milk
1/4 C. sugar
1 t. salt
1/2 C. shortening, melted and cooled
1 envelope dry yeast
1 egg, beaten
3-3/4 C. flour

1/2 C. butter, melted
3/4 C. sugar
1 t. cinnamon
1/2 C. nuts
1/2 C. raisins

Scald milk; add sugar, salt and shortening. Mix well and cool to lukewarm. Add yeast and let sit in warm place about 10 minutes. Add egg and stir. Add flour, mixing well. Turn out on floured board and knead until dough becomes smooth and elastic. Pinch off balls of dough the size of a walnut. Roll in melted butter, then in mixture of sugar and cinnamon. Place in a greased 9" round pan or tube pan, using half of dough for first layer. Add nuts and raisins and then add remaining dough for top layer. Let rise for 1 to 1-1/2 hours and place in 400° oven for 35 minutes, or until golden brown. Serves 8.

ARMENIAN BREAD

2 pkgs. yeast
2 C. warm water
2 T. sugar
1-1/4 T. salt
1/2 C. butter, melted and cooled
6 C. flour
1 egg
1/4 C. cold water
1/4 C. sesame seeds
Salt (optional)

Soften yeast in warm water. Stir in sugar, salt and butter. Add 4 C. of the flour and beat at medium speed for 5 minutes. Add 1-1/2 C. flour by hand to make a stiff enough dough to knead. Turn dough out onto board with remaining 1/2 C. flour and knead until smooth and satiny. (This takes 8 to 10 minutes by hand or 5 minutes if mixer has a dough hook.) Place dough in oiled bowl, turning over to oil both surfaces. Cover and let rise until doubled, about 1 to 1-1/2 hours.

Punch dough down, knead lightly and divide into 12 equal balls. Place on lightly-floured cookie sheet about 1" apart; cover with clear plastic and let rest for 45 minutes. Beat egg and water together for glaze. Roll out one ball at a time to paper-thin consistency, about 12" round. Carefully roll dough onto rolling pin and unroll on ungreased baking sheet. Brush with egg glaze, prick 3 to 4 times with fork, and sprinkle with 1 t. sesame seeds and salt, if desired. Place oven racks so that one is low and one is high. Place on lowest rack in 400° oven.

After baking 4 minutes, or when next sheet is rolled and ready, move first bread to top rack and place next one on lowest rack. Continue this until all are baked to a golden brown—8 minutes in all for each round. Cool on racks and store in plastic bags. To crisp them, place in a 300° oven for 5 to 10 minutes. Makes 1 dozen rounds.

BUTTERHORN ROLLS

1 pkg. yeast
1/4 C. warm water
2 C. milk
1/2 C. sugar
1/2 C. butter
6 to 8 C. flour
1/2 t. baking powder
1/2 t. soda
1 scant t. salt
1/2 C. butter, melted

Dissolve yeast in warm water. Set aside. Heat milk, sugar and butter to a boil; cool and add yeast. Add 6 C. of the sifted flour, baking powder, soda and salt. Knead well, adding only enough flour to achieve a kneadable mixture. Let rise 2 hours. Punch down; cover with a damp cloth, and refrigerate until ready to use. To shape, pinch off 1/4 of dough and roll out as thin as possible. Spread with 2 T. melted butter and cut into pie-shaped wedges. Roll up from wide end into horns. Place on cookie sheet; cover and let rise again for 45 minutes to 1 hour. Bake at 375° for 15 minutes, or until golden brown. Makes 24 to 30 rolls. (Dough may also be used for cinnamon rolls.)

NO-KNEAD POTATO ROLLS

1 pkg. yeast
1/4 C. warm water
1 C. milk
1/2 C. butter
1 C. mashed potatoes
2 eggs, beaten
1/4 C. sugar
1 t. salt
1/4 t. baking powder
5 to 6 C. flour

Dissolve yeast in warm water. Scald milk; add butter to milk, and stir until melted. Add mashed potatoes, yeast, eggs, sugar and salt. Add baking powder and only enough flour to hold dough together—too much flour makes a tough roll. Place in greased bowl. Refrigerate overnight, covered. Divide dough into fourths. On a floured board, roll each piece of dough; cut and shape into rolls. Place in a greased 8" or 9" pan. Let rise 3 hours. Bake at 350° for 15 to 20 minutes. Makes 4 pans. (Dough may also be used for cinnamon rolls.)

MONKEY BREAD

2 pkgs. yeast
1/4 C. warm water
1 C. milk
1/2 C. sugar
1 C. butter
3 eggs, beaten
1 t. salt
3 to 4 C. sifted flour

Soften yeast in warm water. Scald milk and stir in sugar. Add 1/2 of butter, and let it melt as the milk cools. When milk is lukewarm, stir in beaten eggs and yeast mixture. Add salt. Blend flour in gradually, adding enough to make a soft dough. Transfer to a greased bowl and let rise in a warm place (85°) until double in bulk.

Melt remaining butter in shallow pan. Punch dough down and divide into 2 portions for easier handling. Roll out one portion at a time to 1/3" thickness. Cut with a 3" diamond-shaped cookie cutter. Dip each piece of dough in butter; place in tube pan with points overlapping. (There should be about 3 layers, but pan should not be more than 3/4 full.) Let rise until light, about 1 hour. Bake at 400° for 35 minutes, or until golden brown. Turn out on plate while warm and separate into serving pieces with 2 forks. Serves 12.

HONEY-OATMEAL LOAVES

1 C. quick oats
2-1/2 C. boiling water
2-1/2 t. salt
2 T. butter
1/2 C. honey
6 C. flour
2 pkgs. yeast
2 T. butter, melted

Soak oats in boiling water. Cool; add salt, butter and honey. Mix well. Add 2 C. of the flour and yeast. Beat for 2 minutes at medium speed. Add 1 C. flour and beat again for 2 minutes. Knead remaining flour into mixture on floured board. Knead until smooth and elastic. Place in greased bowl and let rise until double in bulk, about 1 hour. Punch down and shape into 2 loaves. Place in greased 9" x 5" bread pans. Let rise until double, or about 30 to 45 minutes. Bake at 350° for 45 minutes. Brush tops with 2 T. melted butter. Makes 2 loaves.

WHOLE WHEAT BATTER BREAD

1-1/4 C. warm water
1 pkg. dry yeast OR baker's yeast
2 T. honey
1 C. whole wheat flour
    OR 1/2 C. whole wheat flour and
    3/4 C. stone-ground wheat flour
2 t. salt
2 T. shortening
2 C. all-purpose flour, sifted
1 to 2 T. butter, melted

Measure water into large bowl; add yeast and stir. Add honey, whole wheat flour, salt and 2 T. shortening. Beat 2 minutes. Add all-purpose flour and beat 2 more minutes. Cover and let rise for 30 minutes. Stir down batter and spread evenly in buttered 9" x 5" bread pan. (Batter will be sticky.) Cover and let rise until batter is 1" from top of pan. Bake at 375° for 40 to 50 minutes, or until bread sounds hollow when tapped on top. Turn out on cooling rack and brush top of loaf with melted butter. Makes 1 loaf.

FRENCH BREAD

1 pkg. yeast
1/2 C. warm water
1 T. oil
1 T. sugar
1 C. warm water
1-1/2 t. salt
4 C. flour

In large mixing bowl, dissolve yeast in 1/2 C. water. Let rest in warm place for 5 minutes. Add oil, sugar, salt and remaining 1 C. water. Mix well. Add flour and mix with wooden spoon. Every 10 minutes mix or stir through dough, 5 different times, letting dough rise between stirrings. Punch down and turn out on floured surface. Divide dough in half and let rest, covered, for 10 minutes. Roll each portion into 9" x 12" rectangle. Roll up tightly, starting at longest side, and seal edge with water. Place loaves on separate baking sheets, seam down, and score top of each loaf 6 times. Cover and let rise 1-1/2 hours. Bake at 400° for 25 to 30 minutes. Makes 2 large loaves.

RYE BREAD

1 C. water	2 C. buttermilk
2/3 C. sugar	2-1/2 C. rye flour
1 T. salt	5 C. all-purpose flour
2 T. butter	2 pkgs. yeast
1/2 C. molasses	1/2 C. warm water
2 t. orange rind, grated	1 t. sugar
1/2 t. soda	2 T. butter, melted

Combine water, sugar, salt, butter and molasses; bring to boil. Add orange rind and cool. Dissolve soda in buttermilk and add. Combine rye flour with all-purpose flour. Put yeast, warm water and sugar in large bowl. Add liquid and flour mixtures, mixing well. Place in buttered bowl and butter top lightly. Cover and let rise until double in bulk, about 1 hour. Punch dough down and divide into 3 parts. Knead lightly, about 12 times each, on a lightly-floured board. Place in three 8" x 4" glass bread pans. Brush top of loaves with melted butter and let rise until double, about 1 hour. Bake in 325° oven for 1 hour. Brush top of loaves with melted butter while warm. Makes 3 loaves.

SWEDISH RYE BREAD

2 C. boiling water	1/4 C. molasses OR dark corn syrup
1/4 C. quick-cooking oats	2 pkgs. yeast
1/3 C. brown sugar	2 C. all-purpose flour
1 T. salt	3 C. rye flour
2 t. anise seed OR caraway seed	1-1/2 C. all-purpose flour
1/4 C. shortening	1/4 C. butter, melted

Pour boiling water over oats, brown sugar, salt, seeds, shortening and molasses. Cool to lukewarm. Sprinkle yeast into mixture and stir well. Add 2 C. all-purpose flour. Beat 2 minutes with mixer. Gradually add rye flour. Let dough rest 10 minutes. Knead in only as much of 1-1/2 C. all-purpose flour as needed to make a smooth, soft, elastic dough. Place in greased bowl; cover and let rise until double. Punch down. Cover and let rise another 30 minutes. Punch down. Turn out on floured board and divide dough in half. Bake in two 9" x 5" loaf pans for 35 to 40 minutes at 375°. Brush with butter. Remove from pans and cover with towel until cool. Makes 2 loaves.

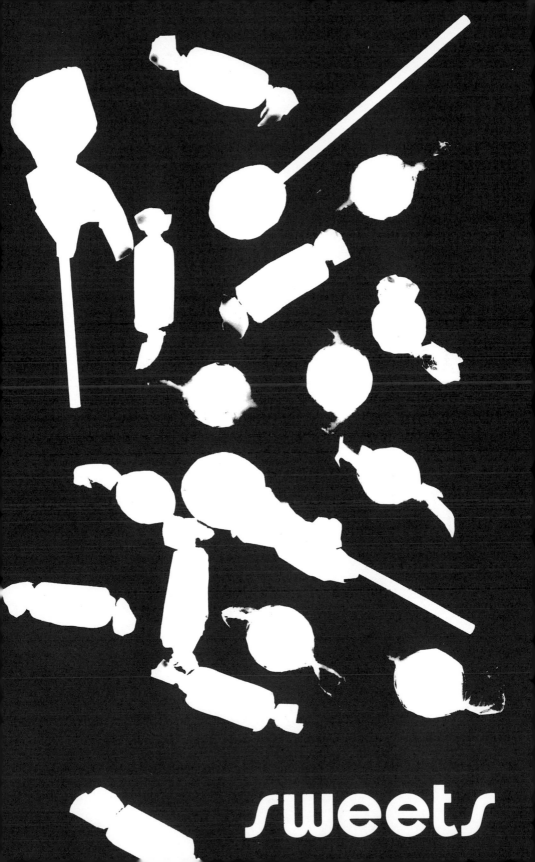

sweets

Dessert—the crowning jewel of a perfect meal—the grand finale. The choice, however, should be dictated by what has gone before, and a light dessert is the best idea following a heavy meal (despite the fact that when waiters roll up heavy-laden dessert carts to a table of diners who have just consumed four enormous courses, the chocolate cream-filled roll is the hands-down favorite)! But a light dessert does not mean a "nothing" dessert. Ice cream seems out of the ordinary if a liqueur is poured over it, and a few chocolate shavings are on top. Even a pineapple sherbet can be served in a stemmed glass accented with a sprig of mint. Desserts seem most festive when presented grandly and served at the table.

For the "let's pull out all the stops" dessert or magnificent cake, the do-ahead plan seems easiest. Cakes look special if they're baked in bundt pans and served on cake stands or elegant platters. Chocolate cake lends itself to a ring of toasted almonds on top; lemon or orange cake to a glaze-type icing and a border of thinly-sliced, halved pieces of the appropriate fruit. For an added attraction, place a few well-washed ivy leaves in a cluster at the base of the cake. A dusting of powdered sugar through a fine sieve is a nice touch to crêpes or dark fruit tarts.

To make a pie into a tart, which is special, indeed, bake the pie in a loose-bottom tart pan. When cool, set the tart on a tin can and carefully slip the ring down from the edge of the tart. Slide the tart onto a pretty platter and, again, add the ivy cluster.

Garnishing food takes it out of the everyday and makes it as special as you wish it to be. You don't need the skill of a cake decorator or ice carver—it's simply going one step further in food preparation, and the results are very rewarding. These suggestions are given in hopes that they will be a springboard for your creativity.

Bon Apetit!

pies

PEACH-BLUEBERRY CUSTARD PIE

9" single pastry shell, unbaked
4 large peaches
3/4 C. fresh blueberries
3 eggs, well-beaten
1-1/2 C. sugar
3 T. flour
1/4 C. vegetable shortening

Peel and slice peaches and place in pastry shell with blueberries. Cream eggs, sugar, flour and shortening and pour over fruit in crust. Bake at 425° for 10 minutes. Reduce heat to 325°, and bake 45 to 50 minutes more. Serves 6.

FRESH PEACH PIE

1/2 C. light brown sugar
1/2 C. flour
6 T. butter
9" unbaked pastry shell
3 C. peaches, peeled and sliced
1-2 T. sugar
1/4 t. nutmeg OR cinnamon
1 egg
2 T. light cream
1 t. vanilla

Combine brown sugar and flour. Cut in butter until mixture is coarse and crumbly. Sprinkle half of crumb mixture in bottom of pastry shell. Add peaches. Sprinkle with mixture of sugar and nutmeg or cinnamon. Combine egg, cream and vanilla and pour over peaches. Cover with remaining crumb mixture. Bake at 400° for 40 minutes. Serves 6 to 8.

LEMON BERRY PIE

1 envelope unflavored gelatin
1 C. sugar
1/2 t. salt
1-1/4 C. milk
4 eggs, separated
3 oz. cream cheese
1/2 C. lemon juice
9" single pie shell, baked
1 pint fresh strawberries

Combine gelatin, 3/4 C. of the sugar and salt in double boiler. Stir in milk and slightly-beaten egg yolks. Cook over boiling water, stirring constantly until thickened slightly and mixture coats a spoon. Divide equally into 2 small bowls (about 1 C. in each bowl). Beat softened cream cheese into 1 part until smooth. Stir in 1/4 C. of the lemon juice. Stir remaining 1/4 C. lemon juice into second part of mixture. Chill both until they begin to thicken. Pour thickened cheese mixture into pie shell. Slice berries over, reserving a few for garnish. Beat egg whites until foamy; gradually add remaining sugar and beat constantly until stiff. Fold in thickened lemon gelatin mixture and spread over chilled first layer. Chill until set and garnish with reserved berries. Serves 8.

RASPBERRY PIE

Crust:
1 C. graham cracker crumbs
1/4 C. butter, melted
2 T. granulated sugar
2 T. brown sugar

Filling:
10 oz. pkg. frozen raspberries
2 T. cornstarch
14 oz. sweetened condensed milk
1/2 C. lemon juice
1 C. heavy cream, whipped
1 t. vanilla
3 T. powdered sugar

Prepare crust by combining crumbs, butter and sugars. Pat into 9" pie pan and bake at 350° for 8 minutes. Cool. Thaw berries; reserve juice and 6 to 8 whole berries for garnish. Mash remaining berries. In saucepan combine reserved juice and cornstarch. Cook until thickened over low heat. Spread over crumb crust. Combine crushed berries, sweetened condensed milk and lemon juice and pour over first layer. Top with whipped cream to which vanilla and powdered sugar have been added. Chill. Drain reserved berries well and garnish each serving with a berry. Serves 6 to 8 .

STRAWBERRY TART

9" single pastry shell, unbaked
3/4 C. dry beans
3-3/4 oz. pkg. Instant Vanilla Pudding
1-1/4 C. light cream
1 C. heavy cream, whipped
2 T. orange peel, grated
1/4 C. Grand Marnier
1-1/2 pints fresh strawberries
4 oz. currant jelly
1 T. Grand Marnier

(Note: makes enough cream filling for 2 pies.) Line pie shell with foil and fill with dry beans. Bake at 450° for 15 minutes. Remove foil and beans and cool crust. Combine pudding and light cream. Beat 1 minute and let stand until thick. Fold in whipped cream, orange peel and 1/4 C. Grand Marnier. Cover bottom of shell with half the cream filling. (Find another use for remaining filling, or make another pie!) Cut berries in half and arrange, cut side up, in circular pattern, pointing outward, over cream filling, using smaller berries in center and larger berries in outer rings. Combine currant jelly and 1 T. Grand Marnier; heat to dissolve jelly. Cool, and with pastry brush, glaze berries and any exposed filling. Chill. Serves 6.

ALASKA MELBA PIE

10 oz. frozen red raspberries, thawed
2/3 C. sugar
1/8 t. cream of tartar
1/2 gallon vanilla ice cream
Single 10" pastry shell, baked

Meringue Topping:
4 egg whites
1/8 t. cream of tartar
1 t. vanilla
1/2 C. sugar

Press raspberries through sieve into small saucepan. Stir in sugar and cream of tartar. Heat quickly to boiling, stirring constantly, and cook for 3 minutes, stirring. Chill.

One day ahead of serving, scoop ice cream in big, flat spoonsful and place 1 layer, petal fashion, in bottom of pastry shell. Drizzle with half of raspberry sauce. Repeat layers, mounding top. Freeze overnight.

Beat egg whites with cream of tartar and vanilla; gradually add sugar and beat until stiff. Spread over ice cream in shell, sealing edges. Return to freezer. Just before serving, place in 425° oven for 5 minutes. Serves 8.

ORANGE CHIFFON PIE

1 envelope unflavored gelatin
1 C. sugar
1/4 t. salt
3/4 C. milk
3 egg yolks, slightly-beaten
1/3 C. orange juice concentrate, undiluted
2 T. fresh orange peel, grated
1/4 C. lemon juice
1/2 t. fresh lemon peel, grated
10" pastry shell, baked
1 C. heavy cream, whipped
Grated orange peel for garnish

Combine gelatin, sugar and salt in saucepan. Add milk and egg yolks. Cook and stir over medium heat until thickened slightly. Remove from heat and add juices and grated peels. Chill until partially set, at least 2 hours. Fold in all except 1/4 C. whipped cream. Chill until mixture mounds. Pile into pastry shell and chill. Garnish wtih remaining whipped cream and grated orange peel. Serves 8.

CHOCOLATE MERINGUE PIE

1-3/4 C. milk
3 T. butter
1-1/2 C. sugar
1/2 t. salt
5 T. flour
2 T. cocoa
4 eggs, separated
1 whole egg
1 t. vanilla
4 t. sugar
10" single pastry shell, baked

Scald milk and butter. Combine sugar, salt, flour and cocoa; add to milk mixture and stir until slightly thickened. Stir a small amount of hot mixture into egg yolks and whole egg, stirring until well blended. Add egg mixture to hot mixture, mixing well. Pour mixture into top of double boiler and cook 20 minutes, stirring occasionally. Add vanilla and cool. Pour into pastry shell. Beat egg whites until frothy, and gradually add sugar, continuing to beat until meringue is quite stiff. Spread over top of filling, sealing edges. Place in 325° oven for 15 to 20 minutes, or until meringue is golden brown. Cool. Serves 8.

MARBLE-TOP CHOCOLATE RUM PIE

1/2 C. sugar
1 envelope unflavored gelatin
Dash salt
1 C. milk
2 egg yolks, beaten
6 oz. semi-sweet chocolate bits

1/4 C. light rum
2 egg whites
1/4 C. sugar
1 C. heavy cream
1 t. vanilla
9" pastry shell, baked

In saucepan, combine 1/2 C. sugar, gelatin and salt. Stir in milk and egg yolks. Cook and stir over low heat until slightly thickened. Remove from heat and add chocolate bits, stirring until melted. Add rum and chill until partially set. Beat egg whites until soft peaks form. Gradually add 1/4 C. sugar, beating until stiff peaks form. Fold into chocolate mixture. Whip cream with vanilla. Layer whipped cream and chocolate mixture in pastry shell, ending with whipped cream. Gently swirl the top to marble. Chill until firm. Serves 6 to 8.

CHEESE-TOPPED PUMPKIN PIE

1-1/2 C. cooked pumpkin
3/4 C. sugar
1/4 t. nutmeg
1/4 t. cloves
1/2 t. ginger
1/2 t. salt
2 eggs, slightly-beaten
1-1/4 C. milk
1 t. vanilla
9" pastry shell, unbaked
8 oz. cream cheese, softened
1/4 C. sugar
1 t. vanilla
Dash salt
2 eggs
6 to 8 pecan halves

Combine pumpkin, 3/4 C. sugar, spices and salt. Blend in 2 eggs, milk and 1 t. vanilla. Pour into unbaked pastry shell. Combine cream cheese, 1/4 C. sugar, 1 t. vanilla and dash salt. Beat in 2 eggs, one at a time. Pour over pumpkin mixture in pastry shell. Bake at 400° for 35 to 40 minutes, or until knife inserted in center comes out clean. Chill and garnish top with pecan halves. Serves 6 to 8.

COFFEE ALASKA PIE

12 chocolate wafers, crushed
1/4 C. butter, melted
1 T. sugar
1 quart + 1 pint coffee ice cream
3 egg whites
1 C. Marshmallow Creme
1 t. vanilla

Chocolate Sauce:
1/4 C. butter
1/2 oz. unsweetened chocolate
1/3 C. cocoa
3/4 C. sugar
1/8 t. salt
1/2 C. milk
1 t. vanilla

Combine wafer crumbs, butter and sugar and press into 9" pie plate. Bake 10 minutes at 350°. Cool crust and pack ice cream into shell. Freeze. Beat egg whites until stiff and add Marshmallow Creme, a large spoonful at a time. Beat until fluffy; add vanilla. Pile into pie, sealing around edges. Place pie plate on board in 450° oven for 3 minutes. Return to freezer, and when solidly frozen, wrap in plastic wrap. To serve, let stand at room temperature for 15 minutes. Drizzle chocolate sauce over each serving. Serves 8.

To make chocolate sauce, stir butter and chocolate over low heat until melted and smooth. Mix cocoa, sugar, salt and milk. Add to butter and chocolate mixture. Bring to low boil, remove from heat and add vanilla. (May be stored in refrigerator. Reheat over hot water.) Makes 1-1/4 C. sauce.

MARVELOUS MOCHA PIE

20 chocolate Oreo cookies, crushed
1/4 C. butter, melted
1 qt. coffee ice cream
3 oz. unsweetened chocolate, melted
1/4 C. butter
2/3 C. sugar
2/3 C. evaporated milk
1 t. vanilla
1 C. heavy cream, whipped
1/3 C. pecans OR almonds, chopped

Combine cookies and melted butter and press into 9" pie plate. Spread ice cream over crust and freeze. Bring chocolate, butter and sugar to a boil. Gradually add evaporated milk and cook until thickened. Cool and add vanilla. Spread over ice cream and return to freezer. When set, top with whipped cream and garnish with nuts. Serves 8.

CHEESE PIE

5 oz. box Lorna Doone Shortbread Cookies
1/4 C. butter, melted
8 oz. cream cheese
1 egg
7 T. sugar
2 t. vanilla
1-1/2 C. dairy sour cream
Fresh sugared strawberries OR blueberries

Crumble cookies, a few at a time, in blender. Mix with butter and press into buttered 9" glass pie pan. Mix cream cheese, egg, 4 T. of the sugar and 1 t. of the vanilla until creamy. Spread on crust and bake at 350° for 15 minutes. Remove from oven. Combine sour cream, remaining 3 T. sugar and 1 t. vanilla and spread over top. Return to oven for 10 minutes. Chill pie for 6 hours or more. Serve topped with berries. Serves 8.

CORONATION BUTTERSCOTCH PIE

1-1/4 C. dark brown sugar
1/3 C. flour
1/2 t. salt
2 C. milk
3 egg yolks
1 T. butter
1 t. vanilla
9" baked pie crust
3 egg whites
1/8 t. cream of tartar
1/3 C. powdered sugar

Blend brown sugar, flour and salt in top of double boiler. Combine milk with egg yolks and add to sugar and flour mixture. Cook until thickened, stirring constantly. Remove from heat. Add butter and vanilla; pour into pie crust. Whip egg whites with cream of tartar. Gradually add sugar and whip until stiff. Spread on filling and bake at 325° for 15 minutes. Serves 6 to 8.

CHESS PIE

1/2 C. butter
1-1/2 C. sugar
3 eggs
1 T. vinegar
6 T. heavy cream
1 t. vanilla
9" unbaked pie shell

Melt butter and sugar in top of double boiler. Cool until firm. Beat eggs until frothy. Continue beating while adding spoonsful of sugar mixture. Add vinegar, cream and vanilla while beating. Pour into unbaked pie shell and bake for 20 minutes at 250°. Turn heat to 350° and bake 25 minutes more. Turn off oven, crack door and let pie remain in oven for an additional 5 minutes. Remove from oven. Serves 8.

OLD-FASHIONED APPLE DUMPLINGS

1 C. sugar
2 C. water
1/4 t. cinnamon
1/4 t. nutmeg
1/4 C. butter
2 C. flour
1 t. salt
2 t. baking powder

3/4 C. shortening
1/2 C. milk
6 small cooking apples,
    peeled and cored
2 T. sugar
Dash cinnamon
Dash nutmeg
2 T. butter

Make syrup by bringing to boil 1 C. sugar, water, 1/4 t. cinnamon and 1/4 t. nutmeg. Stir to dissolve sugar and add 1/4 C. butter. Set aside.

Sift flour, salt and baking powder. Cut in shortening. Add milk all at once and stir until moistened. Roll 1/4" thick and cut into 6 large squares. Center 1 apple on each pastry square. Sprinkle with 1 t. sugar, dash cinnamon and nutmeg. Dot with 1 t. butter. Fold corners of pastry to center over apples, pinching edges together. Place 1" apart in greased pan. Pour syrup over. Bake at 375°, uncovered, for 35 minutes, or until golden brown. Serves 6.

cakes

ORANGE BUTTER CAKE

1 C. butter
2 C. sugar
2 C. less 2 T. flour, sifted
5 eggs
2 T. orange juice
2 T. orange rind, grated
Powdered sugar

Cream butter and sugar. Add flour and eggs alternately to creamed mixture. Add orange juice and rind and bake in a tube pan lined on bottom with wax paper for 25 minutes at 350°. Turn oven to 325° and bake 30 minutes longer. Remove from oven and let stand 5 minutes before removing from pan. Sprinkle with powdered sugar. Serves 12.

BLUEBERRY MAÑANA

1/4 C. butter
2/3 C. sugar
1 egg
2 C. flour
1 T. baking powder
1/2 t. salt
1 C. milk
1 t. vanilla
3/4 C. floured fresh blueberries

Hard Sauce:
3/4 C. butter
1-1/2 C. powdered sugar
1 C. blueberries
1 t. vanilla OR brandy

Cream butter, sugar and egg. Mix and sift flour, baking powder and salt; add alternately with milk to creamed mixture until just mixed. Stir in vanilla and fold in blueberries. Turn into buttered 9" x 9" cake pan and bake for 35 minutes at 350°. To make hard sauce, cream butter and powdered sugar. Fold in blueberries and vanilla or brandy. Serve over warm Blueberry Mañana. Serves 9.

SPRITZ TORTE

4 egg whites
1 C. sugar
18 Ritz crackers, crushed
1 t. vanilla
1 C. pecans, ground
1/2 t. baking powder
2 C. heavy cream, whipped
1/4 C. powdered sugar
Milk chocolate bar for garnish

Beat egg whites until stiff, adding sugar slowly. Stir in cracker crumbs, vanilla, pecans and baking powder. Line 3 cookie sheets with wax paper or brown paper. Shape mixture with spatula into 3 round layers 9" or 10" in diameter and bake at 350° for 10 to 15 minutes. Cool slightly, and peel off paper. Whip cream with powdered sugar. Spread a generous layer of whipped cream between each layer and on top and sides. Refrigerate, covered, for 24 hours before serving. Make chocolate curls or grate chocolate from bar to garnish just before serving. Serves 8.

CHOCOLATE CINNAMON TORTE

1-1/2 C. butter
2 C. sugar
2 eggs
2-3/4 C. flour, sifted
2 T. cinnamon
4 C. heavy cream, whipped

1/3 C. powdered sugar
2 T. cocoa
12 whole red maraschino cherries, well-drained
12 walnut halves
2 oz. semi-sweet chocolate

Select 10 or 12 round cake pans 8" or 9" in diameter for baking cookie-like torte layers. Grease and line cake pans with wax paper and grease again. (This is made easier if a stack of 12 sheets is traced around at once—measurement need not be exact.) Cream butter and sugar. Add eggs and beat until light. Sift flour and cinnamon; add to egg mixture. Spread dough in very thin layers in cake pans and bake at 375° for 8 to 12 minutes, or until golden. Carefully remove to wire rack and cool. Makes 10 to 12 round layers. (May be made ahead and stored in dry place.)

Two hours before serving, whip cream with powdered sugar. Spread whipped cream on layers, stacking torte fashion. Add cocoa to top layer of whipped cream. Decorate top layer by alternating walnut halves and cherries around outside edge. Make chocolate curls from semi-sweet chocolate, using potato peeler, and sprinkle in center of torte. Chill. Serves 12.

WOLFERMAN'S ALSATIAN TORTE

Torte layers:
1-1/8 C. sugar
12 eggs, separated
1-1/2 t. vanilla
3/4 t. salt
1-1/2 C. cake flour

Chocolate shavings for garnish

Icing:
10 T. butter
12 T. margarine
1/2 t. salt
1/2 t. vanilla
9 C. powdered sugar, sifted
1/4 C. sugar
1/2 C. cocoa
1 t. strong instant coffee
4 egg whites, stiffly-beaten

Make torte layers by beating sugar and egg yolks until pale yellow and very thick. Add vanilla and salt. Fold in stiffly-beaten egg whites. Fold in flour and pour into seven 8" tart pans or spring-form pans, filling each pan to level of 1/2". Bake 5 minutes at 400°. Cool layers. Prepare icing by creaming butter, margarine, salt and vanilla until light and fluffy. Add sugars and cocoa while beating on high speed. Add coffee; fold in egg whites. Spread between layers and on top of torte. Garnish top with chocolate shavings. Serves 12.

OATMEAL TORTE

1 scant C. oatmeal, uncooked
1/3 C. coconut
1/3 C. sugar
7 T. butter, melted and cooled
1 C. heavy cream, whipped
12 fresh strawberries OR 1 sliced banana
Milk chocolate bar for garnish

Mix oatmeal, coconut and sugar in bowl and pour melted butter over. Mix well and pat into ungreased 10" round pan. Bake at 375° 10 to 15 minutes, or until light brown. Cool slightly and turn out of pan. Cool thoroughly. Spread with whipped cream and line border with strawberries or bananas. Make chocolate curls or grate chocolate in center to garnish. Serves 8.

CARROT CAKE

1-1/2 C. corn oil
4 eggs
1 t. vanilla
2 C. sugar
2 C. flour
2 t. cinnamon
1/2 t. salt
1 t. baking powder
1 t. soda
3 C. raw carrots, grated

Frosting:
1/2 C. butter
8 oz. cream cheese
1 t. vanilla
1 lb. box powdered sugar
1 C. pecans, chopped

Beat together oil, eggs, vanilla and sugar. Sift together the flour, cinnamon, salt, baking powder and soda. Add carrots to creamed ingredients. Add dry ingredients. Grease and flour three 8" round cake pans or one 9" x 13" pan and bake at 350° for 25 to 30 minutes. To make frosting, blend butter, cream cheese and vanilla. Add powdered sugar and beat well. Add chopped pecans and spread on cake. Serves 12.

DOUBLE CHOCOLATE CAKE

2 oz. unsweetened chocolate
1/2 C. warm water
1/4 C. butter
1 C. sugar
1-1/8 C. cake flour
1-1/2 t. baking powder
1/2 t. soda
1/4 t. salt
1 egg, beaten
1/2 C. hot water
1 t. vanilla

Icing:
1/4 C. butter
2 C. powdered sugar
1/4 C. cocoa
2 to 4 T. coffee

Melt chocolate in top of double boiler. Add warm water and stir until smooth. Add butter and sugar and remove from heat. Sift dry ingredients and blend into chocolate mixture. Add egg, hot water and vanilla. Pour mixture into greased 9" square pan and bake at 350° for 25 minutes, or until toothpick inserted in center is clean. Cool. To make icing, cream butter with powdered sugar and cocoa. Add enough coffee to reach desired spreading consistency. Serves 9.

MAGNOLIA CAKE

18 oz. yellow cake mix
1 C. light brown sugar
1 to 2 T. instant coffee powder
3/4 C. water
2 T. light rum
2 3-1/4 oz. boxes vanilla pudding (not instant)
3 C. milk
2 T. light rum
1 C. heavy cream, whipped
Shaved chocolate for garnish

Bake cake in 2 layers according to package directions. Cool. In saucepan combine sugar, coffee and water; boil for 5 minutes. Cool and add 2 T. rum. Remove cooled cake layers from pans, and spoon rum mixture slowly over both layers, allowing time for it to absorb. Cook pudding according to package directions, using only 1-1/2 C. milk per package. Cool and add 2 T. rum. Set aside 1 C. of pudding and spread remaining pudding between the layers. Refrigerate until 2 hours before serving time. Frost cake with mixture of whipped cream and reserved 1 C. pudding. Sprinkle with shaved chocolate. Chill. Serves 10 to 12.

PRESERVE CAKE

1 C. butter
2 C. sugar
4 eggs
3 C. flour
1 t. cinnamon
1/2 t. ground cloves
1 t. soda
1/2 t. salt
1 C. buttermilk
12 oz. jar peach OR apricot preserves
1 C. pecans, chopped
1 t. vanilla
Powdered sugar

Cream butter, sugar and eggs. Sift dry ingredients and add to creamed mixture alternately with buttermilk. Mix in preserves, nuts and vanilla. Bake in a greased and floured tube pan 1 hour at 350°. Sprinkle with powdered sugar. Serves 12 to 16.

SUNSHINE CAKE

6 eggs, separated
1 C. sugar
2/3 C. flour
2/3 t. cream of tartar
1/4 t. salt

Beat egg whites until frothy. Add sugar gradually, and beat until stiff and dry. Fold in beaten egg yolks. Sift dry ingredients and fold into batter lightly. Bake in ungreased tube pan at 350° for 30 to 40 minutes. Remove from pan when cool. Good filled, iced, glazed, with ice cream and chocolate syrup or plain. Serves 12.

HUNGARIAN DATE CAKE

1 t. soda
1 C. dates, chopped
1-1/4 C. boiling water
3/4 C. shortening
1 C. sugar
2 eggs
1 t. vanilla
1-1/2 C. flour
1 t. cinnamon
1/2 t. salt
1/2 C. pecans, chopped
6 oz. pkg. semi-sweet
    chocolate chips
1/2 C. sugar

Sprinkle soda over dates. Pour boiling water over dates and let stand for 5 to 10 minutes, until dates are plump. Cream shortening and sugar. Add eggs and vanilla. Sift together flour, cinnamon and salt. Add date mixture to creamed mixture alternately with dry ingredients. Pour into greased 9" x 13" pan. Combine pecans, chocolate chips and sugar for topping, and sprinkle over batter. Bake at 350° for 25 to 30 minutes. Serves 12 to 16.

PISTACHIO BUNDT CAKE

18 oz. yellow cake mix
3-3/4 oz. pkg. Instant
    Pistachio Pudding
4 eggs
3/4 C. salad oil
1 C. dairy sour cream
1 C. chocolate syrup

Grease and flour bundt or tube pan. In mixing bowl, combine cake mix, pudding mix, eggs, oil and sour cream. Mix at low speed to combine, then increase speed and beat 4 minutes. Pour half of batter into prepared pan; add chocolate syrup and then remaining batter. Swirl gently with spatula, creating a marbled effect. Bake for 55 minutes at 350°. Cool and remove from pan. Serves 12 to 16.

SWIRL CAKE

1/2 C. butter
1/2 C. shortening
1-1/2 C. sugar
2 t. vanilla
4 eggs
3 C. cake flour
2 t. baking powder
1 t. soda
1/2 t. salt
1-1/2 C. dairy sour cream
5 oz. can chocolate syrup

Glaze:
2 T. cocoa
1 T. vegetable oil
1 T. light corn syrup
2 T. + 1 t. water
1 C. powdered sugar

Cream butter, shortening and sugar; add vanilla. Add eggs, one at a time. Sift dry ingredients and add alternately with sour cream. Pour into well-greased tube pan. Pour chocolate syrup over top, and gently swirl with spatula to make marbled effect. Bake at 350° for 50 to 55 minutes. Cool in pan for 10 minutes and turn out. Make glaze by combining cocoa, oil, corn syrup and water in saucepan. Cook over low heat until smooth. Add powdered sugar and stir until smooth and shiny. Pour over cake and let run down sides. Serves 12 to 16.

CREAM CHEESE POUND CAKE

8 oz. cream cheese
1 C. butter
1-1/2 C. sugar
1-1/2 t. vanilla
4 eggs
2-1/4 C. flour
1-1/2 t. baking powder
1/2 C. golden raisins
1/2 C. walnuts, chopped

1/2 C. sugar
1 T. poppy seeds
2 t. lemon rind, grated
1/2 t. vanilla
1 T. butter
1/2 C. ground walnuts

Blend cream cheese, butter, sugar and vanilla. Add eggs. Sift together flour and baking powder and add to creamed mixture. Stir in raisins and walnuts. Combine 1/2 C. sugar, poppy seeds, lemon rind and 1/2 t. vanilla. Grease bundt or tube pan with 1 T. butter and dust with 1/2 C. ground walnuts. Spoon 1/3 of batter into prepared pan, then 1/2 of poppy seed mixture. Repeat layers and top with last 1/3 of batter. Bake at 325° for 1 hour and 20 minutes. Cool 15 minutes before removing from pan. Serves 12 to 16.

FRESH APPLE CAKE

1-1/2 C. salad oil
2 C. sugar
3 C. flour, sifted
3 eggs
1 C. pecans, chopped
1 t. soda
1 t. salt
1-1/2 t. cinnamon
1/2 t. nutmeg (optional)
1 t. vanilla
3 C. apples, peeled and chopped

Topping:
1/4 C. butter
3/4 C. brown sugar
1/2 C. evaporated milk

In mixing bowl, combine oil, sugar, flour, eggs, pecans, soda, salt, cinnamon, nutmeg, if desired, and vanilla. Blend well. Fold in apples. Pour batter into greased and floured bundt or tube pan and bake at 350° for 1 hour and 15 minutes. Cool and remove from pan. Heat butter, brown sugar and evaporated milk. Stir to dissolve sugar and pour over cake. Serves 16 to 20.

SURPRISE CUPCAKES

Filling:
8 oz. cream cheese, softened
1 egg
1/3 C. sugar
1/2 t. salt
6 oz. semi-sweet
   chocolate chips

Batter:
3 C. flour
2 C. sugar
1/2 C. cocoa
1 t. salt
2 t. soda
1/3 C. vegetable oil
2 C. water
2 T. vinegar
2 t. vanilla

Combine filling ingredients except chocolate chips; beat until smooth and add chocolate chips. Set aside. Sift together all dry batter ingredients. Add all liquids to sifted ingredients and blend until smooth. Fill cupcake tins two-thirds full and drop in a heaping teaspoon of filling. Bake at 350° for 25 minutes. Makes 26 cupcakes.

ENGLISH TOFFEE CAKE

1/4 C. cocoa
1 lb. box angel food cake mix
1 to 1-1/2 t. instant coffee powder (not freeze-dried)
3-5/8 oz. pkg. chocolate pudding (not instant)
1-1/3 C. milk
1 C. heavy cream, whipped
5 English toffee bars (3/4 oz. each)

Add cocoa to dry cake mix, and bake according to package instructions. Cool. Mix instant coffee and pudding in a saucepan. Cook pudding, using only 1-1/3 C. milk. Cool and beat until smooth. Whip cream and fold into pudding. Divide cake into 3 layers. Spread half of the pudding mixture between the layers. With remaining half of pudding mixture, frost top and sides of cake. Crush candy bars (easier if frozen) and sprinkle over cake. Chill. Serves 8 to 12.

MOCHA REFRIGERATOR CAKE

1 doz. almond macaroons, see pg. 273
2 doz. ladyfingers
16 oz. marshmallows
5 t. instant coffee powder
1/4 C. hot water
4 C. heavy cream, whipped
Milk chocolate bar for grating
1 oz. sliced almonds, toasted

Line bottom of spring-form pan with crumbled macaroons. Stand ladyfinger halves around sides, touching pan. Melt marshmallows in top of double boiler. Mix instant coffee with hot water and add to marshmallows. Cool slightly. Whip cream and fold into marshmallow mixture. Pour over macaroon crumbs. Refrigerate overnight. (May be frozen.) To serve, garnish top with grated chocolate and toasted almonds. Serves 12 to 16.

BAKED ALASKA

1 layer yellow cake, any size
4 flavors ice cream of your choice:
  Suggested: Chocolate Almond,
  Vanilla, Strawberry and
  Chocolate Mint
8 egg whites
1/2 t. cream of tartar
1/4 t. salt
1-1/2 t. vanilla
1 C. sugar
1/8 C. rum, warmed
1/8 C. grain alcohol

Sauce aux Marrons:
9-1/2 oz. jar marrons in syrup
1/4 C. rum
6 oz. semi-sweet chocolate chips
1 t. vanilla
1/3 C. butter
1 to 2 T. light cream

Bake layer of cake. Cool on cookie sheet. Line same cake pan with wax paper. Place 4 layers of ice cream in pan and freeze. Make meringue by beating egg whites, cream of tartar, salt and vanilla until frothy. Gradually add sugar, and continue to beat until meringue is stiff and shiny. Remove ice cream from pan, peel off wax paper, and gently place over layer of cake on cookie sheet. Spread quickly with meringue to seal, and bake for 10 minutes or until browned on lower rack of 425° oven. Combine rum and grain alcohol, pour over top and ignite. Serve with warm Sauce aux Marrons.

To make sauce, slice marrons into top of double boiler; add remaining ingredients and heat, adding cream if mixture is too thick. Store in refrigerator.

(As a variation, use Rainbow sherbet instead of ice cream. Serve with Raspberry Sauce or Strawberry Sauce, see pg. 268.) Nine-inch cake serves 12.

ANGEL ORANGE FLUFF

3 egg yolks
1/2 C. sugar
1/3 C. orange juice
1 T. grated orange rind
1-1/2 C. heavy cream, whipped
8 slices angel food cake
Sliced almonds

Mix egg yolks, sugar and orange juice in top of double boiler. Cook over hot water, stirring constantly until mixture thickens, about 15 minutes. Stir in orange rind. Cool. Fold in whipped cream. Spoon over angel food cake and garnish with sliced almonds. Serves 8.

CHOCOLATE FROSTING

3 oz. cream cheese, softened
1 T. coffee
1/4 C. butter, softened
1 oz. unsweetened chocolate, melted
1 t. vanilla
1/8 t. salt
2-1/2 C. powdered sugar, sifted

Blend cream cheese, coffee and butter. Add chocolate, vanilla and salt. Beat well. Add powdered sugar until icing reaches desired spreading consistency. Makes 1-1/2 C. frosting.

BUTTERSCOTCH ICING

1/4 C. butter
1 C. brown sugar, packed
1/4 C. milk
1/8 t. salt
1-1/2 to 2 C. powdered sugar

Melt butter in saucepan. Add brown sugar, milk and salt. Bring to boil and boil for 3 minutes. Cool. Beat and add powdered sugar until desired spreading consistency is reached. Makes 1-1/2 C. icing.

RUM GLAZE

1/4 C. water
1/4 C. butter
1 C. sugar
1 t. vanilla
2 T. rum

Heat all ingredients together, but do not boil. Pour over pound cake, or cake of your choice. (To make chocolate rum glaze, add 3 oz. unsweetened chocolate to above sauce, stirring until chocolate melts.)

CRÊPES SUZETTE

Dessert Crêpes:
6 eggs, well-beaten
1-1/2 t. salt
1-1/2 T. sugar
1-1/2 C. flour
3 T. butter, melted
3 C. milk

Filling:
1 C. butter
1 C. sugar
2/3 C. Grand Marnier
2 T. orange marmalade

Sauce:
1-1/2 C. butter
1-1/2 C. sugar
6 T. orange marmalade
4-1/2 T. orange juice concentrate
1-1/2 C. water
1 T. grated orange rind
1 C. Grand Marnier

2 T. Grand Marnier
2 T. grain alcohol

To make crêpes, combine eggs, salt, sugar, flour, butter and milk and chill overnight. (Batter will be extremely thin.) Slowly heat an 8" skillet until hot. Brush lightly with butter, and pour 2 to 3 T. of batter in pan, rotating pan so that batter covers bottom of pan. Cook for 1 minute; turn and cook other side for 30 seconds. Remove to wire rack to cool. Makes 40 crêpes.

To make filling, cream butter and sugar; add Grand Marnier and orange marmalade. Spread each crêpe with orange butter, fold in half and then in half again. Place in large baking dish. (May be prepared ahead to this point and refrigerated.)

To prepare sauce, combine butter, sugar, marmalade, orange juice concentrate, water, orange rind and 1 C. Grand Marnier and bring to a boil. Simmer 10 minutes. When ready to serve, pour a little warm sauce over crêpes and warm in a 300° oven for 15 to 20 minutes. Warm remaining sauce. Transfer crêpes to chafing dish or flambé pan and pour remaining sauce over. Heat 2 T. Grand Marnier and 2 T. grain alcohol. Pour over crêpes and ignite. Serve flaming. Serves 12.

TRIFLE

3-1/4 oz. pkg. vanilla pudding
1 t. vanilla
1 t. almond extract
1 C. heavy cream
2 T. powdered sugar
8 almond macaroons, crumbled, see pg. 273
2 T. brandy
1/2 pound cake, sliced
1/3 C. dry sherry
1 T. brandy
2 10-oz. boxes frozen raspberries OR strawberries, undrained
6 almond macaroons, crumbled
3 T. sherry
3 T. slivered almonds, toasted

Prepare pudding according to package directions, adding vanilla and almond extract. Set aside. Whip cream with powdered sugar and set aside. In a crystal or glass bowl, assemble Trifle in the following order: 8 macaroons, 2 T. brandy, cake, 1/3 C. sherry, 1 T. brandy, fruit, 6 macaroons, pudding, 3 T. sherry and whipped cream. Refrigerate 24 hours. Serve in stemmed compotes, large wine goblets or on crystal plates. Sprinkle with toasted almonds. Serves 6 to 8.

(Note: To serve 12, make another layer of pound cake, 1/3 C. sherry, 1 T. brandy and fruit before finishing with the macaroons, vanilla, pudding, 3 T. sherry and whipped cream.)

BISCUIT TORTONI

1/2 C. almond macaroon crumbs, see pg. 273
3 eggs, separated
3/4 C. powdered sugar
1/4 t. salt
3 T. Amaretto liqueur
1/2 C. heavy cream, whipped
1/4 C. almonds, toasted

With rolling pin, crumble macaroons and bake in 250° oven 1-1/2 hours, or until very dry. Beat egg yolks with powdered sugar and salt until thick. Add Amaretto and macaroon crumbs. Beat egg whites until stiff and fold into egg mixture. Fold in whipped cream. Spoon into individual ramekins or cupcake papers in muffin tins. Top with almonds. Freeze 2 hours. Serves 8.

BAKLAVA

1 C. sugar
1 C. water
1-1/2 C. honey
2-1/2 C. pecans, walnuts or almonds, ground or finely-chopped
3/4 C. sugar
2 t. cinnamon
1 t. allspice
1 C. butter, melted
1/2 C. butter, melted
1 lb. pkg. filo pastry dough

Combine 1 C. sugar and water and bring to boil; stir until sugar dissolves. Cook over medium heat about 20 minutes, or until quite thick. Add honey and cook 10 minutes longer, watching carefully. Cool.

Combine nuts, sugar, cinnamon and allspice and set aside. Melt 1 C. butter to be used for greasing pan and brushing between sheets of filo pastry. Remove filo pastry from package and wrap in damp towel. (Filo must be kept damp, not wet.) With scissors, cut stack of dough to fit 9" x 13" pan, reserving trimmings.

Lightly grease pan with melted butter. Place 2 sheets of filo in pan and brush with butter. Continue until 10 sheets are used. Spread with 1/3 of nut mixture. At this point, reserve 10 or 12 of best sheets for top layer and work with remainder of sheets, using half for each of next two layers. Continue to layer, buttering every other sheet, using trimmings between full sheets. Add another 1/3 of nut mixture, third layer of dough and third layer of nut mixture, topping with reserved dough. Using a very sharp knife, cut through pastry lengthwise in 6 strips. Turn pan and cut diagonally to make small diamonds.

Heat remaining 1/2 C. butter until frothy and pour over pastry, letting it run into cuts. Bake at 300° (275° for glass pan) 1 hour, until golden. Remove from oven; pour half of syrup over pastry and return to a 400° oven for 3 or 4 minutes, until lightly browned. Remove from oven, pour on remaining syrup and cool. Let stand 3 hours before serving. Serves 30. (May be frozen.)

CRÈME CARAMEL

1/2 C. sugar
3 T. water
8 eggs
5 egg yolks
1 C. sugar
5-1/2 C. milk, heated
1 t. vanilla

1 doz. almond macaroons, see pg. 273
Fresh whole strawberries
Sliced fresh peaches

Heat sugar and water in small pan or iron skillet. Shake and swirl over medium-high heat to dissolve and cook. Do not stir. If sugar crystals start to form, brush down sides of pan with pastry brush dipped in water. Continue shaking until syrup is nut-brown in color. Pour quickly into 2-qt. soufflé dish, tilting so that syrup covers bottom and a little of the sides. Set aside.

Beat eggs and egg yolks until thick. Add sugar gradually; slowly add milk, beating constantly. Add vanilla to mixture and pour through a sieve into prepared soufflé dish. Place dish in larger pan filled with 1" hot water. Bake uncovered for 1 hour and 15 minutes at 325°, or until knife stuck in center comes out clean. (Custard will firm up as it is chilled.) Chill for at least 4 hours.

Break almond macaroons into small pieces. Dry out on cookie sheet in 225° oven for 1-1/2 hours. Cool and crush with rolling pin.

To unmold Crème Caramel, run sharp knife around sides of mold. Place a very large, round platter on top of mold and invert. Just before serving, sprinkle top with macaroon crumbs. Surround with fresh strawberries and peaches. Serves 10 to 12.

COFFEE MOUSSE

33 large marshmallows
1 C. strong coffee
1 C. heavy cream, whipped
2 T. slivered almonds, toasted and chopped

Cut marshmallows in half and melt by stirring in hot coffee. When marshmallows dissolve, add whipped cream and cool. Pour into individual serving dishes and sprinkle with almonds. Serves 6.

CHOCOLATE POTS DE CRÈME

4 oz. German sweet chocolate
2 C. light cream
3 egg yolks
1 egg
3 T. sugar
1 T. Cointreau

1 C. heavy cream, whipped
2 T. powdered sugar

Melt chocolate over low heat. Scald cream and add chocolate, stirring until well blended. Combine yolks, egg and sugar; beat in hot cream mixture. Add Cointreau. Pour into 12 very small pots de crème pots or 6 to 8 medium-sized pots. Place pots in pan of hot water 1/2" deep. Cover entire pan loosely with foil and bake at 350° 30 to 45 minutes, depending upon size of pots. Knife will come out clean when custards are done. Cool and chill. Whip cream with powdered sugar and spoon on top of each pot de crème. Serves 6 to 12.

SURPRISE LIME CRÈME

2 avocados, peeled and diced
1 pint vanilla ice cream
1 pint lime sherbet
Juice of 1/2 lime

2 T. powdered sugar
1 C. heavy cream, whipped
2 T. powdered sugar

Place avocados, ice cream, sherbet, lime juice and 2 T. powdered sugar in blender jar. Blend and turn blender off while there are still bits of avocado in the ice cream. Serve at once in chilled sherbet cups or champagne glasses. Garnish with mixture of whipping cream and powdered sugar. Serves 6.

PUMPKIN FLAN

1/2 C. sugar
3/4 C. sugar
1/2 t. salt
1 t. cinnamon

1 C. pumpkin
5 eggs, beaten
1-1/2 C. evaporated milk
1/3 C. water

Caramelize 1/2 C. sugar in 6 C. ring mold. Combine remaining ingredients and pour over caramelized sugar. Set ring mold in pan of hot water and bake at 350° for 1-1/4 hours. Cool, then chill. To unmold, briefly dip mold in hot water and invert on platter. Serves 8.

MEXICAN CHOCOLATE SOUFFLÉ

1 C. milk
2 oz. unsweetened baking chocolate
1/2 C. sugar
1/2 t. cinnamon
1/8 t. salt
3 eggs
1/2 t. vanilla
1 C. heavy cream, whipped
2 T. powdered sugar

In top of double boiler, heat the milk, chocolate, sugar, cinnamon and salt. Stir to melt chocolate. Add eggs and vanilla, and beat with egg beater for 1 minute. Cover double boiler and cook for 20 minutes without lifting lid. Whip cream with powdered sugar. Serve warm or chilled in dessert dishes garnished with sweetened whipped cream. Serves 6.

EGGNOG CUSTARD

8 egg yolks
2 C. sugar
1 t. salt
1 C. hot water
2 envelopes plain gelatin
1/2 C. cold water
8 egg whites
1 t. nutmeg
1/2 C. dry sherry OR brandy
3 C. heavy cream, whipped
Freshly-grated nutmeg

In double boiler, cook egg yolks, 1 C. of the sugar, salt and hot water until mixture coats a spoon. Dissolve gelatin in cold water. Pour custard over gelatin; mix and cool, but do not refrigerate. Beat egg whites until soft peaks form; gradually add remaining 1 C. sugar and 1 t. nutmeg. Add sherry or brandy and mix lightly. Fold egg white mixture into custard mixture. Fold in two-thirds of the whipped cream. Place in individual serving dishes or in large soufflé dish. Refrigerate. Serve remaining whipped cream on top and sprinkle with freshly-grated nutmeg. Serves 6 to 8.

SOUR CREAM PUDDING

2 C. flour
1 T. baking powder
1/2 t. soda
1/8 t. salt
2 C. dairy sour cream
3/4 C. sugar
1 t. vanilla
1 egg

1-1/3 C. brown sugar
1-1/3 C. dairy sour cream
2 C. light cream

Mix flour, baking powder, soda, salt, 2 C. sour cream, sugar, vanilla and egg. Spread batter into 7" x 11" baking dish. Sprinkle brown sugar over top of batter, and spread 1-1/3 C. sour cream over brown sugar. Bake 30 to 40 minutes at 325°. Serve warm with light cream. (May be made in advance and reheated.) Serves 8.

SWEET POTATO PUDDING

6 large sweet potatoes
6 eggs, separated
1 C. butter
1-3/4 C. fine granulated sugar
2 C. light cream
Rind of 1 lemon, grated
1/2 t. cinnamon
1/4 t. nutmeg
1/4 t. allspice
3 oz. bourbon
Powdered sugar

Bake potatoes; peel and press through fine sieve or potato ricer. Add yolks of 6 eggs, and beat well. Add butter, beating well. Add sugar and cream, beating until very light. Add lemon rind, spices and bourbon and blend well. Beat egg whites to a stiff froth and fold into potato mixture. Place in 3-qt. buttered casserole. Place brown paper or wax paper over top. Bake at 350° for 45 minutes. Remove paper, dust with powdered sugar and bake 15 minutes longer. Serves 10.

FROZEN CHOCOLATE MINT SOUFFLÉ

1 C. butter
2 C. powdered sugar
4 oz. unsweetened chocolate, melted
4 eggs
1 t. peppermint extract
2 t. vanilla
1 C. heavy cream, whipped
1/2 C. pecans, chopped
35 vanilla wafers, crushed
4 T. butter, melted
Chocolate curls for garnish
    OR crushed peppermint candy

Cream butter and sugar; add chocolate, eggs, peppermint extract and vanilla. Fold whipped cream and pecans into chocolate mixture. Toss wafer crumbs with melted butter. Place 2 T. of crumb mixture in bottom of individual ramekins or champagne glasses (or all of crumb mixture in bottom of large soufflé dish).

Top with chocolate mixture and chill or freeze. To serve, garnish each serving with chocolate curls or crushed peppermint candy. Serves 12 to 14.

BRANDY ROYAL

4 dips English Toffee ice cream
4 oz. brandy
2 oz. Crème de Cacao
4 oz. German sweet chocolate bar

Mix ice cream, brandy and Crème de Cacao briefly in blender and pour into stemmed glasses or sherbets. Coarsely grate chocolate bar and sprinkle over top. Serve with straw or spoon. Serves 4. (Note: To vary, spoon ice cream into dishes, pour brandy and Crème de Cacao over top and garnish with grated chocolate.)

LEMON-LIME ICE

1 qt. water
2 C. sugar
2 t. lemon rind, grated
1/8 t. salt
1/2 C. fresh lemon juice, strained (4 to 5 lemons)
1/4 C. fresh lime juice, strained (3 to 4 limes)
3 to 4 drops green food coloring
Grated lime peel for garnish

Combine water, sugar, lemon rind and salt in saucepan. Bring to boil; stir until sugar is dissolved. Boil without stirring for 5 minutes. Remove from heat and cool 1 hour. Add lemon juice, lime juice and food coloring. Pour into 2 ice-cube trays and freeze until mushy, 2 to 4 hours. Place in chilled serving bowl and beat until frothy. Freeze until firm. Garnish with grated lime peel. Makes 1-1/2 qts. (May be served in hollowed-out orange shells garnished with a lime peel curl.)

FROZEN LEMON CRUNCH

2 T. butter
1/2 C. crushed cornflakes
3 T. brown sugar
1/2 C. pecans, chopped
3 egg yolks
1/2 C. sugar
3 T. lemon juice
2 T. lemon rind, grated
3 egg whites
1/4 t. salt
1 C. heavy cream, whipped

Melt butter in skillet; add cornflakes, brown sugar and pecans. Cook and stir until sugar melts and caramelizes slightly. Set aside. In small saucepan beat egg yolks and sugar until light and foamy. Cook over low heat until thick. Add lemon juice and rind. Cool. In large bowl, beat egg whites with salt until stiff. Fold in cooled egg yolk mixture and whipped cream. Place half of cornflake mixture on bottom of spring-form pan. Pour in lemon mixture and top with remaining cornflake mixture. Freeze a minimum of 4 hours. Serves 10.

ORANGE STRAWS

6 oranges OR lemons
12 Russell Stover Honeysuckle Straws

Roll oranges on counter to make juicy. Cut a small, deep hole in top of orange, just large enough to insert Honeysuckle Straw. Do not put candy into orange until ready to serve. Drink juice through candy straw while squeezing orange. Add a second straw as needed. Serves 6.

ORANGE JUBILEE

3/4 C. orange juice
1 C. water
3/4 C. sugar
1/4 C. orange juice
1-1/2 T. cornstarch
6 oranges
1/2 C. slivered almonds, toasted

Peel of 1 orange for garnish
Vanilla ice cream OR sherbet

Combine 3/4 C. orange juice, water and sugar. Bring to boil and simmer 5 minutes. Combine 1/4 C. orange juice and cornstarch and add to hot mixture, stirring until slightly thickened, about 10 minutes. Peel and section 6 oranges and cover with syrup. Sprinkle with almonds and thin slivers of orange peel. Serve over vanilla ice cream or sherbet. Serves 4 to 6.

PEARS CONTINENTAL

16 canned pear halves
2-2/3 T. cocoa
1 egg
1 t. vanilla
2 C. powdered sugar
2 T. butter, melted
1 C. heavy cream, whipped
Chocolate curls OR pistachio nuts for garnish

On day before serving, drain canned pears well and fill cavity of 1 pear half with 1 t. cocoa. Cover with another half, securing with toothpicks if necessary. Repeat with remaining pears. Cover and refrigerate. At least 1 hour before serving, cream egg, vanilla, sugar and butter. Chill and fold into whipped cream. Garnish pears with whipped cream mixture and sprinkle with chocolate curls or pistachio nuts. Serves 8.

CARAMEL SAUCE

1 C. brown sugar
1/2 C. heavy cream
1/4 C. butter

Cook all ingredients in double boiler for 45 minutes without stirring. Remove from heat and beat until smooth and thick. Makes 1 C. sauce.

VANILLA CUSTARD SAUCE

2 C. milk
3-3/4 oz. pkg. Instant Vanilla Pudding
1 C. Cool Whip
1/8 t. salt
1/4 C. Grand Marnier
1 t. orange rind, grated

Combine milk and pudding mix. Beat until mixture reaches consistency of thin custard. Fold in remaining ingredients and chill. Good served over fresh fruit and topped with slivered almonds.

STRAWBERRY SAUCE

2 pints strawberries
3/4 C. currant jelly
1/4 C. Grand Marnier
1 t. lemon juice
1/4 C. to 1/2 C. powdered sugar (optional)

Puree strawberries in blender and pour through a sieve. Heat jelly until melted. Add Grand Marnier and lemon juice to jelly. Cool mixture and beat into strawberry puree. If mixture is too runny, add powdered sugar as needed to thicken. Serve cold.

RASPBERRY SAUCE

1 T. Grand Marnier
10 oz. pkg. frozen raspberries OR strawberries
1 T. cornstarch

Heat Grand Marnier, raspberries and cornstarch, stirring until well thickened. Serve warm or chilled.

FLAMING WESTPORT ROOM CHOCOLATE SAUCE

1/2 C. butter
8 oz. Dutch chocolate
1 C. sugar
1/2 C. to 1 C. canned chocolate syrup
3 T. Cognac

Melt butter in double boiler; add chocolate and sugar. (Mixture will be too thick to stir.) Blend in chocolate syrup until consistency of a smooth sauce is reached. Transfer mixture to chafing dish. Warm Cognac; pour over mixture just before serving and ignite.

CHOCOLATE RUM SAUCE

1/2 C. butter
4 oz. unsweetened chocolate
2-1/4 C. powdered sugar
2/3 C. evaporated milk
2 T. rum OR brandy

Melt butter and chocolate in top of double boiler. Add sugar and milk. Cook over hot water for 30 minutes. Do not stir. Remove from heat and beat well. Add rum or brandy. Serve warm or cold.

BLENDER FUDGE SAUCE

4 oz. unsweetened chocolate, melted
2/3 C. milk, scalded
1 C. sugar
1/4 C. butter
1/4 t. salt
1 t. vanilla

Place all ingredients in blender jar; blend until smooth. Makes 1 C. sauce.

cookies & candies

BROWN LACE COOKIES

1/4 C. butter
2 C. brown sugar, packed
2 eggs, beaten
1 t. vanilla
1/2 C. flour
1 t. baking powder
2 C. pecans, chopped

Cream butter and sugar. Add eggs and vanilla, beating well. Sift flour and baking powder together and add to creamed mixture with nuts. Chill 1 hour. Place sheet of foil on cookie sheet. Drop by half-teaspoonsful 3" apart. (They will spread while baking.) Bake 6 minutes at 400°. Cool before removing from foil. Makes 6 to 7 dozen cookies.

ALMOND WAFERS

1/2 C. blanched almonds, ground
1/2 C. butter
1/2 C. sugar
1 T. flour
2 T. milk

Grease generously and flour teflon cookie sheet. Mix ingredients in saucepan. Cook and stir over low heat until butter melts. Drop by teaspoonsful on cookie sheet at least 3" apart, with no more than 5 to a cookie sheet. (They will spread.) Bake at 375° for 6 minutes, or until lightly browned. Remove from oven and let stand 1 minute. Lift with spatula and roll around handle of wooden spoon. Place on wire rack seam side down. (If they do not roll well, place in oven briefly to reheat.) Grease and flour teflon sheet each time it is used. Reheat cookie mixture if necessary so that butter stays melted. Makes 2 dozens wafers.

WOLFERMAN'S CHOCOLATE DROP COOKIES

3/4 C. sugar
1/2 C. butter
1/4 t. vanilla
1/4 t. salt
1/4 C. light corn syrup
2 eggs
4 oz. unsweetened chocolate,
  melted and cooled
1/2 C. milk
1-3/4 C. flour
1-1/2 t. baking powder
1/4 C. pecans, chopped

Icing:
2 oz. unsweetened chocolate
2 T. butter
1/4 C. milk
2 C. powdered sugar
1 t. vanilla
Dash salt

Cream sugar, butter, vanilla, salt and corn syrup. Add eggs and chocolate. Add milk slowly, and stir in flour and baking powder. Add pecans. Drop by teaspoonful on greased cookie sheet and bake at 325° for 10 minutes. Makes 2 dozen large cookies.

Prepare icing by melting chocolate and butter together. Heat milk and pour over powdered sugar, vanilla and salt. Add chocolate mixture to sugar mixture and mix. Spread on cooled cookies.

BUTTERSCOTCH OATMEAL COOKIES

1 C. butter
3/4 C. brown sugar
3/4 C. granulated sugar
2 eggs, beaten
1 T. hot water
1-1/2 C. flour
1 t. soda
1 C. walnuts, chopped
2 C. oatmeal
1 t. vanilla
6 oz. butterscotch bits

Cream butter and sugars. Add beaten eggs, then hot water. Add flour mixed with soda. Add chopped nuts, oatmeal and vanilla. Stir and add butterscotch bits. Drop by teaspoonful on cookie sheet. Bake at 375° for 8 to 10 minutes. Makes 6 dozen cookies.

CINNAMON OATMEAL CRISPIES

1 C. brown sugar
1 C. granulated sugar
1 C. butter
2 eggs
2 C. flour
1/2 t. salt
1 t. soda
1 t. baking powder
1 t. vanilla
2 C. rolled oats
3 T. sugar
1 T. cinnamon

Cream 1 C. brown sugar and 1 C. granulated sugar with butter. Add eggs. Sift dry ingredients and add. Mix in vanilla and oats. Shape into balls the size of small walnuts. Roll in mixture of 3 T. sugar and 1 T. cinnamon. Place 2" apart on ungreased baking sheet. Press each cookie down with bottom of small glass dipped in sugar and cinnamon mixture. Bake 7 minutes at 350°. Makes 7 dozen cookies.

SOFT GINGER COOKIES

1/2 C. butter
1 C. dark brown sugar
2 eggs
1 C. light molasses
1 C. buttermilk
1 T. soda
Juice of 1/2 lemon
1/2 t. cinnamon
1/2 t. ginger
1/2 t. nutmeg
1/4 t. cloves
4 C. flour, sifted
Sugar

Cream butter and sugar. Add eggs and beat well. Add molasses and buttermilk. Dissolve soda in lemon juice and add. Sift remaining dry ingredients into mixture and mix well. Drop on cookie sheet, and sprinkle each cookie with additional sugar. Bake 10 minutes at 325°. Makes 6 dozen cookies.

FORGOTTEN COOKIES

3 egg whites
1/8 t. salt
1/8 t. cream of tartar
3/4 C. sugar
1/2 C. peppermint candy, coarsely-chopped
    OR 1/2 C. German sweet chocolate, coarsely-chopped

Beat egg whites until foamy; add salt and cream of tartar. When egg whites hold peaks, beat in sugar, 1 T. at a time, beating well after each addition. Fold in peppermint or chocolate. Drop by teaspoonsful onto cookie sheet lined with aluminum foil. Bake at 225° for 2 hours. Turn oven off and let cookies sit in oven until cool, or leave in oven to cool overnight. Makes 2-1/2 dozen cookies.

ALMOND MACAROONS

8 oz. can almond paste
1 C. sugar
3 egg whites
1/2 t. almond extract

Break almond paste into small bits. Add sugar and egg whites. Beat with mixer until smooth and add almond extract. Drop by teaspoonsful onto cookie sheet lined with brown paper and bake for 30 minutes at 325°. Lift brown paper to cooling rack and cool cookies completely before removing paper. (May be frozen.) Makes 2-1/2 dozen cookies.

CHOCOLATE MERINGUE COOKIES

2 egg whites
1/4 t. salt
1/2 C. sugar
6 oz. semi-sweet chocolate chips
7 oz. coconut, shredded
1 t. vanilla

Beat egg whites until stiff, gradually adding salt and sugar. Melt chocolate chips in double boiler; cool and fold into meringue. Gently fold in coconut and vanilla. Drop by heaping teaspoonsful several inches apart on cookie sheet lined with brown paper. Bake in 325° oven for 13 minutes. Cool before removing paper. Makes 3 dozen cookies.

MONTE CARLO SQUARES

3/4 C. butter
1/3 C. sugar
1/8 t. salt
2 egg yolks
1-1/2 C. flour
1 C. apricot preserves
2 egg whites
1/2 C. sugar
2 oz. almonds, sliced

Mix butter, sugar, salt, egg yolks and flour. Pat into 9" x 9" buttered and floured pan. Bake for 20 to 25 minutes at 350°. Remove from oven and spread with apricot preserves. Beat egg whites with sugar until stiff and spread over apricot preserves. Sprinkle with almonds and return to oven for 25 to 30 minutes. Cut into 16 squares. Cool before removing from pan.

WATSON'S BROWNIES

3 oz. unsweetened chocolate
1 heaping T. cocoa
2 C. sugar
1/2 t. salt
1/2 C. butter
2 t. vanilla
4 eggs, beaten
1 C. flour
2 C. pecans, chopped

Melt chocolate, cocoa, sugar, salt and butter in double boiler. Cool and add vanilla and eggs. Stir in flour, then pecans. Pour into buttered 9" x 13" pan and bake for 25 minutes at 350°. Makes 32 brownies.

TOFFEE NUT BARS

1/2 C. butter
1/2 C. brown sugar
1 C. flour, sifted
2 eggs, well-beaten
1 C. brown sugar
1 t. vanilla
2 T. flour
1 t. baking powder
1/2 t. salt
1 C. coconut, shredded
1 C. almonds, sliced OR pecans, chopped

Cream butter and 1/2 C. brown sugar. Mix in flour and press into ungreased 9" x 13" baking pan. Bake at 350° for 10 minutes. Cool. Combine eggs, 1 C. brown sugar and vanilla. Add flour, baking powder and salt. Add coconut and almonds, and spread mixture over first layer. Return to 350° oven for 20 to 25 minutes or until topping is golden brown. Cool and cut into 24 bars.

FONDANT SQUARES

1/2 C. butter	*Filling:*	*Glaze:*
1/4 C. sugar	2 T. vanilla pudding mix	1 T. butter
5 T. cocoa	(not instant)	3 oz. unsweetened
1 egg	3 T. milk, warmed	chocolate
1/2 C. pecans, chopped	1/4 C. butter	
2 C. graham cracker crumbs	2 C. powdered sugar	

Heat butter, sugar, cocoa and egg until butter melts. Cool slightly and add pecans and graham cracker crumbs. Mix thoroughly and press tightly into 8" x 8" square pan.

Add pudding to warm milk. Add to butter alternately with powdered sugar, beating until smooth. Spread over first layer, covering completely. Refrigerate.

Melt butter and chocolate in small saucepan. Pour over filling, spreading smoothly with spatula. Chill. One hour before serving, cut into 1" squares and return to refrigerator until serving time. Makes 80 one-inch squares.

ALMOND TOFFEE

4 oz. blanched almonds, slivered
Dash salt
1 C. sugar
1 C. butter
1/2 t. cream of tartar
12 oz. milk chocolate bar

Butter a 7" x 11" pan. Sprinkle with almonds, and salt almonds lightly. In a large, heavy skillet, cook sugar, butter and cream of tartar until mixture reaches the hard-crack stage. Quickly pour over nuts in pan. Break milk chocolate bar into pieces and immediately place on top of toffee. As chocolate melts, spread it evenly to cover surface of toffee. Cool at room temperature, refrigerate, and when well chilled, break into irregular pieces. Store in refrigerator.

HEAVENLY HASH

1 C. butter
2 C. sugar
4 eggs, slightly-beaten
3/4 C. cocoa
1 C. flour
1 t. vanilla
1 lb. bag miniature marshmallows

Icing:
1/2 C. butter
1/4 C. cocoa
1/3 C. milk
1 lb. box powdered sugar

Cream butter and sugar. Add eggs, cocoa, flour and vanilla. Pour into 9" x 13" buttered pan and bake for 35 to 40 minutes at 325°. Remove from oven, cover with marshmallows and return to oven for 1 minute. Remove from oven and cool for 10 minutes. Make icing by melting butter in saucepan. Add cocoa and milk. Blend in powdered sugar. Beat well and pour over marshmallows. Cool and cut into 1" squares and place in bon-bon cups. Makes 5 dozen squares.

ICED ALMONDS

1 C. whole blanched almonds
1/2 C. sugar
2 T. butter
1/2 t. vanilla
3/4 t. salt

In heavy skillet over medium heat, cook almonds, sugar and butter, stirring constantly, until almonds are toasted and sugar is golden brown, about 15 minutes. Stir in vanilla. Spread on sheet of aluminum foil and sprinkle with salt. Cool and break into clusters. Makes 1-1/2 C. almonds.

index

281

285